T0318254

ADAM SMITH'S SCIENCE OF MORALS

ADAM SMITH'S SCIENCE OF MORALS

T.D. CAMPBELL

Volume 3

Routledge
Taylor & Francis Group

LONDON AND NEW YORK

First published in 1971

This edition first published in 2010
by Routledge
2 Park Square, Milton Park, Abingdon, Oxon, OX14 4RN

Simultaneously published in the USA and Canada
by Routledge
605 Third Avenue, New York, NY 10017

*Routledge is an imprint of the Taylor & Francis Group, an
informa business*

First issued in paperback 2012

British Library Cataloguing in Publication Data
A catalogue record for this book is available from the
British Library

ISBN 13: 978-0-415-56199-0 (hbk)
ISBN 13: 978-0-415-52154-3 (pbk)

Publisher's Note
The publisher has gone to great lengths to ensure the quality of
this reprint but points out that some imperfections in the original
copies may be apparent. The publisher has made every effort to
trace copyright holders and welcomes correspondence from those
they have been unable to contact.

UNIVERSITY OF GLASGOW SOCIAL
AND ECONOMIC STUDIES

General Editor: Professor D. J. Robertson

21

ADAM SMITH'S SCIENCE OF MORALS

UNIVERSITY OF GLASGOW SOCIAL
AND ECONOMIC STUDIES

New Series

General Editor: *Professor D. J. Robertson*

ADAM SMITH'S
SCIENCE OF MORALS

T. D. CAMPBELL

Lecturer in Moral Philosophy
University of Glasgow

London
GEORGE ALLEN & UNWIN LTD
RUSKIN HOUSE MUSEUM STREET

FIRST PUBLISHED IN 1971

ISBN 0 04 192027 9

PRINTED IN GREAT BRITAIN
in 10 *point Times Roman*
BY T. AND A. CONSTABLE LTD.
HOPETOUN STREET, EDINBURGH

For Ailsa

PREFACE

This book is based on a Ph.D. thesis submitted to the University of Glasgow in 1969. I have special cause to thank Professor D. D. Raphael who supervised my work for this thesis. Not only did he direct my attention to Smith's *Theory of Moral Sentiments*, but he also provided me with much helpful criticism and encouragement.

The Carnegie Trust for the Universities of Scotland has given generous financial assistance towards the publication costs of this book; I am most grateful for this help. I should also like to thank the University of Glasgow for including this book in its *Social and Economic Studies*.

T. D. C.

CONTENTS

Contents

with abbreviations and notes on those editions which are referred
to in the text

1. *The Theory of Moral Sentiments* (1st edn. 1759). 6th edn, with considerable additions and corrections, 2 vols, London: A. Strahan and
T. Cadell, and W. Creech and J. Bell and Co., 1790.
Short title: *Moral Sentiments.*
Abbreviations used in footnotes: T.M.S., I.i.1 (I.1) is an abbreviation
for *Moral Sentiments*, 6th ed. part one, section one, chapter one
(volume one, page one).

2. *An Inquiry into the Nature and Causes of the Wealth of Nations* (1st edn,
1776), 5th edn (1789), 2 vols, ed. by Edwin Cannan (1904), London:
Methuen, 1961.
Short title: *Wealth of Nations.*
Abbreviations: W.N., I.x.1 (I.112) is an abbreviation for *Wealth of
Nations*, 5th edn, book one, chapter ten, part one (volume one, page
112).

3. *Essays on Philosophical Subjects*, ed. by Dugald Stewart, London:
T. Cadell Jun. and W. Davies, and W. Creech, 1795.
Short title: *Essays.*
Abbreviations: (*a*) E.P.S. is an abbreviation for *Essays.*
(*b*) 'Account' is an abbreviation for 'Account of the Life and Writings
of Adam Smith, LL.D.', an essay by Dugald Stewart published in the
Essays.
(*c*) H.A. is an abbreviation for 'The Principles which lead and direct
Philosophical Enquiries; illustrated by the History of Astronomy'.
Short title: *On the History of Astronomy.*
(*d*) H.A.P. is an abbreviation for 'The Principles which lead and direct
Philosophical Enquiries; illustrated by the History of Ancient Physics'.
(*e*) H.A.L. & M. is an abbreviation for 'The Principles which lead and
direct Philosophical Enquiries; illustrated by the History of Ancient
Logics and Metaphysics'.

4. 'Considerations concerning the first Formation of Languages', appended to the third and subsequent editions of the *Moral Sentiments.*
Short title: Considerations.

5. *Lectures on Justice, Police, Revenue and Arms*, delivered in the University
of Glasgow, reported by a student in 1763 and edited with an introduction and notes by Edwin Cannan, Oxford: Clarendon Press, 1896.
Short title: *Lectures on Jurisprudence.*
Abbreviation: L.J.

N.B.—Another, somewhat fuller, version of these lectures, also based
on students' notes, was discovered by Professor J. M. Lothian in 1958,
and is in the possession of the University of Glasgow. I have been
permitted to read a typescript of these lectures but have been asked not

to quote passages from them before the text is published in the University's edition of the Works of Adam Smith.

6. *Lectures on Rhetoric and Belles Lettres*, a copy of students' notes taken down in 1762-3, edited with an introduction and notes by John M. Lothian, London: Nelson, 1963.
   Short title: *Lectures on Rhetoric*.
   Abbreviation: L.R.B.L.

INTRODUCTION

Adam Smith is renowned as an economist. To those who take specialization for granted Smith's importance as the author of the *Wealth of Nations* implies that he is unlikely to be very competent in, or concerned with, other subjects. This is a common view of Adam Smith. The same polite comments are made about his non-economic works as are used to acknowledge a great scientist's excursion into the realm of philosophy or a famous conductor's efforts as an instrumentalist: in view of the maestro's great work his other activities are treated with good-natured but unenthusiastic respect. In this way Smith's economic theory is frequently given the place of honour while his lesser known moral and legal theories receive only minimal attention.[1]

From a general historical point of view this is quite justified. The *Wealth of Nations* has had a practical influence probably unsurpassed by any other book of modern times. Its extraordinary historical significance marks it off quite distinctly from the rest of Smith's work. But, unless influence is equated with truth, this does not imply that it is equally superior as a contribution to knowledge. The *Wealth of Nations* was adopted as the ideology of early liberal capitalism and its popularity may have been due as much to the way in which it accorded with the economic and political prejudices of the emergent bourgeoisie as to its intrinsic merits as a scholarly work. That it has such merits is not in doubt; it is one of the very first systematic studies in political economy; but the relative historical insignificance of Smith's other work has perhaps detracted from a fair assessment of its quality. Yet for some years before the *Wealth of Nations* appeared, in 1776, Smith had enjoyed international fame as the author of *The Theory of Moral Sentiments* (1759).

This book was a development of lectures which he delivered as professor of Moral Philosophy in the University of Glasgow, an

---

[1] Cf. J. Bonar, *The Moral Sense* (New York, 1930), p. 168: 'It has needed all the fame of the second (the *Wealth of Nations*) to keep alive the memory of the first (the *Moral Sentiments*)'; and R. B. Haldane, *Life of Adam Smith* (London, 1887), pp. 13f: 'It is as an economist that Adam Smith will be remembered . . . he was also a writer on Ethics . . . His contribution to Ethics was, as we shall see, unimportant.'

appointment he held from 1752 to 1764 after a short spell as professor of Logic and Rhetoric in the same university. It is a work which has not continued to receive general acclaim. Sometimes it is mentioned as an aid to the interpretation of the *Wealth of Nations*, but it is infrequently given much consideration in its own right. Yet Adam Smith himself is reported to have considered it superior to the *Wealth of Nations*[1] and took the trouble to revise and expand it for a sixth edition which was published in 1790, the year of his death.

There is no doubt that the *Theory of Moral Sentiments* is important for the understanding of *The Wealth of Nations* for it presents a broader picture of Smith's social theory, of which the work on economics is only a specialized part. Regarding the matter in the light of this logical relationship between the two books it would be more justified to consider the *Moral Sentiments* in isolation from the *Wealth of Nations* rather than to follow the more usual practice of giving exclusive attention to the latter work. However, both of these works have to be looked at in the perspective of a programme of research which Smith planned but never completed. For large as were Adam Smith's achievements, they fell far short of his aspirations. His published work represents only a part of his intended writings. At his own insistence sixteen volumes of manuscripts were destroyed shortly before his death.[2] He is reported to have expressed regret that 'he had done so little', and the destroyed manuscripts must have contained the 'materials in my papers, of which I could have made a great deal', mentioned in Dugald Stewart's 'Account of the Life and Writings of Adam Smith, LL.D'.[3]

Some manuscripts did survive and are contained in the posthumous collection *Essays on Philosophical Subjects*. His literary executors, Messrs Joseph Black and James Hutton, declared these to be a part of a larger collection of material designed to fulfil 'a plan he once had formed, for giving a connected history of the liberal sciences and elegant arts'.[4] This project probably grew out of his studies at Balliol and his lectures on rhetoric and *belles-lettres*, which were delivered in the first place at Edinburgh in 1748-9 and elaborated in his Glasgow lectures. For a long time it was thought that all trace of these lectures had been lost, but recently a copy of students'

---

[1] Sir Samuel Romilly, *Memoirs*, vol. I, p. 403; quoted in J. Rae, *Life of Adam Smith* (London, 1895), p. 436.
[2] Rae, *Life of Adam Smith*, p. 434.
[3] E.P.S., p. lxxxix.
[4] E.P.S. ('Account'), p. iii.

notes, taken down in 1762-3, has been discovered and this has added valuable, if not entirely reliable, evidence as to their content.[1]

This 'connected history of the liberal sciences and elegant arts' does not, however, represent Smith's main projected work. He himself described his unfulfilled plans in a letter to the Duc de la Rochefoucauld, in these words:

'I have likewise two other great works upon the anvil; the one is a sort of Philosophical History of all the different branches of Literature, of Philosophy, Poetry and Eloquence; the other is a sort of theory and History of Law and Government.'[2]

The second and more important scheme which Smith failed to complete was this systematic work on politics, jurisprudence and sociology. At the end of the first edition of the *Moral Sentiments*, published in 1759, he wrote:

'I shall in another discourse endeavour to give an account of the general principles of law and government, and of the different revolutions they have undergone in the different ages and periods of society, not only in what concerns justice, but in what concerns police, revenue, and arms, and whatever else is the object of law.'[3]

In the Advertisement to the sixth edition, published in 1790, he expanded on this:

'In the *Enquiry concerning the Nature and Causes of the Wealth of Nations*, I have partly executed this promise; at least so far as concerns police, revenue, and arms. What remains, the theory of jurisprudence, which I have long projected, I have hitherto been hindered from executing, by the same occupations which had till now prevented me from revising the present work. Though my very advanced age leaves me, I acknowledge, very little expectation of ever being able to execute this great work to my own satisfaction.'[4]

The missing section of this work, dealing with justice, has not, however, been entirely lost to us since it appears in outline, together with some material which later found a place in the *Wealth of Nations*, in *Lectures on Justice, Police, Revenue, and Arms*. These

---

[1] *Lectures on Rhetoric and Belles Lettres*. Edited with an Introduction and Notes by John M. Lothian (London, 1963).

[2] First published in the *Athenaeum*, December 28, 1895, and reprinted in *The Economic Journal*, VI (1896), pp. 165f.

[3] T.M.S. (1st edn), p. 551. Cf. T.M.S. (6th edn) VII.iv (II.399).

[4] T.M.S. (I.vii).

17

lectures exist in the form of a copy of notes taken down by a student probably in 1762-3 or 1763-4.[1]

To assist in relating Smith's two main works and the *Lectures on Jurisprudence* we have an important summary of the content of Smith's moral philosophy lectures provided by John Millar and quoted by Dugald Stewart in his 'Account'.[2] By comparing this with the content of the three sources we can reconstruct the lectures roughly as follows:

1. *Natural Theology.* No record of this survives but Millar reports that in it 'he considered the proofs of the being and attributes of God, and those principles of the human mind upon which religion is founded'.
2. *Ethics.* This covers Smith's general theory of morality and an introduction to justice as a part of this theory. This was published as the *Moral Sentiments*.
3. *Jurisprudence.* Millar wrote that 'In the third part he treated at more length of that branch of morality which relates to *justice*'. This represents the projected work in jurisprudence parts of which are outlined in those sections of the *Lectures on Jurisprudence* dealing with Justice and the Laws of Nations.
4. *Economics.* Millar reported this to be in substance the work he published as the *Wealth of Nations*, which means that it is the same as those parts of the *Lectures on Jurisprudence* which do not feature as part of Jurisprudence, namely the sections on Police (that is 'Cleanliness and Security' and 'Cheapness or Plenty'), Revenue and Arms.

From this it can be seen that the progress from the *Moral Sentiments* to the *Wealth of Nations* is partly one of increasing specialization and partly a change of emphasis from morality to economics. The *Lectures on Jurisprudence* form a bridge between the two main works; they connect with the *Moral Sentiments* in that justice is part of morality, and they connect with the *Wealth of Nations* not only because this latter work is summarized in the lectures but also because Smith considered economic matters to be included in 'the four great objects of law', which are given as 'justice, police, revenue and arms'.[3]

The aim of the present work is to examine the ethical and, to a lesser extent, the legal theories of Adam Smith as contributions to

[1] Edited by Edwin Cannan, Oxford, 1896. Another, somewhat fuller version of these lectures, taken down in 1762-3, was found by John Lothian in 1958, but has yet to be published.
[2] E.P.S. ('Account'), pp. xvi-xix.   [3] L.J., p. 3.

the scientific study of morals and law. Attention will therefore be focused on those parts of his work which deal with moral and legal rather than economic theory, but the systematic unity of his work will be assumed and reference will be made to all his writings.[1] In practice this means that the *Moral Sentiments*, and those parts of the *Lectures on Jurisprudence* which deal with justice as such, will be subjected to detailed analysis, while the *Wealth of Nations*, the *Essays on Philosophical Subjects* and the *Lectures on Rhetoric and Belles Lettres* will feature less directly, and the 'Considerations concerning the first Formation of Languages' hardly at all.

The justification for approaching Smith's moral and legal studies as works of science rather than of philosophy is exegetical. This is the way in which they can best be understood from the vantage point of the twentieth century. Purely as an aid to enlightened interpretation, it is better to regard Smith as presenting a sociological and psychological but not a philosophical theory of morals and law. Much confusion and misrepresentation arises from the assumption that there is a close similarity of approach and method between Smith's 'moral philosophy' and contemporary moral philosophy. If comparisons are to be made it is between Smith and those of today who concern themselves with the psychology and sociology of morals and law. Despite the normative framework of all his studies which can be summed up as 'giving advice to statesmen', his basic preoccupation is with the correct description of social facts and the explanation of human behaviour through relating these facts to general laws and scientific theories. While he raises and deals with philosophical questions of logic, epistemology and metaphysics as he goes along, his chief concern is with causal and not with logical relationships, with the origins and function of moral judgments rather than with the clarification or criticism of moral language. He does not, of course, lack presuppositions about the moral value of natural processes and the epistemological foundations of knowledge, but the bulk of his work has the logic of a science and can be properly understood only as such.

In this connection it is interesting to note that the most damning criticisms of the *Moral Sentiments* have come from those who

---

[1] This unity has often been called in question; the alleged incompatibility between the *Moral Sentiments* and the *Wealth of Nations* has become known as 'the Adam Smith problem' (cf. A. Oncken, 'The Consistency of Adam Smith', *The Economic Journal*, VII (1897), pp. 443-50). Instead of attempting a general discussion of what I regard as a largely unnecessary controversy I shall deal with specific issues within the general debate as they become relevant.

consider that Smith failed to provide an answer to the most pressing philosophical problem of eighteenth-century ethics: the need to find a non-theological method of justifying moral judgments. This can be called a problem of *normative epistemology*. For instance Leslie Stephen lists Adam Smith amongst those who tried to answer the question: 'How . . . should morality survive theology?' and then goes on to deliver the patronizing judgment that, when reading the *Moral Sentiments*, 'we are not listening to a thinker really grappling with a difficult problem, so much as to an ambitious professor who found an excellent opportunity for displaying his command of language, and making brilliant lectures'.[1] This sort of criticism is frequently voiced by those who have assumed that Smith is trying to justify moral convictions or to defend their epistemological status.[2]

In contrast, those who interpret Adam Smith as offering sociological and psychological analyses and explanations of the moral consciousness of the ordinary man tend to take him more seriously and consider, like Selby-Bigge, that the *Moral Sentiments* 'deserves more attention than it has recently received from the sociologist, the psychologist, and the moralist'.[3] Sidgwick's ambivalent judgment that the quality of Smith's work declines when 'he passes from psychological analysis to ethical construction' does at least imply admiration for his contribution to the psychology of morals, although he also criticizes Smith for failing to 'provide a criterion or standard of right conduct'.[4] Less qualified praise comes from men, such as Edward Westermarck, William McDougall and Frank Giddings, whose chief interests lay in the social sciences. Their favourable assessments are supported by modern historians of thought who have found it illuminating to regard the work of Adam Smith, including the *Moral Sentiments*, as part of, and not simply a prelude to, modern social science.[5]

The *Moral Sentiments* has certain defects of style; it contains

[1] *History of English Thought in the Eighteenth Century* (London, 1876), ix. 2 and ix. 80.
[2] Cf. *Jouffroy's Ethics*, Translated by W. H. Channing (Boston, 1841), vol. 2, p. 167; Thomas Brown, *Lectures on Ethics* (Edinburgh, 1846), p. 143; and James McCosh, *The Scottish Philosophy* (London, 1875), p. 170.
[3] *British Moralists* (Oxford, 1879), vol. 1, p. lxii.
[4] *History of Ethics* (6th edn, London, 1931), p. 223.
[5] G. R. Morrow, *The Ethical and Economic Theories of Adam Smith* (New York, 1922); A. Salomon, 'Adam Smith as a Sociologist', *Social Research*, XII (1945); D. Forbes, ' "Scientific" Whiggism: Adam Smith and John Millar', *Cambridge Journal*, VIII (1955), pp. 643-70; and J. A. Schumpeter, *History of Economic Analysis* (New York, 1954).

much repetition, looseness of terminology and imprecision of statement and it is undoubtedly a difficult book to grasp as a whole. But I shall argue that those who, like McCosh, find that the book 'wanders like a river amidst luxuriant banks' so that 'it is not easy to define its course'[1] have usually failed to see the unifying scientific purpose which determines the course and content of the work. Despite Smith's intense interest in practical affairs it is clear that the *Wealth of Nations* and, even more, the *Moral Sentiments* are attempts to apply his understanding of Newtonian scientific methods to the study of society. Much that seems obscure or irrelevant in the *Moral Sentiments* falls into place when this book is regarded as an explanation of the social origin and function of moral rules. I shall therefore spend some time enquiring into Smith's conception of scientific method on the grounds that an understanding of Smith's scientific purpose is of fundamental importance for the just assessment as well as the correct interpretation of his moral theory.

The present study does not seek to deal with historical questions of dependence and influence except in so far as they have a bearing on the interpretation of Smith's ideas. The aim is to understand these ideas rather than to determine their origin and effects. Reference to Smith's forerunners, contemporaries and followers, and to the general context of his work, will be made only where it is necessary to carry out the prior aim of analysing and clarifying Smith's own theories of morals and law.

This is not to imply that historical interest in Smith's moral and legal theories would be misplaced. Whatever its wider historical significance, the *Moral Sentiments* has considerable historical significance within the context of eighteenth-century Scotland. This period of intense scholarly activity in Scotland has often been noted for its anticipations of modern social science[2] and, in this context, Smith's work on moral and legal theory is an important contribution to the objective study of the function of morality and law in society and the explanation of their nature and content. It has a developed theoretical basis which provides a stable viewpoint for Smith's acute observations of individual behaviour and of the interactions of individuals in society. It is in this latter aspect that Smith made his most distinctive addition to eighteenth-century moral and legal theory since he stands out from his more individualistically oriented contemporaries and goes some way towards rectifying the in-

[1] *The Scottish Philosophy* (London, 1875), p. 168.
[2] Cf. G. E. Bryson, *Man and Society* (Princeton, 1945) and Roy Pascal, 'Property and Society', *The Modern Quarterly*, 1938-9, pp. 167-79.

21

adequacies of their methodological assumptions. The present work may, therefore, make an indirect contribution toward the thesis that eighteenth-century Scotland saw the beginning of the idea and practice of social science and help to indicate the part which Smith's moral and legal theories played in this fascinating period of Scottish intellectual history.

PART I
THE SCIENCE OF SOCIETY

CHAPTER 1

PHILOSOPHY AND SCIENCE
IN ADAM SMITH

Two hundred years is not a long period in the history of human thought, and the eighteenth-century mind, particularly in its most critical and urbane manifestations, does not seem alien to the modern reader. The key terms of the eighteenth century may not be so dominant today but, for the most part, they are still current and are readily understood. A straightforward summary of Adam Smith's writings, without any translation into twentieth-century idioms of thought, would not, therefore, be met by the incomprehension of the general reader. Yet such a procedure would often result in a superficial understanding of Smith's work, and, in some cases, might lead to serious misinterpretations. For, although most eighteenth-century terminology has an accepted place in our own vocabulary, the actual concepts represented by these familiar terms are often significantly different from those with which we operate today. A trivial example to illustrate this difficulty is the eighteenth-century use of the word 'commonwealth' to refer to the polity of particular states or nations,[1] rather than to some form of association between independent states. Both uses still occur but the latter is now the generally accepted connotation of the word.

Of more importance for the present discussion is the fact that, in the eighteenth century, the terms 'philosophy' and 'science' had a more general significance than they have today. These words were then used almost interchangeably of any systematic attempt to understand the world and man's place in it,[2] whereas nowadays they tend to be taken as denoting distinct types of study with differing aims and methods. To ask of any piece of work 'is this philosophy or science?' is thus a question which would have been unintelligible to an eighteenth-century person. Yet, if the modern distinction is valid, it is a question which must be asked, whenever the issue is in doubt, before any work can be correctly interpreted and critically assessed.

[1] T.M.S., II.ii.1 (I.201).
[2] Thus, for Smith, optics is 'the philosophy of vision', cf. T.M.S., III.3 (I.332), and metaphysics is a branch of 'science', cf. W.N., V.i.3 (II.292).

I. PHILOSOPHY

Science is a descriptive and explanatory discipline whose purpose is to provide causal theories which can be tested by reference to observable matters of fact. Philosophy is much harder to define since what constitutes a philosophical question is itself a disputed issue within philosophy; such consensus as exists at the present time on this matter is largely on the negative description of philosophy as a study concerned with general questions about the world, and man's place in it, which cannot be answered by the methods of science. As more and more subjects break away from their philosophical origins and establish their independence, philosophy has become a residual category which continues to deal with those issues which remain beyond the scope of particular sciences.

Classifying these issues in a summary and dogmatic way, we can say that they consist, on the one hand, of speculations about the nature of the world of a quasi-factual type which science either cannot *yet* deal with, or perhaps cannot deal with in principle; and, on the other hand, discussions of various normative issues which are logically inappropriate for the methods of science. The first we may call metaphysics, the second normative philosophy. This latter may be strongly normative, making and seeking to support general evaluative judgments about correct standards of reasoning (logic), reliable sources of knowledge (epistemology), acceptable moral rules and ideals (moral philosophy), and standards of artistic appreciation (aesthetics); or they may be weakly normative, aiming only to describe and analyse what is involved in adopting and employing various forms of normative discourse. It is now common to deny the possibility of objective and rational normative disciplines in the strong sense, and, in consequence, the various departments of philosophy mentioned above are often interpreted as being different spheres for the deployment of the skills of logical clarification and analysis, which involve no evaluative commitment on the part of the analyst.

Yet, although the descriptive analysis of linguistic practices is a distinctive feature of modern philosophy, it is best regarded as one philosophical method, rather than as a defining aim of all philosophical activity. Without denying that purely descriptive analyses of discourse can be undertaken for their own sakes, it has to be noted that such analyses are also instrumental in discussions of the traditional normative and metaphysical problems of philosophy, and, perhaps more significantly in this context, the clarification and logical analysis of concepts are also integral parts of many scientific

26

researches, especially in the social sciences. There is some justification, therefore, for saying that the important distinction to be
borne in mind when classifying theories of morality, for instance,
is the distinction between those that are philosophical in purpose, in
the sense that they aim to analyse the logical structure of fundamental
moral concepts with a view to elucidating, and perhaps suggesting
solutions to, certain problems connected with the justification of
moral judgments, and, on the other hand, those theories which are
scientific, in that they attempt to erect a theory of morality which can
provide causal explanations for the moral judgments characteristically made by different types of person and in different social groups.
These are, in many important respects, exclusive alternatives, and,
although they are far from being the only possible types of moral
theory, they do embody, as we shall see, the major alternative
interpretations of the *Moral Sentiments*.

In the long process of determining whether Smith's moral theory
falls into the category of philosophy or that of science, it is as well
to begin by considering his own statements about the nature of
these two activities. For the reasons which we have been discussing
it is not possible to do this by examining his use of the terms
'philosophy' and 'science'. Instead we must employ the modern
distinction between the two disciplines and see if there is a comparable distinction to be found in the writings of Smith. For instance,
we get no nearer an answer to our question by discovering that
Smith regards himself as a 'philosopher' since this is a name he
applies to Newton and to other founders of modern science. When
Smith does distinguish between these terms it is to make philosophy
the more abstract and theoretical activity and science the more
practical and immediately useful one; something like the modern
distinction between pure and applied science.[1] However this does
not necessarily mean that he, and other eighteenth-century thinkers,
were unconscious of the modern contrast between philosophy and
science, but only that they did not use these labels to mark this
particular conceptual distinction. This can be demonstrated from
Smith's own writings.

In the *Wealth of Nations*, for instance, he notes with approval the
Greek division of 'philosophy' or 'science' into 'physics or natural
philosophy; ethics, or moral philosophy; and logic'.[2] It is therefore
tempting to think that, in modern terms, he should be understood
to mean that natural philosophy is science, and that moral philosophy

[1] T.M.S., VII.iii. Introd. (II.325); VII.iii.1 (II.326f.); and W.N., I.i. (I.14).
[2] W.N., V.i.3.art.2 (II.290).

27

together with logic go to make up philosophy. But this is too simple a solution: at a time when social science had not yet separated itself from its philosophical origins, moral philosophy and logic embraced economics, sociology, political science and psychology as well as the logical and epistemological issues of modern philosophy. The boundary between science and philosophy is, therefore, to be found *within* eighteenth-century moral philosophy and logic, and not between these subjects and natural philosophy. In fact I shall argue that, in Adam Smith's case, moral philosophy is largely of a scientific nature, and that he was well aware of this himself.

Smith's concept of philosophy, in the modern sense of a discipline which is independent from science, is rarely made explicit. His discussions of metaphysics are largely historical in character and represent it as a forerunner and a rival to science as much as a distinct type of study. He classifies Plato's theory of Ideas, for instance, as metaphysics, and criticizes it for involving an *a priori* method of searching for knowledge about the world.[1] A similar point is made, not about metaphysics as such, but about excessive concentration on metaphysics, in the *Wealth of Nations*, where he discusses the content of university education. Here metaphysics is made out to be the study of invisible things, allied to theology, in contrast to physics which studies visible objects or 'bodies'. Smith laments that the study of bodies, which is 'The proper subject for experiment and observation, a subject in which a careful attention is capable of making so many useful discoveries', had been 'almost entirely neglected'; whereas 'the subject in which, after a very few simple and almost obvious truths, the most careful attention can discover nothing but obscurity and uncertainty, and can consequently produce nothing but subtleties and sophisms', was being 'greatly cultivated'.[2] The scarcely concealed implication is that metaphysics is an unimportant pre-scientific activity of significance only to those who have an interest in theology.

As regards the other branches of philosophy, Smith seems to have been in no doubt that logic is 'the science of the general principles of good and bad reasoning',[3] a normative study whose purpose is to determine which types of argument are valid and which are fallacious, although he does not appear to have thought that there was a great deal which needed to be said on this subject. We shall be concerned later with Smith's detailed views on moral philosophy, but for the moment we will simply note his awareness that ancient moral

1 E.P.S. (H.A.L. & M.), p. 123.
2 W.N., V.i.3.art.2 (II.293).
3 W.N., V.i.3.art.2 (II.292).

28

philosophy had attempted to answer both quasi-normative and empirical questions. For, although he asserts that the question 'Wherein consisted the happiness and perfection of a man'[1] was central to the thought of ancient moral philosophers, he also points out that the ancients attempted to apply the methods of natural philosophy to the study of morality, so that 'the maxims of common life were arranged in some methodical order, and connected together by a few common principles, in the same manner as they had attempted to arrange and connect the phenomena of nature'.[2]

II. TYPES OF DISCOURSE

We have passed fairly quickly over what Smith has to say about the various branches of what would today be recognized as philosophy, for it would be difficult, and anachronistic, to try to demonstrate that he has a particularly modern view of the nature of philosophy. But this is much less the case with respect to his understanding of science. The evidence for this contention, which is fundamental to the thesis that the *Moral Sentiments* is a self-conscious attempt to formulate a scientific theory of morality, is to be found in his *Lectures on Rhetoric and Belles Lettres*, and, more particularly, in his *Essays on Philosophical Subjects*. Seen together these books provide important guidelines for the analysis of Smith's principal works.

The *Lectures on Rhetoric* outline the different types of discourse and the style of presentation most appropriate to each of them, while the *Essays* discuss in detail the development of a few examples of a particular type of discourse, the scientific one. The essay which deals with the history of astronomy is particularly important because it shows Smith's acute insight into the nature of the advances which had been made up to that time in a subject which was, even then, indisputably scientific in the modern sense. An examination of this early work indicates that it is quite wrong to suggest that, even if Smith was scientific in his method, he did not have the explicit awareness of the nature of science which is necessary to produce a systematic scientific treatise.[3]

The united theme of the *Lectures on Rhetoric* is the need to adapt the style of writing to the intentions of the author:

'. . . the perfection of style consists in express[ing] in the most

---

[1] W.N., V.i.3.art.2 (II.293).
[2] W.N., V.i.3.art.2 (II.291); cf. p. 51f.
[3] This contention is put forward by Jacob D. Hollander, in an essay 'The Dawn of Science' in *Adam Smith, 1776-1926*.

concise, proper, and precise manner the thought of the author, and that in the manner which best conveys the sentiment, passion, or affection with which it affects—or he pretends it does affect—him, and which he designs to communicate to his reader.'[1]

These different intentions show themselves in different types of discourse. Smith classifies these by means of two important distinctions. The first distinction is between historical narrative and what could be called 'reasoned discourse'. Historical narrative confines itself to relating particular facts of interest and importance and placing these in a temporal or causal sequence. What I have called reasoned discourse argues to a conclusion or conclusions.

The second important distinction is within reasoned discourse. On the one hand there is the objective type of discourse which presents arguments for and against a conclusion and discusses their relative weight: this Smith calls didactic discourse.[2] On the other hand, if the argument is one-sided and aims at persuasion rather than a critical assessment, then this is called rhetoric:

'Every discourse proposes either barely to relate some fact or to prove some proposition. The first is the kind of discourse called a narrative one; the latter is the foundation of two sorts of discourses, the didactic and the rhetorical. The former proposes to put before us the arguments on both sides of the question in their true light, giving each its proper degree of influence, and has it in view to persuade no further than the arguments themselves appear convincing. The rhetorical, again, endeavours by all means to persuade us, and for this purpose it magnifies all the arguments on the one side, and diminishes or conceals those that might be brought on the side contrary to that which it is designed that we should favour.'[3]

Philosophy and science, therefore, must both be forms of didactic discourse. History may also be didactic if it presents conflicting arguments about the accuracy and truth of alleged historical facts.[4] In this case the distinction between philosophy and science on the one hand and history on the other is that history deals with particular events while philosophy and science deal with types of event.[5]

[1] L.R.B.L., p. 51.
[2] This should not be confused with the modern concept of 'normative'.
[3] L.R.B.L., p. 58.
[4] L.R.B.L., pp. 84ff.
[5] E.P.S. (H.A.L. & M.), p. 117: 'In every case, therefore, Species, or Universals, and not Individuals, are the objects of Philosophy.'

The *Lectures on Rhetoric* do not help us to distinguish between science and philosophy but they do have something to say about the style of presentation suited to didactic discourse and thus to both science and philosophy. Smith considers that a didactic discourse may either start by presenting a collection of facts about different specific subjects and proceed to explain these facts by reference to separate principles, or begin with a few general principles and go on to illustrate and prove these in different areas:

'Either, first, we lay down one or a very few principles by which we explain the several rules or phenomena, connecting one with the other in a natural order; or else we begin with telling that we are to explain such and such things, and for each advance a principle either different or the same with those which went before.'[1]

The former Smith calls the 'Newtonian method'. He declares it to be the 'more philosophical' if we, like Newton, 'lay down certain principles, primary or proved, in the beginning, from whence we account for the several phenomena, connecting all together by the same chain',[2] and adds that 'in every science, whether of morals or natural philosophy' this method is 'vastly more ingenious'.

But this does not mean that he restricts this style of presentation to science in the modern sense. The 'Newtonian method' applies to all didactic discourse and this includes the *a priori* methods of Descartes as well as the empirical ones of Newton; it is the method of presentation which is most appropriate to any objective argument which sets out to establish the truth of a proposition, whether scientific or otherwise. It would appear to have been the method at which he aims in the *Moral Sentiments* which begins with a statement of the principle or principles of sympathy which he then goes on to apply to different areas of social life. The *Wealth of Nations* is nearer to the alternative method which Smith calls 'Aristotelian'.

Smith took more from Newton than his form of presentation; he also saw what it was about Newton's general method that made his approach particularly important. It is in the *Essays* that we can see just how far Smith saw empirical science as a distinct species of didactic discourse. These essays are primarily an attempt to give a scientific explanation for the progress of science by reference to the

[1] L.R.B.L., p. 139.
[2] L.R.B.L., p. 140.

31

psychological needs and the social environment which prompt and permit men to undertake scientific investigations. However, in the course of his discussion Smith arrives at an interpretation of the nature of science which corresponds closely to what is now called the hypothetico-deductive model of the nature of scientific inquiry.[1] This theory holds that science progresses through testing hypothetical generalizations about the connections between observed events. A proposition is scientific if it is possible to deduce from it other propositions which state under what conditions a particular observable event will take place;[2] if, given the conditions, the event does occur then the proposition is corroborated; if it does not occur as prediction, then the proposition is falsified; if no predictions can be deduced from the proposition, or if the predictions, like those of the astrologer, are so vague as to be compatible with any combination of observable events, then it is not a scientific proposition at all. This is usually presented as a logical thesis, designed to bring out what is distinctive and central to the scientific method of proof,[3] but Smith incorporates it in a psychological and sociological explanation of the development of science.

'The clew that is most capable of conducting us through all the labyrinths of philosophical history' Smith wrote in the 'History of Astronomy', is that all generally accepted scientific theories have owed their success to their ability to 'sooth the imagination'.[4] Unfamiliar and unexpected objects and events disturb the imagination: 'What is new and singular, excites that sentiment which, in strict propriety, is called Wonder; what is unexpected, Surprise'.[5] Both these emotions are unpleasant and even, on occasion, painful to the extent of manifesting themselves in alarming physical

[1] For recent discussions of Smith's method which take into account the evidence of the *Essays*, cf. H. J. Bittermann, 'Adam Smith's Empiricism and the Law of Nature', *Journal of Political Economy*, vol. XLVIII (1940), pp. 487-520 and 703-37; O. H. Taylor, *A History of Economic Thought* (New York, 1960); J. F. Becker, 'Adam Smith's Theory of Social Science', *Southern Economic Journal*, vol. XXVIII (1961), pp. 13-21; H. F. Thomson, 'Adam Smith's Philosophy of Science', *Quarterly Journal of Economics*, vol. LXXIX (1965), pp. 212-33; and J. L. Lindgren, 'Adam Smith's Theory of Inquiry', *Journal of Political Economy*, vol. LXXVII (1969), pp. 897-915.

[2] In a stronger sense of 'science' these predictions must be part of a system of propositions which have actually been corroborated.

[3] Cf. K. Popper, *The Logic of Scientific Discovery* (London, 1959).

[4] E.P.S. (H.A.), p. 21. Smith was particularly pleased with this essay and wished it to be published. Originally written in the 1750s, it was probably revised after 1773 and can, therefore, be taken as important evidence for his methodological outlook; cf. Rae, *op. cit.*, p. 262.

[5] E.P.S. (H.A.), p. 2.

symptoms.[1] In seeking to free themselves from these disturbing mental states men try to find explanations for the phenomena whose appearances have caused them distress. The function of an explanation is to restore the imagination to its usual smooth and tranquil state.[2] Further, if the explanation is sufficiently comprehensive, it will give rise to the pleasing emotion of admiration, which is aroused by contemplation of 'what is great or beautiful'. These sentiments of wonder, surprise and admiration combine to provide the psychological motivation for scientific research.[3] Wonder and surprise trouble the imagination and develop scientific curiosity; scientific theories serve to quieten the imagination; and the whole enterprise is crowned with the pleasing sentiment of admiration.

These psychological spurs to scientific endeavour do not bear fruit unless the social conditions are suitable. To account for the emergence of science at particular times and places Smith adds to his theory of the psychology of science, the sociological theory that scientific progress cannot take place 'before the establishment of law, order, and security'.[4] In the 'first stages of society' and in disturbed periods such as that which followed the fall of the Roman empire[5] men did not have that combination of physical security, leisure and wealth, which are required to provide a suitable environment for scientific work. More pressing and obvious distresses overshadowed the uneasy sensations of wonder and surprise while 'those more magnificent irregularities, whose grandeur he [the savage] cannot overlook' impel him to suppose 'that they proceed from some intelligent, though invisible cause'[6] but do not lead to scientific speculation. Benign events give rise to a belief in favourable deities and terrifying ones to a belief in evil spirits. Thus the same emotions of wonder and surprise that stimulate scientific reasoning

---

[1] Ibid., p. 12: 'It is this fluctuation and vain recollection, together with the emotion or movement of the spirits that they excite, which constitute the sentiment properly called *Wonder*, and which occasion that staring, and sometimes that rolling of the eyes, that suspension of the breath, and that swelling of the heart, which we may all observe, both in ourselves and others, when wondering at some new object, and which are the natural symptoms of uncertain and undetermined thought.'

[2] Ibid., p. 20: Tranquillity, as we shall see, is an important psychological state in Smith's theory. The influence here is probably Locke's; cf. *An Essay Concerning Human Understanding* (1690), II.xxi.Sec. 33f.

[3] Ibid., p. 26: 'Wonder, therefore, and not any expectation of advantage from its discoveries, is the first principle which prompts mankind to the study of Philosophy.'

[4] E.P.S. (H.A.), p. 23. A similar precondition is given for the development of commerce, cf. W.N., IV.vii.2 (II.76).

[5] E.P.S. (H.A.), p. 46.   [6] E.P.S. (H.A.), p. 26.

in more settled and prosperous times account for the prevalence of polytheism in primitive societies. It was not until the political and economic conditions which were attained in 'Greece and the Greek colonies in Sicily, Italy and the Lesser Asia'[1] that the scientific outlook could flourish, and it is from this era that Smith begins his historical survey of astronomical and physical theories.

III. THE FAMILIARITY THEORY

In the course of this survey Smith expounds an interesting version of the familiarity theory of explanation; this theory postulates that an event is explained when it has been classified as, or compared to, something with which we are familiar. However, in Smith's case, this turns out to be a psychological version of the regularity or covering-law theory. This latter theory states that an event has been explained when it has been shown to be an instance of a general law; or, expressing this in the terms of the hypothetico-deductive theory, which is a type of covering-law theory, an event is explained if its occurrence could have been deduced from an established empirical hypothesis which states under what conditions such events take place.

What is familiar, Smith points out, does not require an explanation; it is accepted as being in the nature of things.[2] To explain the novel and uncommon phenomena which excite wonder and surprise it is necessary, therefore, to relate them to something that *is* familiar. Men 'naturally explained things to themselves by principles that were familiar to themselves'.[3] This is why classification helps to explain these things, for 'it is evident that the mind takes pleasure in observing the resemblances that are discoverable betwixt different objects'.[4] Even although such classifications add nothing to our knowledge of the object concerned 'yet we are apt to fancy that by being able to do so, we show ourselves to be better acquainted with it, and to have a more thorough insight into its nature'.[5] Just as the uneasy wonder aroused by the appearance of an unfamiliar object is allayed by the discovery that this object is similar to a more familiar one, so the surprise which is occasioned by an event which, however familiar in itself, does not fit into a common sequence of events, requires to be mollified by showing that it is part of a sequence of events similar to one with which we are familiar.

Both these tendencies, the tendency to classify and the tendency to relate one object to another in a familiar type of sequence, are explained by the theory of the association of ideas. Smith includes

[1] E.P.S. (H.A.), p. 26.   [2] E.P.S. (H.A.), p. 19.   [3] E.P.S. (H.A.), p. 22.
[4] E.P.S. (H.A.), p. 10.   [5] E.P.S. (H.A.), p. 11.

34

amongst the fundamental principles of the human mind the tendency for the imagination to pass from one idea to another similar idea or to one which has been frequently presented to the senses in close temporal and spatial proximity to the first idea. This latter 'habit of the imagination' is strengthened by the constant repetition of the sequence of events and, when it is established, takes place without effort or mental disturbance.[1] This is the condition of tranquillity: a state of smooth operation rather than rest. Because the speed of this operation is greater than that of the succession of external objects, the perception of the first object leads, by the smooth operation of the imagination, to the anticipation of its successors. We might say that the association of ideas involves the imagination in the subconscious prediction of the immediate future. It is only when these expectations cannot continue because some unknown object presents itself to the senses or the anticipated events do not take place because events present themselves in an unusual order, that the flow of ideas is halted and the mind seeks for some explanation which will return the imagination to its normal course.

In presenting this familiarity theory of the nature of scientific explanation Smith does not claim that scientific explanations are straightforward expressions of the truth. His intention is to explain *why* science is explanatory, that is, why the mind is satisfied with scientific explanations: this is a psychological question and Smith provides a logically appropriate type of answer: 'philosophy', he declares, is 'one of those arts which address themselves to the imagination'.[2] He does not, therefore, claim any ultimate metaphysical validity for the established hypotheses of science, any more than, in his essay 'Of the External Senses', he claims that sense perception is to be trusted beyond its usefulness in the practical affairs of life.[3]

Yet despite this stress on the causal explanation of scientific

---

[1] E.P.S. (H.A.), p. 14. In a passage in which Smith comes closest to Hume's theory of the association of ideas he writes: 'When two objects, however unlike, have often been observed to follow each other, and have constantly presented themselves to the senses in that order, they come to be so connected together in the fancy, that the idea of the one seems, of its own accord, to call up and introduce that of the other.'   [2] E.P.S. (H.A.), p. 20.

[3] One of the essays contained in the posthumous collection entitled *Essays on Philosophical Subjects*. On p. 227 Smith writes, on the lines of Berkeley's *New Theory of Vision*: 'As, in common language, the words or sounds bear no resemblance to the things which they denote, so, in this other language, the visible objects bear no sort of resemblance to the tangible object which they represent.' cf. J. R. Lindgren 'Adam Smith's Theory of Inquiry', *Journal of Political Economy*, vol. 77 (1969), pp. 897-915. Lindgren is right to stress that Smith is not an epistemological realist, but wrong to imply that this undermines Smith's clear distinction between observation and imagination.

progress and his relative indifference to the ultimate truth value of science, Smith's theory turns out to be paralleled, in most respects, by logical theories of the nature of science. For instance, Smith notes the psychological tendency to anticipate familiar sequences of events and the irritation that results if we cannot do this. Science steps in to help, when common sense fails to aid the imagination, by relating the unfamiliar to the familiar: for this reason he defines 'philosophy' as 'the science of the connection principles of nature'.[1] Translated into logical terms this is identical to the view that science establishes general statements of the form 'If *a* then b' where *a* is one type of event or set of events, and *b* is another type of event or set of events. Thus, instead of the psychological law that, when the mind perceives *a*, the imagination passes to the idea of *b*, we have a generalization of the form 'if *a*, then *b*' from which it is possible to predict when *b* will occur, but instead of saying that the occurrence of *b* is explained if the sequence 'whenever *a* then *b*' is a familiar one, the covering-law theory requires that the generalization has been tested and shown to be true. Since this involves the observation of many instances of *a* being followed by *b* and no instances in which *a* has not been followed by *b* this amounts to very much the same thing as saying that the sequence must be a familiar one. We may say, therefore, that the regularity theory and the familiarity theory adopted by Smith complement each other, the former giving the logical requirements of a scientific explanation and the latter giving the psychological reasons why scientific explanations are accepted.

In making the everyday activities of classification and generalization the initial steps in scientific thinking Smith does full justice to the continuity of scientific and common sense explanations. The principles involved are substantially the same as those which feature in his 'Considerations concerning the first Formation of Languages'. Moreover he is conscious of the place which inductive procedures have at this elementary level in science. The association of ideas leads men to believe that if *b* has followed *a* in the past it will do so in the future, that is, it accounts for the fact that men who have observed that on many occasions *b* had followed *a*, tend to conclude that *a* is *always* followed by *b*. In logical terms this psychological process becomes the inductive procedure of arguing from the some to all, a procedure which is justified by inductive logic, and called simple enumeration, because it consists of the accumulation of many observations which confirm a generalization. Smith assumes that inductive procedures of this sort are one of the

[1] E.P.S. (H.A.), p. 20.

normal operations of reason[1] and are the basic methods by which we learn from experience.[2]

However, while induction enables men to escape from the particular to the general and to make limited predictions about the future from experience of the past, the explanatory power of such generalizations is limited. To explain that *this* piece of wood floats in water because *all* pieces of wood float in water, merely leads on to the next question; why does wood float? Another source of dissatisfaction with low-level generalizations of this sort is that they are not connected together, but seem haphazard and fragmentary. Everyday inductive procedures are therefore insufficient to provide the 'connecting principles' which are required to explain common-sense generalizations.

Smith indicates how science transcends the limitations of simple inductive procedures by pointing out that the scientist is not content with a sequence of observed events if, however familiar that sequence is in itself, it is not similar to other observed sequences. The example he gives is that of the piece of iron which moves along the table towards a lodestone.[3] Familiarity with this happening does not fully overcome the difficulty which the imagination feels in passing from the idea of a magnet being placed on a table to the idea of the movement of a piece of iron toward it: the movement may be expected but it is not fully explained, for the imagination is not able to relate this phenomenon to others with which it is even more familiar. In order to do this science has to leave behind the method of simple induction and resort to a hypothesis which will explain this phenomenon by suggesting how it is related to others. In terms of the covering-law theory it is necessary to explain scientific facts, which state regularities observed to hold between observable events, by establishing a more general connection between phenomena from which such facts can be deduced;[4] it is necessary to move

---

[1] T.M.S., VII.iii.2 (II.337): 'The general maxims of morality are formed, like all other general maxims, from experience and induction. We observe in a great variety of particular cases what pleases or displeases our moral faculties, what these approve or disapprove of, and, by induction from this experience, we establish those general rules. But induction is always regarded as one of the operations of reason.'

[2] E.P.S., pp. 229ff discusses the role of observation and experience in the co-ordination of perceptions in infants.   [3] E.P.S. (H.A.), p. 15.

[4] Smith expresses the matter in this way in W.N., V.i.3.art.2 (II.291) in comparing the aims of moral philosophy and physics where he says of ancient moral philosophy that it tended 'to multiply the number of those maxims of prudence and morality, without even attempting . . . to connect them together by one or more general principles, from which they were all deducible, like effects from their natural causes'.

from the level of describing facts to formulating laws, which are at once more abstract and more general.

The move to a higher level of abstraction and generalization is, for Smith, a move from placing an event in sequence with another event, to comparing sequences of events themselves. In order to do this the scientist has to go beyond relating observed phenomena and suggest hypotheses about the unobserved connections between events. Returning to the example of the lodestone, a scientific hypothesis is one which connects the two ideas, that of the lodestone and that of the movement of the iron towards it, by suggesting an invisible chain of events which act as a bridge over which the imagination can pass. To be effective as a bridge the hypothesis must suggest an invisible sequence of events which is comparable to a visible sequence of events with which we are very familiar; in this way the strange sequence of events is explained by being shown to be an instance of a more common and more general type of connection:

'. . . when, with Des Cartes, we imagine certain invisible effluvia to circulate round one of them, and by their repeated impulses to impel the other, both to move towards it, and to follow its action, we fill up the interval betwixt them, we join them together by a sort of bridge, and thus take off that hesitation and difficulty which the imagination felt in passing from the one to the other. That the iron should move after the lodestone seems, upon this hypothesis, in some measure according to the ordinary course of things. Motion after impulse is an order of succession with which of all things we are the most familiar.'[1]

A good hypothesis thus 'fills the gap' between seemingly unconnected events. A series of related hypotheses constitutes a 'system' because they enable us to connect a large number of disparate events and reduce them to some sort of coherence.

This shows that Smith knew the importance of theorizing in science; that is, he saw the need for a complete scientific explanation to go beyond the recording of observable relations and to suggest a model from which a wide variety of observable events can be deduced.[2] Smith describes how, in astronomy, the 'system' or theory of concentric spheres, taught in Italy before the time of Aristotle, held that the sun, the moon, the five planets and the

---

[1] E.P.S. (H.A.), p. 16.
[2] Cf. The economic theory of the *Wealth of Nations* enables him to counter the simple minded mercantilist argument that because prosperity has followed the introduction of mercantilist laws that these laws must be the cause of the prosperity. W.N., IV.v (II.50).

remainder of the stars each had a solid sphere to which they were attached. The virtue of this theory was that 'though rude and in-artificial, it is capable of connecting together, in the imagination, the grandest and the most seemingly disjointed appearances in the heavens'.[1] By providing 'a connecting chain of intermediate events'[2] between observed phenomena, the imagination can find a satisfactory link between the movements of the heavenly bodies, and by positing unobserved mechanisms and chains of invisible connections which are 'the mere inventions of the imagination',[3] science goes far beyond the compilation of observed connections between events. This is the creative element in scientific progress. It represents Smith's version of the 'bold ideas, unjustified anticipations and speculative thought' which Popper believes to be 'our only way for interpreting nature'.[4]

IV. SCIENTIFIC CRITERIA

Smith's history of astronomical theories demonstrates that he considers one theory to be superior to another if it is more successful in soothing the imagination. But he also sees that it must accord more exactly with observed phenomena than any alternative theory. In the end this last condition is the decisive one, although all theories must go some way towards pleasing the imagination, and, other things being equal, the theory which is the most pleasing to the imagination is preferred. As far as the psychological criteria are concerned the basic test of a theory is whether or not it connects as large as possible a number of observed events in the simplest and most familiar way. The first criterion of a good scientific theory is, therefore, that it connects or renders more coherent a large number of apparently dissimilar phenomena. On this score the 'system of concentric, and that of eccentric spheres' which suggested that some of the spheres did not have the earth for their centre, and thus explained many of the motions of the planets which were 'irregular' in that they did not fit in with the original theory of concentric spheres, was preferred to that of Cleanthes and the Stoics who were 'at a loss to connect together the peculiarities that are observed in the motions of the other heavenly bodies'.[5] At a later time the theory of Copernicus replaced that of Ptolemy partly because 'this new

---

[1] E.P.S. (H.A.), pp. 31f.   [2] E.P.S. (H.A.), p. 16.
[3] E.P.S. (H.A.), p. 93; cf. p. 44. 'A system is an imaginary machine invented to connect together in the fancy those different movements and effects which are already in reality performed.'
[4] *The Logic of Scientific Discovery*, p. 280.
[5] E.P.S. (H.A.), p. 42.

account of things render[ed] the appearances of the heavens more completely coherent than had been done by any of the former systems'.[1]

The second criterion is that a hypothesis or system must be *simple*. Since one of the primary functions of a scientific theory is to reduce the complexities of nature to a few familiar principles, any theory which becomes so complex that the imagination no longer finds it of any assistance has to be abandoned in favour of a more simple theory. A good theory, like a new machine, may start off being fairly complex but, as it improves, it should become more stream-lined.[2] But if, on the other hand, a simple theory has to be subjected to many modifications, then this creates the need for a new theory. The theory of concentric spheres started as a simple theory, but, in order to fit in with the appearances of the heavens, the number of spheres had to be increased to seventy-two, and the attractiveness of the theory was reduced until it could be simplified again by the introduction of the hypothesis of eccentric spheres.[3] Similarly the theory of Copernicus which made the earth move round the sun not only accounted for more observed facts than previous theories but 'it did this, too, by a more simple and intelligible, as well as more beautiful machinery'.[4]

Thirdly, a theory which is to be acceptable to the imagination must suggest a simple hypothesis of a type which is *familiar;* the invisible chains which it uses to bind events together must be of a sort which have common visible counterparts. In practice this is a demand that all scientific theories must suggest some mechanical analogy, an invisible *machine* behind the scenes whose workings result in the motions of visible objects.[5] This is the criterion which Smith stresses most when he is explaining the psychological causes of the acceptance and rejection of theories: 'No system, how well soever in other respects supported, has ever been able to gain any general credit on the world, whose connecting principles were not such as were familiar to all mankind.'[6] He attributes the failure of chemistry to its inability to discover such connecting principles.[6] And, again, the theory of Copernicus was rejected for a long time because it seemed to go against many of the familiar evidences of the senses which imply that the world is at rest.[7] It was not until Galileo

---

[1] E.P.S. (H.A.), p. 54. [2] E.P.S. (H.A.), p. 44.
[3] E.P.S. (H.A.), p. 36: 'This system had now become as intricate and complex as those appearances themselves, which it had been invented to render uniform and coherent.'
[4] E.P.S. (H.A.), p. 54. [5] E.P.S. (H.A.), pp. 44f.
[6] E.P.S. (H.A.), p. 21. [7] E.P.S. (H.A.), p. 64.

related the theory to familiar examples of objects moving relative to the earth, but not to each other, that it gained wide acceptance.[1]

By insisting that all scientific theories must stick to familiar mechanisms of nature Smith was encouraged by the success of Newton's system and the extreme familiarity of the phenomenon of gravity. Like many thinkers of the period he assumed that this would be the model for all scientific theories. This enabled him to avoid addressing himself to the major problem of the familiarity theory of explanation, namely the difficulty it has in accounting for the emergence of new types of explanatory theory. For Smith a new theory is explanatory only if it is based on an analogy with a familiar mechanism. The progress of science has demonstrated that this is too constricting a requirement, and in particular that the demand that all theories should be a type of mechanical analogy became in the end a sterile methodological principle. However, it should be noted that Smith emphasized the familiarity criterion most in the context of explaining the popularity of scientific theories and, as we shall see, it drops into the background when he discusses the experts' attitude to their investigations.[2]

Smith's essay 'On the History of Astronomy' does not confine itself to stressing the qualities which a scientific theory must have in order to appeal to the imagination. This, in itself, would leave the field open for uncontrolled speculations which, because of their subjective nature,[3] would result in extensive and incorrigible disagreements. But Smith notes that, however well a theory satisfies imaginative and therefore aesthetic criteria, it is rejected if it does not fit the observed facts. The creative aspect of scientific endeavour, suggesting hypotheses and formulating theories, is controlled by the ability of the scientist to demonstrate that his intellectual inventions can be used to describe and predict appearances in the world of sense perception. Imaginative appeal is necessary for a theory, but it is by no means sufficient.

The close relationship that Smith builds up between theory and observation begins with the assertion that it is on account of the wonder and surprise aroused by the visible and tangible world that

[1] E.P.S. (H.A.), p. 65.
[2] E.P.S. (H.A.), p. 83: 'When the observations of Cassini had established the authority of those laws, which Kepler had first discovered in the system, the philosophy of Des Cartes, which could afford no reason why such particular laws should be observed, might continue to amuse the learned in other sciences, but could no longer satisfy those that were skilled in Astronomy.'
[3] E.P.S. (H.A.), p. 18: 'such orders of succession are familiar to the one, and strange to the other'.

41

scientific explanations are sought in the first place. The purpose of theory is to explain the appearances of nature. In the first stages of science the curiosity which is aroused by unusual phenomena and the desire to find unnoticed regularities in nature, leads to much closer scrutiny of phenomena. This, in turn, results in the observation of more irregularities and surprising events. The scientist comes to wonder at, and be surprised by, things which the casual observer takes for granted. The botanist sees more differences as well as more similarities between plants.[1] The astronomer notices that the planets do not move in perfect circles and other 'irregularities' of the heavens,[2] while 'A philosopher, who has spent his whole life in the study of the connecting principles of nature, will often feel an interval betwixt two objects, which, to more careless observers, seem very strictly conjoined.'[3] These detailed observations are challenges to further scientific thinking; they are one cause of the creative stage of hypothesis and theory formation.

However, the observation of natural processes is not merely the beginning of scientific theorizing, it is also its logical conclusion. Scientific theories are *tested* by their power to predict observed events. The more numerous and accurate their predictions, the more satisfactory the theory. As Smith develops the history of astronomy from its commonsense beginnings to its most sophisticated achievements, this requirement comes to the fore. Thus the early form of the system of concentric spheres could not account for the motions of the sun and moon, which are 'such as cannot be discovered but by the most attentive observation', and, after extensive modifications to accommodate the theory to these observations, it had to be abandoned.[4] Similarly the tables of Ptolemy 'having, upon account of the inaccuracy of the observations on which they were founded, become altogether wide of the real situation of the heavenly bodies', became useless.[5] The system of Copernicus was not only more simple than its predecessors, it also coincided with the observed irregular movements of the planets.[6] Smith acknowledged the advances made in science by the development of new and more precise instruments of observation,[7] and by the ability to discover numerical relationships between observed events and so enable more precision to be introduced into hypotheses and predictions.

[1] E.P.S. (H.A.), p. 11.   [2] E.P.S. (H.A.), p. 82.

[3] E.P.S. (H.A.), p. 20.

[4] E.P.S. (H.A.), p. 34. Smith realized that theories are not often falsified by a single observation but suffer death from a thousand modifications.

[5] E.P.S. (H.A.), p. 49.   [6] E.P.S. (H.A.), p. 54.

[7] E.P.S. (H.A.), p. 47; cf. pp. 79, 93 and 66: 'His [Copernicus] telescopes rendered the phases of Venus quite sensible.'

Astronomy is not, or at least was not until the advent of man-made satellites, a subject which lends itself to experiment in the sense of the creation of a controlled situation for the purposes of observing what will happen or for testing hypotheses. Yet it has its logical equivalents in the practices of making observations from different places on the earth's surface and in predicting uncommon appearances in the heavens. Smith stresses several important examples of this sort of 'experiment'. He notes, for instance, that 'the observations of Astronomers at Lapland and Peru have fully confirmed Sir Isaac's system',[1] and discusses the prediction, advanced from theory, that since Venus and Mercury revolved round the sun they would show the same phases as the moon, which was confirmed by the observations of Galileo.[2] Similarly the mathematical relations which Kepler suggested might hold between the periodic times of the planets and their distances from the sun, although they had little appeal for the imagination, were nevertheless established by the observations which confirmed them.[3]

In another interesting example which shows that Smith realized the extent to which accurate prediction is more important than facile imaginative satisfaction, he describes how the yearning of the imagination for nature to conform to perfect circles, which supported the system of Descartes, was overruled by observations which showed that the circles of the planets were irregular: this confirmed the system of Copernicus from which these irregularities could be deduced.[4]

It is clear, therefore, that, like Popper, Smith saw that science was 'imaginative and bold conjectures or anticipations . . . carefully and soberly controlled by systematic tests'.[5] His account of the development of astronomy, which illustrates the continuous dialectic between imaginative hypotheses and observations of irregularities, concludes with an outline of the superiority of Newton's system over all previous ones. In this he shows that Newton's theory had all the virtues which attract the imagination: simplicity, comprehensiveness, and familiarity. Newton is said to have made 'the greatest, and most admirable improvement in philosophy . . . when he discovered that he could join together the movements of the planets by so familiar a principle of connection, which completely

---

[1] E.P.S. (H.A.), p. 88.   [2] E.P.S. (H.A.), p. 66.
[3] E.P.S. (H.A.), p. 68.
[4] E.P.S. (H.A.), p. 82: Descartes 'had never himself observed the Heavens with any particular application', and his theory connected the motions of the planets 'in the gross; but did not apply to them, when they were regarded in the detail'.
[5] K. Popper, *The Logic of Scientific Discovery*, p. 279.

removed all the difficulties the imagination had hitherto felt in attending to them';[1] the principle was, of course, 'the simple and familiar fact of gravitation'.

But the superiority of Newton's system lay even more in the precision with which the appearances of the heavens could be deduced from the invisible mechanism which he suggested: 'Sir Isaac Newton computed the difference of the forces, with which the Moon and the Earth ought, in all those different situations, according to his theory, to be impelled towards one another; and found, that the different degrees of their approaches, as they had been observed by Astronomers, corresponded exactly to his computations.'[2] These different forces are in precise mathematical terms and the deduction of the appearances from the principles are not 'general and loose' but are 'the most precise and particular that can be imagined'.[3] They have frequently been confirmed and Smith notes that, at the time of writing, astronomers are waiting to see if the predicted appearance of a comet actually takes place; a later footnote is inserted to report 'that the return of the comet happened agreeably to the prediction'.[4]

Smith's admiration for Newton's theory draws from him the admission that, in this case at least, a scientific theory may be describing 'the real chains which Nature makes use of to bind together her several operations.'[5] This seems to follow from its power to make detailed and accurate astronomical predictions. There are other places in the essay where he hints that, while psychological laws determine if a theory will receive popular acceptance, it is the extent to which a theory accords with observed facts that determines its truth. In explaining that chemistry has been 'disregarded by the generality of mankind' because of the unfamiliarity of its principles, he does not suggest that these are not 'agreeable with experience'.[6] Again, while the mathematical connections between planetary movements suggested by Kepler were for a long time too 'intricate and difficult to be comprehended' and this delayed their acceptance, Smith relates how observation eventually showed them to be true.[7] Moreover, the imaginative criteria, while necessary for the advance of science, can be positively misleading in that they encourage men to assume that the world is more regular and simple than it really is.[8]

---

[1] E.P.S. (H.A.), p. 84.   [2] E.P.S. (H.A.), p. 86.
[3] E.P.S. (H.A.), p. 92.   [4] E.P.S. (H.A.), p. 90.
[5] E.P.S. (H.A.), p. 93. This point, and the general requirement that a scientific theory account for *detailed* observations, seems to have been overlooked by H. F. Thomson, *op. cit.*, pp. 219ff and J. L. Lindgren, *op. cit.*, pp. 903ff.
[6] E.P.S. (H.A.), p. 20.   [7] E.P.S. (H.A.), pp. 72f.   [8] E.P.S. (H.A.P.), p. 99.

We can say, then, that when Smith moves from explaining the popular progress of scientific knowledge to an assessment of the reasons which are, in the last analysis, decisive for scientific truth, he stresses the importance of detailed correspondence between the deductive consequences of theories and observations of the phenomena which they purport to explain. This does not mean that he thought that science could ever outgrow the need for creative theorizing, but only that these theories which satisfy the imagination must also accord with the observed facts if they are to gain widespread and lasting acceptance by those experts who are intimately acquainted with the relevant subject matter. The aesthetic criteria which are met by those theories which allay the puzzlement of wonder and evoke the admiration of the scientist require to be supplemented by the more objective tests of precise empirical observation.

The repeated stress which Smith places on the criterion of familiarity and the connection of this with the doctrine of the association of ideas are the main ways in which his account diverges from the consensus of modern philosophy of science. Simplicity and comprehensiveness are still frequently mentioned as features of a good scientific theory, and the place of imaginative conjecture in guiding empirical observation is widely accepted. But the requirement that an explanation be given in terms of what is familiar to the layman is usually confined to analyses of the nature of commonsense explanations and is more characteristic of popularizations of science than of its sophisticated theories. Nevertheless, we have seen how much of what Smith puts in terms of 'familiarity' can be translated into the logical terms of the covering-law theory. Where this is not the case, as with Smith's insistence that all scientific theories must consist of mechanical analogies drawn from everyday experience, it has to be admitted that his imaginative foresight into the nature of future scientific progress was, understandably, limited. This does not affect his basic insight into the role of theorizing as a link between the observations which provoke scientific hypotheses and those which confirm them. Even if we might want to say that science appeals more to the intellect than to the imagination, Smith's analysis of the nature of scientific progress is sufficiently modern for us to say that he had a remarkable grasp of the logic of scientific method.

CHAPTER 2

SOCIAL SCIENCE OR SOCIAL PHILOSOPHY?

Adequate evidence had now been presented to justify the view that Adam Smith was sufficiently aware of the nature of modern science to make it reasonable to ask whether he saw his own work, and particularly the *Moral Sentiments,* as (social) science or (social) philosophy, or as some combination of the two. The final answer to this question must wait on the analysis of the contents of the *Moral Sentiments* which is contained in part two of the present work. However, since a basic unity of purpose and method lies behind all Smith's writings, it will be helpful to begin with a preliminary survey of his other books in order to gain an overall impression of his aims and methods. Such a survey reveals that the main rival to my own view of the *Moral Sentiments* is the interpretation of that book as a strongly normative study designed to set forth the ideals and practices appropriate to the best form of society.

The paucity of overt methodological statements which can be found in Smith's writings means that the main burden of evidence concerning the logical status of his theories must come from an examination of his actual practice. Yet there are some important passages in which he reveals his hand. By and large, these appear to imply a normative purpose for his studies in morality, law and economics. But there are other passages which indicate a scientific approach and, in any case, I shall argue that his stated aims are often misleading descriptions of the actual content of his work and, at best, give only a partial picture of its scope.

I. SPECULATIVE OR PRACTICAL?

Dugald Stewart, noting Smith's early interest in mathematics and natural science, infers that he came to prefer the study of society as a result of his desire to be of practical assistance with human problems. 'The study of human nature', Stewart wrote, 'gratified his ruling passion, of contributing to the happiness and the improvement of society.'[1] This fits well with Smith's often stated preference for studies of practical import. For instance, he was very much aware of the need to involve universities in practical affairs and considered it of great importance that an academic study should be able to prove its usefulness to society. It was for this reason that he passed quickly over the traditional study of ancient logic and metaphysics in his early Glasgow lectures[2] and, probably with his experience of Oxford in mind, castigated the universities in general for failing to prepare their students for 'the real business of the world'.[3] In general he is strongly opposed to 'abstract and speculative reasonings which perhaps tend very little to the bettering of our practice'.[4]

The 'more interesting and useful' matters to which Smith turned his attention in his Logic lectures were rhetoric and *belles-lettres*. The analysis of the different types of discourse which these contain has already been outlined,[5] but it should be stressed, in this context, that one fundamental purpose of this analysis is the practical one of determining which mode of expression is most appropriate to each type of discourse, whether historical, scientific or poetic. The lectures contain guidance on how to present a balanced or a persuasive argument and how to describe and stimulate emotions. It is thus a psychological study of the means of communication approached from the point of view of the person who wishes to convey his thoughts or sentiments. This is of a piece with other parts of the available material which was to make up his 'sort of Philosophical History of all the different branches of Literature, of Philosophy, Poetry and Eloquence', namely the *Essays*, where Smith advises on the most effective way of presenting scientific theories. In so far as these essays are historical, tracing the development of science, they may be said to conform to the practical sort of history, which Smith commends in the *Lectures on Rhetoric*, the purpose of which is to enable men to learn from experience and so conduct their affairs better; Thucydides is praised for adopting this method in his history of the Peloponnesian war since, 'by recording in the truest manner the various incidents of that war, and the causes that produced [it], posterity may learn how to produce the like events or shun others, and know what is to be expected from such and such circumstances'.[6]

The same interest in practical affairs can be seen in some of Smith's explicit remarks about the nature of moral philosophy. At

---

1 E.P.S. ('Account'), p. xii.
2 This is John Millar's report: E.P.S. ('Account'), p. xvi.
3 W.N., V.i.3.art.2 (II.295).
4 L.R.B.L., p. 37.   5 Cf. pp. 29ff.   6 L.R.B.L., p. 102.

the end of the *Moral Sentiments* he wrote that 'The two useful parts of moral philosophy' are 'Ethics and Jurisprudence',[1] with the implication that these are the only proper objects of study in this field. In the context of this particular statement the contrast is with casuistry which, he argues, while it may have a practical aim, is in fact useless in helping men to decide specific moral questions. In the wider context Smith is comparing the utility of ethics and jurisprudence with the non-utility of theories about the nature of the moral faculty.[2] Ethics is useful because its descriptions of virtue and vice 'inflame our natural love of virtue, and increase our abhorrence of vice' and so help to 'correct and to ascertain our natural sentiments with regard to the propriety of conduct'.[3] This is the 'science which is properly called Ethics' and it accomplishes 'whatever precept and exhortation can do to animate us to the practice of virtue'. The examples he cites are the *Offices* of Cicero and those practical parts of Aristotle's ethics where he 'points out to us the different habits by which he would have us regulate our behaviour'.

Similarly jurisprudence is useful because it provides 'a theory of the general principles which *ought* to run through and be the foundation of the laws of all nations'.[4] This would seem to betoken an evaluative exercise in the tradition of those natural law theorists who seek to establish a base from which to criticize positive law. Finally, the division between moral philosophy and economics comes when Smith passes, in Millar's words,[5] from justice to expediency, from considering what laws a state ought to enforce in order to maintain justice, to an enquiry into the content of those laws which are most beneficial to the advancement of a country's wealth, for 'Political economy, considered as a branch of the science of a statesman or legislator, proposes two distinct objects . . . to enrich both the people and the sovereign'.[6]

By considering Smith's descriptions of his own writings and taking into account his professed and reported preoccupation with practical concerns, it is easy to arrive at a picture of his work very far removed from that of the detached observing scientist, seeking to explain but not to evaluate, and to agree with Eli Ginzberg that Smith 'was

---

[1] T.M.S., VII.iv (II.394).   [2] T.M.S., VII.iii.Introd. (II.324f.).

[3] T.M.S., VII.iv (II.364): In particular Smith considered that part six of the *Moral Sentiments* ('Of the Character of Virtue') contained a 'practical system of morality'; cf. W. R. Scott, *Adam Smith as Student and Professor* (Glasgow, 1937), p. 309.

[4] T.M.S., VII.iv (II.398); my italics; cf. L.J., p. 1.

[5] E.P.S. ('Account'), p. xviii.

[6] W.N., IV.Introd. (I.449).

first and foremost a moralist',[1] although a moralist as much concerned with means as with ends. The *Moral Sentiments* might, therefore, be expected to provide a general outline of virtue and vice designed to encourage the one and condemn the other; we should then proceed to the 'science of the statesman' for a consideration of the moral content of the law, under the heading of 'justice', followed by further recommendations designed to increase the prosperity and security of the nation. This would provide a coherent and logical system of moral and prudential recommendations, a normative and practical study which aims to tell us what is virtuous, just and desirable, and how to achieve those ends in practice.

Yet a more detailed inspection of the actual content of Smith's work, and a look at some other passages in which he outlines his method, give a very different impression. At the beginning of Part VII of the *Moral Sentiments* he says that there are two questions to be considered in treating of the principles of morals:

'First, wherein does virtue consist? Or what is the tone of temper, and tenor of conduct, which constitutes the excellent and praiseworthy character, the character which is the natural object of esteem, honour, and approbation? And, secondly, by what power or faculty in the mind is it, that this character, whatever it be, is recommended to us? Or in other words, how and by what means does it come to pass, that the mind prefers one tenor of conduct to another; denominates the one right and the other wrong; considers the one as the object of approbation, honour, and reward, and the other of blame, censure, and punishment?'[2]

The first part of this outline could be taken to cover the general picture of virtue and vice which constitutes 'the science which is properly called Ethics', but the second part does not fit the description he has given of the useful purpose of moral philosophy. In fact he admits that:

'The determination of this second question, though of the greatest importance in speculation, is of none in practice. The question concerning the nature of virtue necessarily has some influence upon our notions of right and wrong in many particular cases. That concerning the principle of approbation can possibly have no such effect. To examine from what contrivance or mechanism within, those different notions or sentiments arise, is a mere matter of philosophical curiosity.'[3]

---

[1] *The House of Adam Smith* (New York, 1935), p. 242.
[2] T.M.S., VII.i (II.196f.).   [3] T.M.S., VII.iii.Introd. (II.324f.).

This would lead us to expect a secondary and subordinate investigation appended to a vivid description of virtue and vice, but this is not borne out by an examination of the actual content of the *Moral Sentiments*. The 'mechanism' by which we come to make judgments of approval and disapproval, is, in fact, the main theme of the book; the 'contrivance' of sympathy with all its ramifications is the chief subject of study.[1] Further, the outline of men's opinions concerning virtue and vice is mainly used to test the theory that all moral distinctions are derived from sympathy, and the concept of sympathy, as we shall see, is given a purely empirical content.

It turns out, therefore, that the practical aspect of his moral philosophy is incidental to its main aim which is theoretical and scientific. In this it follows the programme given in the *Wealth of Nations* where Smith dates the origin of moral philosophy at the time when 'The maxims of common life were arranged in some methodical order, and connected together by a few common principles, in the same manner as they had attempted to arrange and connect the phenomena of nature', and adds that 'the science which pretends to investigate and explain those connecting principles, is what is properly called moral philosophy'.[2] This can be taken as Smith's most accurate statement of the relationship between the two parts of his ethical theory, the first part describing and classifying opinions concerning the content of virtuous and wicked behaviour, and the second explaining these opinions by reference to the constitution of human nature and the social processes by which men come to make judgments of approval and disapproval. It argues for a scientific rather than a normative purpose for the book.

Support for this view of Smith's moral philosophy is to be found in an important footnote at the end of Part II of the *Moral Sentiments* where Smith answers the complaint that his analysis of the sense of ill-desert in terms of resentment is a degradation of that sense by asserting:

'Let it be considered too, that the present inquiry is not concerning a matter of right, if I may say so, but concerning a matter of fact. We are not at present examining upon what principles a perfect being would approve of the punishment of bad actions; but upon what principles so weak and imperfect a creature as man actually and in fact approves of it.'[3]

[1] W. R. Sorley, *Ethics of Naturalism* (London, 1885), makes this point, p. 85: 'Especially among the later English Moralists—Adam Smith, for instance—the question of the end or the standard came almost to drop out of sight in the midst of the controversy regarding the nature of the "moral sense" or "moral faculty".'
[2] W.N., V.i.3.art. 2 (II.291). Cf. p. xx.   [3] T.M.S., II.i.5 (I.189).

Coming, as this does, in the middle of the main exposition of Smith's moral theory, it is a comment which provides justification for strengthening W. C. Swabey's tentative conclusion that 'it is possible to interpret Adam Smith as making no ethical statements at all, that is, solely as a moral psychologist engaged in analysing and explaining acts of approval and disapproval'[1] and to say that this is the correct interpretation of the *Moral Sentiments* (provided that the term 'psychologist' is not taken to exclude a sociological approach).

A similar contrast between stated aims and actual practice is to be found in the *Lectures on Jurisprudence*. Although Jurisprudence is introduced to us as the study of the rules by which civil government *ought* to be directed, in practice the subject is treated almost entirely descriptively, and in the case of justice we are provided with a summary of the rights which applied in eighteenth-century Britain, with an account of the development of justice through different types of society, and explanations of its less obvious benefits. This fits his promise, at the end of the *Moral Sentiments*, to 'give an account of the general principles of law and government, and of the different revolutions they have undergone in the different ages and periods of society'.[2] The *Wealth of Nations* is an expansion of part of the *Lectures on Jurisprudence* and, despite its more frequent pleas for alterations to the law in accordance with the system of 'natural liberty', it contains the same abundance of descriptive detail together with historical and sociological explanation. It deals primarily with the causes and effects of the division of labour and the development of economic production and only secondarily with criticisms of those institutions which retard this progress. For the most part Smith is explaining what had to happen and what will happen, however misguided legislators have been in the past and, regrettably, will be in the future.[3] Similarly, in the *Essays on Philosophical Subjects*, it is possible to ignore Smith's passing comments on the advantages to be gained by different methods of presentation, and see him as a detached observer explaining *why* science and theology have pro-

---

[1] *Ethical Theory from Hobbes to Kant* (London, 1961), p. 179.

[2] T.M.S., VII.iv (II.399); cf. p. 17.

[3] Cf. O. H. Taylor, 'Economics and the Idea of *Jus Naturale*', *The Quarterly Journal of Economics*, XLIV (1929), p. 231: 'Smith's theory of the natural economic order differed from that of the Physiocrats in being less a theory of an ideal order to be achieved by a rational plan of reform than a theory of an existing order among economic events'. Also J. Viner, 'Adam Smith and *Laissez-Faire*', *Journal of Political Economy*, XXXV (1927), p. 198, and even W. Bagehot, *Economic Studies* (ed. by R. H. Hutton, 1953), p. 107. Also H. F. Thomson, 'Adam Smith's Philosophy of Science', *Quarterly Journal of Economics*, vol. LXXIX (1965), especially pp. 229-33.

51

gressed to their present state. Here, as elsewhere, Smith's interests are more 'speculative' or theoretical than he is sometimes prepared to admit.

Nevertheless there does seem to be an inconsistency or at any rate an ambivalence in Smith's stated purposes. I have indicated that the actual content of his work would lead us to attach more weight to those places where he puts a straightforward scientific and non-normative interpretation on his writings. In some measure we can reconcile this with his insistence that all studies should have practical uses by likening his studies to applied science concerned with means rather than ends. This fits much of the *Wealth of Nations* where his recommendations for free trade are based on the facts of economic behaviour as he sees them, taking for granted the desirability of high individual consumption. Such advice, as is the case with all recommendations suggested by applied science, is hypothetical: if you wish to increase the prosperity of the citizens and the sovereign, he suggests, then you must free industry and commerce from certain legal restrictions. But even in the *Wealth of Nations* there is a great deal of material which describes and explains processes which have taken place and will continue in the future, without reference to the 'science of a statesman', since statesmen are powerless to change them; and in the *Moral Sentiments*, as we shall see, there is even less practical advice to be found, and even more explanation of unalterable social processes.

Some commentators have assumed that the *Moral Sentiments* is more evaluative than the *Wealth of Nations* because it established the system of values which the *Wealth of Nations* takes for granted.[1] This would mean that, with the assistance of the *Moral Sentiments*, the hypothetical imperatives of the *Wealth of Nations* could be turned into categorical obligations. But in fact the *Moral Sentiments* explains *why* men make the moral judgments they do, and this is logically quite distinct from providing a moral justification of values. The *Moral Sentiments* tells us a good deal about Smith's theory of human behaviour which helps with the interpretation of the *Wealth of Nations*, but those who expect to find in it a moral justification for the economic system described in the *Wealth of Nations* will be disappointed.

[1] A. Small, *Adam Smith and Modern Sociology* (Chicago, 1907), pp. 18 and 40ff. Small suggests that the *Moral Sentiments* evaluates the economic aspect of society by putting persons at the centre of life, and so provides 'a theory of ends which the means should serve' and embodies 'the discovery of a standard of life to which economic technology must be conformed'.

II. NATURE AND NATURAL LAW

There remains, therefore, especially in the case of Ethics and Jurisprudence, a discrepancy between the various statements which Smith makes concerning the nature of his work, some of them preparing us for straightforward hortatory evaluations and others suggesting a science of society as detached as Newton's theory of motion. Even if we consider that Smith's practice is modelled more on the latter than the former approach, there is still a need to account for the coexistence of these apparently contradictory purposes in Smith's mind. The explanation is, perhaps, to be found in his view of the relation between what is and what ought to be. Broadly speaking, the position he adopts is that, for the most part, whatever in the long term is, is right. Human choices may, to some extent and for some time, lead to changes and delays in the inevitable course of events, but the underlying, average and long-term tendencies are as inescapable as the movements of the planets, and their consequences are, on the whole, good. Men may either go along with or resist these processes; they are not, therefore, absolutely powerless, or without responsibility. Nevertheless the modifications which they can bring about in their own behaviour and in the development of society are neither far-reaching nor prolonged. Their actions are governed by the forces of instinct, and environmental necessities, almost as surely as material objects are subject to the law of gravity, and this works out, in the main, to their advantage.

The concept which holds together the factual and the ideal world is that of 'nature'. Nature was, for Smith as for most eighteenth-century theorists, both an object to be studied and an ideal to be brought into existence. This is an ambiguity which goes back to classical times and can be found in Plato, Aristotle and the Stoics as well as in Roman law and mediaeval theories of natural law; it is associated with the concept of the law of nature as a term used to denote both factual generalizations and moral or legal imperatives. The resuscitation of natural law theory in the seventeenth and eighteenth centuries was part of an attempt to establish a theology which was independent of revelation and a morality which was independent of religion. As such it tended to draw more on pre-Christian concepts of nature than on mediaeval theory and to take up those elements of natural law which originated in Greek thought and became embodied in Roman and hence European law. Smith was part of this movement.[1] Sometimes it is thought that to admit

[1] Cf. A. L. Macfie, *The Individual in Society* (London, 1967), p. 25, etc.

this is to accuse him of confusing the normative and the factual, and to find him guilty of relying on *a priori* methods in all his work.[1] Buckle, for instance, presents Smith as following the Cartesian method of dividing a problem into its ultimate elements, clearly and distinctly perceived, from which he then goes on to deduce truths about the world and prescriptions for human action.[2]

To some extent these critics are misled by Smith's method of presentation. We have seen from the *Lectures on Rhetoric* that Smith admires the Newtonian method of laying out a theory as a deductive system and it is clear that he follows this model in the *Moral Sentiments*, starting with his analysis of sympathy, and going on to demonstrate its operation in various social phenomena. But we have also seen, from the *Essays*, that he is fully aware of the place of observation and induction in the framing and testing of hypotheses. The *Moral Sentiments* contains ample evidence that he did not forget the need for an empirical base on which to build and test his explanations of morality. At each stage he bases his contentions on an appeal to common experience, sometimes citing a variety of 'observations', sometimes claiming that 'no instance is necessary' to prove the presence or effect of some disposition or instinct.[3] Smith, no doubt, relied too much on second-hand accounts and tales from classical literature, and his use of introspection and everyday casual observation may seem subjective, unsystematic and lacking in the rigour that would be required of the social scientist today. He tends to assume, somewhat optimistically, that the evidence upon which moral philosophy is based is much more familiar and therefore less open to dispute than that on which natural philosophy has to rely.[4] But this optimism does not go so far as to make him think that it is unnecessary to gather and present a great deal of supporting evidence for his theories about human society. The illustrations which he gives go beyond what is required for clarifying his meaning, and are intended to represent samples of the sort of evidence on which he relies and on which he can call if his theories are questioned.[5]

Smith's ability to provide apt examples has often been noted, but

---

[1] Cf. T. E. C. Leslie, *Essays in Political and Moral Philosophy* (London, 1879), p. 149; J. K. Ingram, *History of Political Economy* (Edinburgh, 1888), pp. 90f; and W. D. Grampp, 'Adam Smith and the Economic Man', *Journal of Political Economy*, LVI (1948), pp. 315-36.

[2] H. T. Buckle, *History of Civilisation in England* (Oxford, 1904), vol. III, pp. 305ff.

[3] T.M.S., III.3 (I.370).

[4] T.M.S., VII.ii.4 (II.320f.); cf. p. 64f.

[5] Cf. E. Roll, *History of Economic Thought* (London, 1938), p. 147, and L. Stephen, *English Thought in the Eighteenth Century*, ix.73.

critics who have mistaken his purpose find much of the material in the *Moral Sentiments* out of place and talk of his examples as 'embellishments'.[1] This is particularly true of Smith's discussions of the 'irregularities' and 'corruptions' of the moral sentiments. To dismiss these as interesting irrelevances is to miss the importance which Smith attaches to the power of a scientific theory to account for 'irregular' phenomena in the sense of unexpected departures from an even pattern of events. In the *Essays* he notes the superiority of those astronomical theories which could account for small variations in the regular movements of the stars, and he regards it as an important factor in favour of his own theory that it can explain certain aspects of the moral sentiments which are unexpectedly different from the normal run of moral attitudes.[2] Far from being irrelevant, these irregularities are, for Smith, crucial tests for his theory, and the more of them he can explain the more secure he regards its empirical basis.

It is also important to realize the importance which Smith attaches to simplicity and familiarity in a scientific theory,[3] since this explains his effort to present his conclusions in terms of uncomplicated and well-known phenomena; in this there are direct parallels between his use of sympathy, self-interest and even, to some extent, following Hutcheson, benevolence, and the place of gravity in Newton's system.[4] This may seem to lay him open to Viner's charge that 'in his earlier work Smith was a purely speculative philosopher, reasoning from notions masquerading as self-evident verities'[5] since a familiar and simple empirical truth may often be made to appear 'self-evident', but this is, on the whole, an unfair charge and certainly mistakes Smith's own purpose. It may, however, be true, as Stewart alleged, that Smith does tend to oversimplify in his effort to attain the Newtonian ideal,[6] although Smith himself is aware of this danger.[7]

To pursue this further it is necessary to take a closer look at Smith's use of the term 'nature' and the related idea of natural law. Since the discovery, in 1895, of the *Lectures on Jurisprudence*—

---

[1] J. Bonar, *The Moral Sense* (New York, 1930), p. 175; cf. J. Viner, *Adam Smith, 1776-1926*, p. 118, and J. A. Farrer, *Adam Smith* (London, 1881), pp. 18f.
[2] Cf. p. 41f.   [3] Cf. p. 40f.
[4] Cf. E. Halevy, *The Growth of Philosophical Radicalism*, trans. by Mary Morris (London, 1928), p. 100. Millar described Smith as the Newton of the study of civil society (*Historical Review of English Government*, 1812, pp. 429f.).
[5] J. Viner, *Adam Smith, 1776-1926*, p. 136.
[6] E.P.S. ('Account'), p. xxxviii.
[7] E.P.S. (H.A.), p. 68; cf. p. 40.

a copy of a student's lecture notes taken down in 1762-3, a year before Smith's visit to France when he is alleged to have come under the influence of the Physiocrats (which has greatly weakened the argument that he modelled the *Wealth of Nations* on the semi-rationalistic methods of some of his French contemporaries)—those who classify Smith as an *a priori* natural law theorist have tended to concentrate their attacks on the *Moral Sentiments* where the concept of 'nature' is most evident.

The term is certainly grossly over-used in this work and this leads to many ambiguities and obscurities, but a study of its multiple uses shows that Smith, following in the Aristotelian tradition, is able to give it an empirical cash value. What is natural, for Smith, is either what normally happens,[1] or, more typically, that which normally takes place, or would take place, in the absence of some distinctively human factor. In this latter sense the term is, therefore, logically incomplete, and each occurrence of it requires to be interpreted according to the particular factor in question. Usually it is some exercise of human choice which involves reflection and effort.[2] By his endeavours a man may change the behaviour which comes 'naturally' or spontaneously, and, if these endeavours are repeated, this can permanently modify his spontaneous or 'instinctive' behaviour. In this case what is 'natural', in the sense of 'untaught' and 'undisciplined' is contrasted with what becomes natural, in the sense of spontaneous, as the result of 'habit, custom and education'.[3] Smith does not, therefore, tie the concept of nature to the idea of some pre-governmental state of nature. What is 'natural' may be opposed to behaviour which is influenced by religion,[4] extensive utilitarian reflection,[5] or 'violence and artifice' from a source external to the individuals concerned.[6] Its meaning is always relative to the particular contrast Smith has in mind and to the stage of development of the individual or the society concerned.

Spontaneous and instinctive behaviour is, for Smith, not only natural but normal. He believes that, for the most part, whatever factor inhibits the natural processes can only do so temporarily and partially. 'Natural sympathy', for instance, is not only 'immediate and instinctive', it is also 'necessary' in that it always influences behaviour.[7] Similarly, in the *Wealth of Nations* the 'natural price' is

---

[1] This point is made by J. A. Schumpeter, *History of Economic Analysis*, p. 112.
[2] Cf. T.M.S., I.i.4 (I.35f. and 37f.); I.ii.3 (I.75); III.3 (I.361) and II.ii.3 (I.227).
[3] W.N., I.ii. (I.19f.).   [4] T.M.S., III.6 (I.444).
[5] T.M.S., II.i.2 (I.172) and IV.2 (I.487).
[6] W.N., I.xi.3 (I.256).
[7] Cf. T.M.S., II.i.2 (I.172); VII.ii.1 (II.264); III.3 (I.364); and W.N., V.i.3.art (II.324).

a consequence of the 'ordinary and average rates ... of wages, profit and rent at the time and place in which they commonly prevail', so that 'The natural price is, as it were, the central price, to which the prices of all commodities are continually gravitating'.[1] It is almost always possible to render Smith's use of 'natural' by the word 'actual' provided it is realized that he means what is normally the case. Laughter is 'natural' when it is caused by something which we would normally find amusing.[2] Tranquillity is the 'natural' state of mind because it reasserts itself after some unexpected occurrence has disturbed it.[3] Wealth and greatness are the 'natural' objects of respect because they 'almost constantly obtain it'.[4] The entire *Moral Sentiments* is concerned with the normal moral judgments of the 'bulk of mankind' which indicate, for Smith, what is 'naturally' approved and disapproved of.

In the *Wealth of Nations* Smith is more prepared to admit that the 'natural' course of events may be quite different from the normal; for instance, Book III illustrates how, in Europe, the natural precedence of agriculture in the process of economic development has been reversed by laws which favoured the towns. In parts of the book it sometimes appears that the all-important system of 'natural liberty' is a potential ideal system not actualized in any real state, the deviations from the natural course of events being due to inappropriate institutions and laws. In such cases the natural courses of events is what *would* happen in the absence of restraints. To this extent the system of natural liberty is hypothetical, but it is not unempirical, for it rests on the claim that certain economic forces are operative even if they are being thwarted in certain respects. Yet, on the whole, Smith does believe that the economic system of natural liberty is *largely* in operation: its main features can never be obliterated and only in minor respects can it be hindered over a long period of time. A typical conclusion of the *Wealth of Nations* is one concerning the development of wealth; Smith writes that 'though the profusion of government must, undoubtedly, have retarded the natural progress of England towards wealth and improvement, it has not been able to stop it'.[5] And even the marginal

---

[1] W.N., I.vii (I.65). Note the Newtonian metaphor.

[2] T.M.S., I.i.3 (I.26).   [3] E.P.S. (H.A.), p. 20.

[4] T.M.S., I.iii.3 (I.149).

[5] W.N., II.iii (I.367); cf. IV.v (II.49): 'The natural effort of every individual to better his own condition, when suffered to exert itself with freedom and security, is so powerful a principle, that it is alone, and without any assistance, not only capable of carrying on the society to wealth and prosperity, but of surmounting a hundred impertinent obstructions with which the folly of human laws too often incumbers its operations.'

effects which government can have on an economic system are less pronounced in the case of morality and justice.

Attempts to place Smith in the *a priori* natural law tradition make some of their strongest points in relation to his jurisprudence, with its explicit premise that the laws which ought to be contained in the law codes of all countries can be known and stated with the precision of grammar.[1] In particular it is noted that he admired Grotius as the person who first attempted to establish a system of 'natural jurisprudence' 'without regard to the particular institutions of any one nation'.[2] Yet Grotius himself is far from being a pure rationalist and Smith is a long way from being an unreserved admirer of his work.[3] Indeed if identity of views is proved by expressed admiration, there is more reason to say that Smith followed Hume in his attack on the natural law tradition.[4] Similar points can be made about Adam Smith's alleged dependence upon Pufendorf. And even if Grotius and Pufendorf are regarded as Cartesians, we should remember Smith's explicit rejection of the Cartesian method,[5] and the scorn with which he treats concepts such as the 'social contract' which are fundamental to Grotius, Pufendorf and Hobbes. Smith denies that reason plays a central part in human behaviour in general and in moral judgment in particular. This shows in his rejection of casuistry,[6] his argument against utility as the ground of approbation[7] and his repeated insistence that reason cannot provide a motivational basis for morality.[8] In jurisprudence his main interest lies in describing the content of positive law and explaining its origin and development. In so far as this is carrying on the tradition of *ius gentium*, it does so in the most empirical meaning of this concept. When, for instance, he contrasts laws that are in accordance with nature with those that depart from this 'norm' he simply means that the latter

---

[1] T.M.S., III.6 (I.442f.).

[2] T.M.S., VII.iv (II.398); cf. L.J., p. 1.

[3] Cf. L.J., p. 1: 'His treatise On the Laws of War and Peace, *with all its imperfections*, is perhaps at this day the most complete work on this subject' (my italics). Dugald Stewart says that Smith had Grotius and Pufendorf in mind when he attacked the universities of his day for remaining sanctuaries for 'exploded systems': *Dissertations on the Progress of Metaphysical, Ethical and Political Philosophy*, in *Collected Works*, ed. by Sir W. Hamilton, I.178.

[4] Cf. H. J. Bittermann, 'Adam Smith's Empiricism and the Law of Nature', *The Journal of Political Economy*, XLVIII (1940), pp. 487-520 and pp. 703-34, and P. Stein, 'Legal Theory in Eighteenth Century Scotland', *Juridical Review* (1957), pp. 1-20.

[5] L.R.B.L., p. 140.   [6] T.M.S., VII.iv (II.391).

[7] T.M.S., IV, *passim*. Cf. Chap. 5, pp. 116-119.

[8] T.M.S., VII.iii.2 (II.332ff). Cf. Chap. 3, pp. 64ff.

do not accord with the consensus of moral opinions in that type of society.

It might be said that, even if Smith does, in his jurisprudence, identify the law of nature with what men in general believe ought to be in the law, rather than with his own views as to what ought to be the content of positive law, he still muddles up the idea of prescriptive and descriptive law. Consider the following passage:

'All general rules are commonly denominated laws: thus the general rules which bodies observe in the communication of motion, are called the laws of motion. But those general rules which our moral faculties observe in approving or condemning whatever sentiment or action is subjected to their examination, may much more justly be denominated such. They have a much greater resemblance to what are properly called laws, those general rules which the sovereign lays down to direct the free actions of men: they are prescribed most surely by a lawful superior, and are attended too with the sanction of rewards and punishments.'[1]

This indicates that Smith distinguishes prescriptive and descriptive law and that he takes the former to be the more fundamental, although the latter is also rightly called law since descriptive generalizations express the purposes of God. He is arguing, also, that moral rules are felt as commandments and are supported by sanctions so that they are properly called laws in the most basic meaning of the word 'law'. But this does not mean that these rules cannot be explained by showing that they can be accounted for by laws in the secondary sense of descriptive generalizations. Smith considers that such generalizations about human behaviour are part of nature's 'unalterable laws'.[2] Men, he believes, move according to 'a principle of motion of their own', which human laws cannot alter,[3] and which are, therefore, similar to the 'laws of motion' which physical bodies observe.[4] The processes by which men come to possess their moral sentiments are part of human behaviour, and can be subsumed under descriptive laws. This is not affected by the fact that these moral sentiments, once established, give rise to moral rules which are laws in the more immediate and fundamental sense of prescriptions which are experienced as imperatives and are accompanied by sanctions. Men, Smith allows, may fail to obey these commandments without their ceasing to be laws, but they cannot fail to feel them as commandments; their feelings are determined, and may therefore be described by means of laws in the secondary sense of generaliza-

[1] T.M.S., III.5 (I.412f.). [2] T.M.S., III.3 (I.364).
[3] T.M.S., VI.ii.2 (II.110). [4] T.M.S., III.5 (I.413); cf. L.J., p. 83.

tions known through empirical observation. The *Moral Sentiments* is an attempt to establish laws in this latter sense which, Smith believes, explain why societies have the prescriptions which are embodied in their moral codes.

III. DEISM

What is different about this approach, which distinguishes it from that of the modern social scientist, is the way in which he endorses the theological belief that all laws, prescriptive and descriptive, are, in the end, to be regarded as the commandments of God. It might be thought, therefore, that his belief in natural religion provides him with a non-empirical method of determining the content of both types of law, which overcomes his openness to factual evidence. But this is not so. His belief in an all-wise Author of nature is certainly an important presupposition of his thought; it encourages him to look for systematic aspects in society and leads him to adopt, as we shall see, a method of explanation similar to modern functionalist theory. But he does not draw on this belief for information about the world. The *Essays* show that he regarded theism as an outcome rather than a logical presupposition of scientific study. It is admiration, the emotion which *follows* on a scientific explanation, that prompts belief in God, and it is the advanced study of nature, which shows it to be one immense machine, that confirms this faith.[1] Belief in a god, even when based on the argument from design, is certainly an extra-empirical faith, but of all the arguments for God's existence, that from design is most dependent on the assessment of empirical evidence; if nature cannot be shown to exhibit a systematic order, or have beneficial consequences for man, then the argument fails, although, as Hume showed, it need not succeed even if these facts and their consequent moral evaluation are accepted.[2] Therefore, while we may admit that Smith's theology led him to expect nature to exhibit the signs of a creator, we should regard his faith as a consequence, and not a cause, of his study of nature. This is not an assertion about the sources of his religious belief but about the arguments he uses to support it and, more importantly, the place it holds in his system of thought: he does not deduce facts from his theology but makes theological statements on the basis of facts independently ascertained.[3]

The two passages in which Smith mentions the 'invisible hand' have misled some commentators into thinking that Smith believed in

[1] E.P.S. (H.A.P.), p. 107; and T.M.S., III.5 (I.408ff.).
[2] *Dialogues concerning Natural Religion.*
[3] This is discussed more fully in chapter 11.

some direct intervention, by the Deity, in the causal sequence of events.[1] But Smith uses this term as a metaphor and, even then, only to summarize his conclusion that the consequences of the mechanism of nature are, on the whole, beneficial, even where these benefits are not intended by men. The 'invisible hand' is no capricious intervener in the natural course of events, but is a figure of speech used to suggest that the total operations of nature betoken the ultimate planning of a benevolent God. It involves no suggestion of a *deus ex machina* brought in to establish the principle of the harmony of interests. It is the total 'economy of nature' which has this result, and thus demonstrates the work of a divine maker. The analogy is explicitly drawn between the universe and a watch: the working of blind causes produces a result of which the parts of the mechanism are unaware.[2] The invisible hand makes the watch but does not intervene in its operation.

Smith frequently emphasizes the error of mixing up final and efficient causes:

'But though, in accounting for the operations of bodies, we never fail to distinguish in this manner the efficient from the final cause, in accounting for those of the mind we are very apt to confound these two different things with one another. When by natural principles we are led to advance those ends, which a refined and enlightened reason would recommend to us, we are very apt to impute to that reason, as to their efficient cause, the sentiments and actions by which we advance those ends, and to imagine that to be the wisdom of man, which in reality is the wisdom of God.'[3]

This is in line with his general tendency to play down the place of reason in human conduct and to emphasize that human behaviour is subject to general laws in the same way as other phenomena. It also stresses that these general laws must be discovered and explained in terms of efficient causes conceived in terms of constant conjunction; explanations in terms of the will of God have no place in determining the efficient causes of behaviour, but enter at a later stage once the scientific investigation is completed. In fact, it is possible to remove the theological terminology and Smith's reflections about a benevolent Deity and not affect the empirical content of his work.[4]

---

[1] W.N., IV.2 (I.477) and T.M.S., IV.1 (I.464); cf. p. 71f.
[2] T.M.S., II.ii.3 (I.217).   [3] T.M.S., II.ii.3 (I.218).
[4] There is some evidence that his theological enthusiasms waned in later life, but although this led to alterations in some of his more dogmatic deistic statements, and perhaps to the withdrawal of the atonement passage, this did not lead him to revise the substance of the *Moral Sentiments* in the last edition of the work. Cf. p. 228.

It is more difficult to reconcile Smith's deism with his normative than with his scientific aims. If he conducts an empirical investigation to discover what are the consequences of human action, or the 'ends of nature', and concludes that these are the ends of a benevolent deity, then is he not precluded from suggesting improvements in the behaviour of individuals and states? Even if he is not guilty of theological naturalism, and does not simply assume that the ends of nature must be good but makes an independent valuation of their worth, he would seem to be debarred from recommending any tampering with such a well-designed mechanism unless he can make out that such tampering is itself part of the design. However, our analysis of his concept of nature has shown that his judgment that the intentions of 'Nature' are benevolent need only mean that on the whole the *normal* course of events show a providential ordering, and, in particular, it enables him to discount those events which are consequences of human intervention in what would have resulted had the immediate impulses of human nature been permitted to achieve their objects. His argument from design therefore only commits him to the view that, when human will does not change the spontaneous behaviour of men in society, the usual consequences of such behaviour are beneficial to most members of that society. This leaves him scope for encouraging spontaneous behaviour and even suggesting that men improve on the economy of nature by remedying some of the defects of a system that is on the whole good, but may have incongruous and unhappy consequences on occasion. Smith regards this as a form of co-operation between man and God.

CHAPTER 3

SMITH'S SOCIAL THEORY

Even if it can be established that Smith's normative interests do, in practice, take second place to his factual analyses of social behaviour, it could still be argued that his moral theory is of a type with the sort of non-normative but non-scientific logical and epistemological analysis which is characteristic of modern philosophy. The positive case in favour of the scientific interpretation of Smith's theories must, therefore, include evidence which demonstrates that the questions which he is asking are scientific ones, and that the answers which he gives to these questions are of a logically appropriate kind.

In the light of the first two chapters it is reasonable for us to postulate that Adam Smith did attempt to apply his understanding of Newtonian scientific methodology to his study of society. This may not have been his exclusive concern, but it does indicate his main interest. There is no evidence that he thought there to be a logical dichotomy between the natural and the social sciences, or that the methods of 'natural philosophy' are, in some way, not applicable to 'moral philosophy'. He was conscious of the fact that our ability to know something of the motives for human action, what he calls the 'internal facts, to wit the thoughts and sentiments or designs of men which pass in their minds',[1] provides the social scientist with a more immediate type of evidence than is available to the student of nature. But, far from concluding that this makes the methods of natural science inappropriate, he uses this point to argue that the student of society is less at the mercy of erroneous theories than is the natural scientist.[2] In a direct reference to his essay 'On the History of Astronomy', he writes, in the *Moral Sentiments:*

[1] L.R.B.L., p. 59.
[2] Smith is, however, somewhat optimistic about our ability to 'observe' human motives. While admitting that human action cannot be defined in terms of external movements alone (T.M.S., II.iii (I.231)), he assumes that we can know the motives of other people through observing their visible manifestations (T.M.S., I.i.1 (I.7), L.R.B.L., p. 71 and T.M.S., VII.iv (II.363)).

'A system of natural philosophy may appear very plausible, and be for a long time very generally received in the world, and yet have no foundation in nature, nor any sort of resemblance to the truth. The vortices of Des Cartes were regarded by a very ingenious nation, for near a century together, as a most satisfactory account of the revolution of the heavenly bodies. Yet it has been demonstrated to the conviction of all mankind, that these pretended causes of those wonderful effects, not only do not actually exist, but are utterly impossible, and if they did exist, could produce no such effects as are ascribed to them. But it is otherwise with systems of moral philosophy, and an author who pretends to account for the origin of our moral sentiments, cannot deceive us so grossly, nor depart so very far from all resemblance to the truth.'[1]

The parallel between natural and moral philosophy, which Smith takes for granted in this passage, is of more significance than the difference to which he draws our attention. Both seek to discover the connecting principles of nature by establishing the causes of the phenomena in question. In the case of moral philosophy, Smith argues:

'The author who should assign, as the cause of any natural sentiment, some principle which neither had any connexion with it, nor resembled any other principle which had some such connexion, would appear absurd and ridiculous to the most injudicious and inexperienced reader.'[2]

It is the moral sentiments in particular which Smith has in mind here, and we shall see, in Part II, how he formulates his own causal analysis of these sentiments by reference to the familiar phenomenon of sympathy. But, first, it is necessary to present an outline of the total social theory in which this analysis features in order to demonstrate that Smith possessed the sort of conceptual apparatus which is necessary for the creation of a social theory which can hope to provide the right kind of answers to the scientific questions which he is asking.

I. MOTIVES AS CAUSES

It is not difficult to demonstrate that Smith regarded himself as enquiring into 'causes'[3] and 'origins',[4] or that he is seeking for explanations of *types* of social phenomena rather than of particular

---

[1] T.M.S., VII.ii.4 (II.319f.).   [2] T.M.S., VII.ii.4 (II.322).
[3] Cf. the full title of Smith's economic work, *An Inquiry into the Nature and Causes of the Wealth of Nations*.   [4] Cf. T.M.S., VII.i (II.195).

historical events. The *Moral Sentiments*, as a study of men's attitudes towards human conduct, necessarily includes a working theory of action. This theory is conceived almost entirely in causal language. Smith's analysis divides an act into (1) its cause or occasion, (2) its sentiment, passion or motive, (3) its intention and its actual effects,[1] and (4) the various processes of perception, imagination and reason which play a part in connecting cause to motive, motive to intention, and intention to effects. Actions are principally determined by the passions or sentiments; these are the motives, in the sense of the motive powers, which lie behind all human behaviour and are its fundamental causes. They are not, however, the sufficient causes of behaviour, and the complete analysis of action requires reference to the situations which arouse the passions (which Smith is inclined to speak of as *the* causes of action), as well as to the processes of perception, imagination and reason which are necessary to stimulate the motives and translate them into actions.

Occasionally, the relationship between stimulus, sentiment and intention is said to be 'immediate' or 'instinctive', but the ways in which the faculties enter into this process can be exceedingly complex. In particular, the imagination, by its capacity to reproduce copies of sense impressions, frees the agent from being able to respond only to those stimuli which are present to his senses. The ideas which are formed by the imagination are 'weaker in degree, but not altogether unlike'[2] the original impressions from which they derive. The mental operations involved in these processes do not introduce a non-causal element into the analysis of action because, Smith believes, they can be described in terms of certain mechanistic laws which, as we shall see, he uses extensively in his theory of the moral sentiments.

The activities of reason are not so easy to fit into a causal theory of action as those of the imagination. An act may be said to be rational if it is done because the agent believes that it is a means to a desired end. In Smith's scheme of action this element is played down in that the typical act is considered to be the spontaneous consequence of stimulated desire. He certainly rules out long-term calculations as an element in normal behaviour. However he does allow that the agent acts in the light of what he considers to be in his *immediate* interests. This is an essential factor in economic behaviour and is amply illustrated in the *Wealth of Nations*. It is particularly a feature, therefore, of commercial society, for, as Smith says 'the very intention of commerce is to exchange your own commodities

---

[1] Cf. T.M.S., I.i.3 (I.28).   [2] T.M.S., I.i.1 (I.3ff.); cf. (I.6).

for others you think will be more convenient for you'.[1] The 'trucking disposition' does involve 'reason and speech', but it is a response to immediate rather than long-term self-interest. This is made quite clear by Smith's well-known insistence that men do not engage in trade and manufacture in order to produce all the many economic benefits of the division of labour, but in order to satisfy their immediate needs and conveniences: 'It [the division of labour] is the necessary, though slow and gradual, consequence of a certain propensity in human nature which has in view no such extensive utility'.[2] Behaviour at this level of rationality is not far removed from that which is 'caused' by the perceiving or imagining of a desired object.

Behaviour is also rational in so far as it is based on knowledge which the individual has acquired through learning. Smith takes induction to be one of the chief functions of reason;[3] the ability to generalize has already been referred to in our account of Smith's philosophy of science, and we shall see later how it features in his discussion of moral rules. With respect to the means-end relationship Smith assumes that most knowledge about causal relationships which is useful in everyday life is the consequence of trial-and-error learning. On the basis of their experience men are able to formulate certain rules of thumb which embody the fruits of such learning and enable them to act from habit. These rules are interpreted as inductive generalizations from the individual's experience of what he finds pleasant and painful, and the methods which he has found to be successful in obtaining the former and avoiding the latter.

Because men are able to act in accordance with general rules of practice they are able to pursue consistent lines of action in relative independence of the immediate promptings of the sentiments. But Smith considers that it is absurd to think that reason can have any influence on conduct which is not derived from the emotions; reason may help men to obtain their goals, but 'nothing can be agreeable or disagreeable for its own sake, which is not rendered such by immediate sense and feeling'.[4] Nothing Smith says about economic rationality alters this basic premise.

The fundamental causes of human behaviour are, therefore, the passions. These are conceived on the analogy of physical forces and

[1] L.J., p. 204; cf. L.J., p. 160, and W.N., I.ii (I.18).
[2] W.N., I.ii (I.17).   [3] T.M.S., VII.iii.2 (II.337).
[4] T.M.S., VII.iii.2 (II.338); cf. T.M.S., VII.iii.2 (II.339). Smith acknowledges Hutcheson as the first person to delineate clearly the powers of reason and sentiment (cf. II.340) but he is also restating Hume's position (*Treatise*, III.1).

may be regarded as the principles of movement in the human constitution. Smith's attempt to indicate the relative strength of the passions is an important part of his general theory. He does so by means of what is basically a pleasure-pain theory of human behaviour, for 'pleasure and pain are the great objects of desire and aversion'.[1] Without saying that pleasure and pain are always the direct aims of action, he assumes that the explanation of human conduct requires the discovery of operative motives which can be interpreted as instances of the desire to escape discomfort, to maintain a pleasant state of body or mind, or to seek something which is believed to be pleasant. Not only are the objectives which the instinctive passions prompt men to seek pleasurable, but the passions themselves have hedonic qualities: it is painful to experience hunger or resentment, but pleasurable to experience joy or benevolence.

One of the chief causes of happiness is the uninterrupted functioning of a set pattern of activity, and, conversely, disturbances of these activities cause pain. However, rest is also pleasant, while work, which involves effort, is not. The bodily passions or natural appetites connected with eating, drinking and sexual activity impel men to act in the most literal sense; these 'immediate instincts' are strong but spasmodic, as are a certain range of highly charged emotions like envy, malice and resentment.[2] More persistent are the continuous but less violent desires, like those for ease and comfort, and these determine the main lines of human behaviour. Happiness, in Smith's view, is as much a mental as a physical state, and, in particular, the mental condition which tends to establish itself and which men seek to maintain is one of 'tranquillity'; this is partly a condition of rest, but is also connected with the smooth functioning of the mental processes.[3] This general theory is filled in by a series of generalizations concerning the precise things that men find pleasant and painful.

An important distinction, upon which Smith frequently insists, is that between 'original' and 'secondary' passions. The original passions are those which cannot be 'derived from' other passions; they are the raw material or basic human nature from which other passions are developed through individual and social experience, and are therefore present in all human beings to much the same degree.[4] The original passions are 'The unalterable principles of

1 T.M.S., VII.iii.2 (II.338); cf. T.M.S., II.i.5 (I.191).
2 W.N., V.i.2 (II.231).
3 E.P.S. (H.A.), p. 20; T.M.S., III.4 (I.400) and III.3 (I.365).
4 T.M.S., I.i.1 (I.16).

human nature' which 'though they may be somewhat warpt, cannot be entirely perverted'.[1] They include the fundamental bodily desires, but also essentially social desires such as the wish for approval, the fear of disapproval and the desire for company. They are contrasted with secondary desires which arise from the operations of the imagination and the processes of learning; thus fear, hope and despair become associated with men's efforts to satisfy their original desires. The ability to imagine what it would be like to be in some situation different from that of the present moment gives rise to many secondary passions, of which the most significant is the desire for the 'imagined' pleasure of wealth which is manifested in the 'uniform, constant, and uninterrupted effort of every man to better his condition'.[2]

Of equal significance in the hierarchy of human motives is the desire to obtain the approval of other men, and this desire gives rise to numerous secondary passions: 'Bring him [a solitary man] into society, and all his own passions will immediately become the causes of new passions.'[3] In society a man learns what is approved and disapproved of, and, because he has an original desire to please his fellows, he strives to obtain those things and behave in such ways as will gain this approval. This supposition frees Smith from a narrowly individualistic psychology and makes his theory, as it has been set out above, a type of social psychology. It also leads to some complexity in expounding the distinctions which Smith draws between unsocial, social and selfish passions.[4]

The unsocial passions, which chiefly derive from the imagination, are directed against other human beings: hatred, anger, resentment, and envy are the main examples given.[5] The social passions include 'all . . . benevolent affections' such as 'generosity, kindness, compassion, mutual friendship and esteem' and 'the sentiment of love'.[6] The selfish passions are those 'conceived upon account of our own private good or bad fortune' whether these are thought of in terms of bodily or 'imaginative' needs. The social passions are not strong except with respect to a man's family and close friends.[7] But they do obtain social approval and are, to this extent, reinforced. The unsocial passions can be extremely powerful, but they evoke such strong disapproval that men have forcible motives for controlling them. Within these limitations the dominant human passions are those of self-interest: 'Every man . . . is much more deeply interested

---

[1] T.M.S., V.2 (II.19).
[2] W.N., II.iii (I.364).
[3] T.M.S., III.1 (I.279).
[4] T.M.S., I.ii.3, 4 and 5 (I.74ff.).
[5] T.M.S., I.ii.3 (I.77, 82 and 84).
[6] T.M.S., I.ii.4 (I.88f.) and 5 (I.93).
[7] T.M.S., VI.ii (II.66ff.).

in whatever immediately concerns himself, than in what concerns any other man'.[1] Yet, because his own happiness is bound up with the approval and disapproval of others, ambition to obtain their approbation is one of the chief objects of self-interested action once immediate bodily needs have been satisfied.[2] Avarice is an element within this ambition, since wealth is one of the best known methods for obtaining the attention and admiration of other men.

Those who find a contradiction between the doctrines of the *Moral Sentiments* and the *Wealth of Nations* often argue that in the former Smith gives pride of place to the social passions while in the latter work he assumes that self-interest is the dominant human motive. This is true only to the extent that Smith argues in the *Moral Sentiments* that social passions are approved and applauded more than selfish ones, but he never says that selfish passions are not, in their proper degree, approved of, and, more important, he does not deny that they are the most efficacious motives. By arguing that benevolence is regarded as being of superior moral worth Smith is not committed to the view that it is the chief motive for action. The fact that men are primarily concerned with their own affairs is accepted as a matter of fact, and one which calls forth neither strong approval nor disapproval. Where self-interest leads men to injure others, then strong disapproval is expressed, but in both Smith's major works he accepts that self-interest is restricted by the need to avoid injuring other men.

It should also be noted that the selfish passions are not selfish in that they always aim at the welfare of the self at the expense of others. The operations of sympathy, which will be described in detail later, make it possible for a man to feel something for the good of others, and desire their happiness as part of his own. By making the pleasure of sharing the happiness of others and obtaining their approval two of the principal ingredients of human happiness Smith ensures that there is nothing essentially anti-social in 'selfish' behaviour.

II. FUNCTIONALISM

This general theory of human behaviour, as I have outlined it so far, would justify us in regarding the *Moral Sentiments* as the work of at least a would-be social psychologist if not of an actual

[1] T.M.S., II.ii.2 (I.205); cf. VII.ii.1 (II.69) and W.N., I.ii (I.18) and II.iii (I.371).
[2] T.M.S., I.iii.2 (I.120ff.); cf. W.N., V.i. (II.231).

practitioner of that science. However Smith's network of explanatory approaches includes more than the search for the 'efficient causes' of human behaviour; he also attempts to establish, by an investigation of the consequences of certain patterns of action, explanations in terms of 'final causes'. It is this concern with final causation which makes Smith a sociological theorist. The addition of a teleological framework to his social psychology is not to be dismissed as an unfortunate theological accretion; for, I shall argue, it enables Smith to address himself to the sort of functionalist questions which are fundamental to modern sociology.

Part II section iii of the *Moral Sentiments* deals with man's tendency to make moral judgments in the light of the actual consequences of an action rather than its intended consequences. Smith's explanation of this phenomenon is typical of his general approach and is conveniently summarized at the beginning of the section:

'This irregularity of sentiment, which every body feels, which scarce any body is sufficiently aware of, and which nobody is willing to acknowledge, I proceed now to explain; and I shall consider, first, the cause which gives occasion to it, or the mechanism by which nature produces it; secondly, the extent of its influence; and, last of all, the end which it answers, or the purpose which the Author of nature seems to have intended by it.'[1]

This scheme combines the strict curtailment of explanations in terms of human purposes and intentions with the introduction of a different level of explanation in terms of the purposes and intentions of Nature or God. The theological explanation is offered, not as a substitute for causal explanation, but as supplementary to it. Once the causal pattern of events has been exhibited, the end result or state towards which the pattern tends is alleged to have some benefit which was not foreseen by any human agent and on account of which it is intelligible and explanatory to say that the whole process exhibits a plan and therefore implies a planner. I have mentioned Smith's use of this line of argument when it is used as an argument for the existence of God. But, if God's existence is taken for granted, then His intentions can be used within 'final' explanations of causal processes. This is not to introduce the operation of the divine will into the causal process; rather it adds to the causal explanation of events a different type of explanation, a teleological one. The last part of Smith's explanatory scheme is not, therefore,

[1] T.M.S., II.iii.Introd. (I.233f.).

independent or self-sufficient but is supervenient upon his prior causal analysis.

The position of Smith's teleological explanations as logically sequential upon his causal explanations does not mean that they play an unimportant part in his total theory. It is a recurring theme in all his works that men are an unwitting part of a larger system and that the intended consequences of their acts have, mainly beneficial, consequences for themselves, for other people, and for the order, stability and prosperity of their society. This 'economy of nature'[1] is, for Smith, a constant source of wonder, and its discovery represents the climax of his scientific endeavours.[2] He takes particular satisfaction in demonstrating the inter-relationships of morality, law, religion and economic life, and in pointing to unsuspected connections between patterns of individual behaviour and the welfare of society as a whole, especially when these patterns seem 'irregular', pointless or even harmful. This represents a development of the idea of a 'system' as applied to societies with which he would be familiar from the writings of Shaftesbury,[3] Hutcheson,[4] and Butler,[5] with particular emphasis on Mandeville's favourite theme, the unintended beneficial consequences of self-interested behaviour.

The most famous examples of this are to be found in the *Wealth of Nations*, where Smith argues that the self-interested actions of individuals serve the economic interests of society as a whole. It is in this context that we come across the only mention of the invisible hand in that book; while discussing the activity of the capitalist Smith writes:

'He generally, indeed, neither intends to promote the public interest, nor knows how much he is promoting it. By preferring the support of domestic to that of foreign industry, he intends only his own security; and by directing that industry in such a manner as its produce may be of the greatest value, he intends only his own gain, and he is in this, as in many other cases, led by an invisible hand to promote an end which was no part of his intention. Nor is it always the worse for the society that it was no part of it. By

---

[1] T.M.S., II.i.5 (I.190).   [2] Cf. p. 32f.

[3] Cf. *An Inquiry Concerning Virtue, or Merit* (1699). In D. D. Raphael, *British Moralists* (Oxford, 1969), §195: 'How hard it is to give the least account of a particular part, without a competent knowledge of the whole.'

[4] Cf. *Concerning Moral Good and Evil*, (4th ed 1738). In D. D. Raphael, *op. cit.*, especially §332.

[5] Cf. *Fifteen Sermons* (1726). In D. D. Raphael, *op. cit.*, §376: 'the idea of a system, economy or constitution of any particular nature, or particular anything . . . it is an one or a whole made up of several parts'.

pursuing his own interest he frequently promotes that of the society more effectually than when he really intends to promote it.'[1]

The other 'invisible hand' passage occurs in the *Moral Sentiments* where he goes even further by suggesting that economic activity is motivated not simply by self-interest but by mistaken self-interest, in that men have a false idea of the pleasure to be derived from wealth and greatness, yet 'it is this deception which rouses and keeps in continual motion the industry of mankind'.[2] Thus the landlord strives to increase the productivity of his land but 'the capacity of his stomach bears no proportion to the immensity of his desires' and he is forced to distribute what he produces above his own needs to those around him:

'They are led by an invisible hand to make nearly the same distribution of the necessaries of life, which would have been made, had the earth been divided into equal portions among all its inhabitants, and thus without intending it, without knowing it, advance the interest of the society, and afford means to the multiplication of the species.'[3]

Smith's motive in pointing out these causal connections is not in the first instance to promote a free-trade economic policy, but to offer an explanation of the economic system. At the heart of the *Wealth of Nations* is the argument that the motive of self-interest, manifested in man's pursuit of his own immediate economic advantage, produces a self-adjusting economic system. By following utility in the sense of their individual material interests, men unwittingly serve utility in the sense of the general interest. This approach is endorsed in the *Moral Sentiments:*

'society may subsist among different men, as among different merchants, from a sense of its utility, without any mutual love or affection; and though no man in it should owe any obligation, or be bound in gratitude to any other, it may still be upheld by a mercenary exchange of good offices according to an agreed valuation.'[4]

This passage has been frequently misinterpreted. It does not mean that men maintain their social relationships because they are aware of the necessity of such relationships for the general happiness; it is their own immediate self-interest, as embodied in acts of barter and trading, that binds them to society. Nor is this motive sufficient for

[1] W.N., IV.ii (I.477f.). [2] T.M.S., IV.1 (I.464).
[3] T.M.S., IV.1 (I.466). [4] T.M.S., II.ii.3 (I.214).

social cohesion; it requires to be supplemented, as the context makes abundantly clear, by the moral and legal constraints of justice. This is an assumption which is taken for granted in the *Wealth of Nations*.

The phrase 'invisible hand' is an unfortunate one in that it suggests that God intervenes in a course of events that, left to itself, would have unfortunate consequences, but the hand in question is the designer and creator of the total system, not the mechanic who comes to the rescue when the machine goes wrong. The metaphor of the 'invisible hand' is brought in to cap a causal explanation with a teleological one, not to introduce an unverifiable intervention by a *deus ex machina* designed to bolster up a shaky causal explanation.[1]

The *Moral Sentiments* contains many other examples of the same reasoning. When men judge by the consequences rather than the intentions of actions they prevent unfulfilled evil intentions from provoking hostile reactions and they are encouraged to put their good intentions into deeds: this is a demonstration of 'the wisdom and goodness of God even in the weakness and folly of men'.[2] Or, again, the disposition men have to admire the rich and the great which results from their imaginative identification with the pleasures of the great, is said to be 'necessary both to establish and to maintain the distinction of ranks and the order of society',[3] and this ensures the maintenance of justice which in turn promotes commerce.[4] It is a presupposition of Smith's whole theory that when men act under the direction of their immediate and short-sighted impulses, this works out to their own benefit, to the benefit of others and in the interests of the whole structure of society. To show this is the crowning aim of his explanatory endeavours.

It might be thought that to stress the theological idea of God's purpose as one of the central organizing principles of Smith's social theory is to remove it from the realm of science and to subordinate his scientific generalizations to unverifiable theological presuppositions. Yet many of Smith's statements about final causation have a remarkable similarity to modern functionalist theories, and this should make us hesitate before dismissing them as irrelevant to social science. Smith's concern to exhibit 'unintended consequences' has much in common with the search for 'latent functions' in the

---

[1] Cf. D. Emmet, *Function, Purpose and Powers* (London, 1958), p. 90: 'it [the invisible hand] is a metaphor to express his sense of how remarkable it was that individual forces in society should balance one another'.

[2] T.M.S., II.iii.3 (I.267).   [3] T.M.S., I.iii.3 (I.146).

[4] W.N., IV.vii.2 (II.76).

modern study of society.[1] Such theories assume, as does Smith, that society is a bounded system, not unlike an animal organism, with complex inter-relations between its parts, so that each makes a contribution to the other or to the system as a whole. Modern theorists talk of the social system instead of an 'immense machine',[2] but the idea is the same, the organization of parts in a whole which is more than an aggregate because each part contributes something distinctive to the operation of the whole. This is the theme of the entire *Wealth of Nations* which outlines the economic system which results from men's short-sighted desire to look after their own interests, and produces results which no 'human wisdom' could achieve.[3] It is also the over-arching perspective of the *Moral Sentiments.*

Can we then select from Smith's statement of his explanatory scheme the assertion that he is seeking, in his teleological explanations, to show 'the end which it answers' and ignore the alternative formulation, 'the purpose which the author of nature seems to have intended by it', and thereby turn it into a respectable sociological method? This might seem to be artificial but it has the advantage of helping us to see the continuity between eighteenth-, nineteenth- and twentieth-century studies of society.[4] To remove the theological framework and turn divine teleology into latent functionalism may have the effect of taking the explanatory power out of Smith's statements of final causation. The alleged logical inadequacies of functional explanation in the social sciences are a continuing problem for all functional theorists and raise more issues than can possibly be considered here. What can be said is that those functional explanations which assert that a particular pattern of social behaviour is essential for the survival of a society are more serious contenders for the status of being regarded as a distinct type of explanation than those which simply point that this behaviour is 'functional' in the sense that it has consequences which are beneficial to some social institution of which it is not itself a part.

It is possible to interpret the most important 'final cause' explanations in the *Moral Sentiments* according to the first model. Again and again Smith argues that justice, and to a lesser extent social stratification, are necessary to the existence of society; and by

---

[1] Cf. R. K. Merton, *Social Theory and Social Structure* (New York, 1949) chap. 1.

[2] Smith also writes of 'one immense and connected system', T.M.S., VII (II.253).

[3] W.N., IV.ix (II.208).

[4] For a similar attempt in the case of Newton, cf. E. Mach, *The Science Mechanics* (1883).

this he does not simply mean that they are necessary conditions for the continuance of that particular society, he means that they are essential to the survival of any society whatsoever. Certain aspects of religion are contributory to this function: the fear of death, for instance, 'while it afflicts and mortifies the individual, guards and protects society' by making men fear the unpleasant consequences of the injustices they inflict on others.[1] The 'law of retaliation', based on the immediate instinct for revenge, is 'sacred and necessary' because 'the very existence of society requires that unmerited and unprovoked malice should be restrained by proper punishments',[2] for society 'cannot subsist among those who are at all times ready to hurt and injure one another'.[3] These assertions are the clearest examples in the *Moral Sentiments* of the belief that certain patterns of behaviour are necessary for the existence of society. They do not provide a complete explanation of these patterns of behaviour, but Smith does not pretend that they do, since they are appended to psychological accounts of such behaviour. But by showing that justice is a necessary condition of existence for any society he may be said to have contributed to its explanation within the bounds of science.

Further questions need to be asked: when does society cease to exist? When its members are 'dissipated and scattered abroad'?[4] Why do societies exist at all? Because they are necessary for the survival of man? If some further explanation for society's existence is required, Smith must retreat into his belief that all things work towards the two 'favourite ends of nature', 'self-preservation and the propagation of the species'.[5] For Smith this is ultimately explanatory because of his theological beliefs, but as these have been replaced in the science of biology by the theory of natural selection, a similar step can be made in the science of society. If it is at all plausible to suggest that human groups have gone through a process of natural selection in the early history of human society it is possible not only to see a continuity between Smith's explanation of revenge as a motive necessary to the survival of man in society and modern functional theory, but to give some sort of justification for this type of theory as a whole.

However, not all functional explanations involve a reference to the necessary conditions of existence for the system concerned. If, in the place of mere survival, there is posited some normal state of

[1] T.M.S., I.i.1 (I.14).   [2] T.M.S., II.i.3 (I.172); cf. T.M.S., II.i.5 (I.189f.).
[3] T.M.S., II.ii.3 (I.214).   [4] T.M.S., II.ii.3 (I.214).
[5] T.M.S., II.i.5 (I.190 and 191).

the system which tends to re-establish itself whenever it is disrupted, then parts of the system are said to be functional to the extent that they contribute to the attainment or continuity of this normal state. It is a common feature of many biological organisms, and of some machines, that they have such states of equilibrium which are associated with various 'feed-back' mechanisms whereby any deviance from the equilibrium is corrected. The most common examples are the bodily mechanisms which maintain an even blood temperature in animals, or the ball-cock on a water tank which ensures that the level of water in the tank remains constant. Some of these homeostatic controls are necessary conditions for the existence of organisms but others are functional for a normal state which is only very indirectly related to survival. The random movements of animals which cease only when they reach a 'comfortable' resting place certainly help to keep them within an environment conducive to survival, but in higher animals these movements persist to degree far beyond what is necessary to achieve this end.

It would be too much to suggest that Smith had any clear idea of this sort of functionalism, yet we may still compare parts of his explanatory scheme with modern equilibrium theory. Many of his functional statements can be taken as referring to homeostatic ends which go beyond the necessary conditions for the survival either of individuals or of society. Hunger is an instinct which is clearly functional for the survival of the individual, as sex is functional for the survival of the species,[1] but in addition to these primary ends Smith believes that nature 'intended the happiness and perfection of the species'.[2] Justice is necessary to society but the moral sentiments are concerned with more than mere justice; they encourage the exercise of benevolence and mutual kindness which is conducive to the harmony of social relationships:[3] for instance, mutual kindness is necessary for happiness, therefore our moral sentiments approve of rewarding kindness with kindness.[4] Or, again, to judge actions by their consequences, not their intentions, has as its final cause the happiness of the species.[5] As we shall see, Smith's whole moral system is designed to show how the moral sentiments arise out of the mutual adjustment of sentiments which is sufficient for the harmony of society. Since this harmony is necessary for the happiness of individuals, we may say that the ultimate end which all morality tends to establish is the happiness of mankind:

[1] T.M.S., II.i.5 (I.191).   [2] T.M.S., II.iii.3 (I.265).
[3] T.M.S., I.iii.1 (I.113).   [4] T.M.S., VI.ii.1 (II.88).
[5] T.M.S., II.iii.3 (I.270).

'Nature, indeed, seems to have so happily adapted our sentiments of approbation and disapprobation, to the conveniency
both of the individual and of the society, that after the strictest
examination it will be found, I believe, that this is universally
the case.'[1]

Functional explanations of this sort can be tied in with Smith's
hedonistic motivational theory to provide an explanation for the
congruence between human nature and social life in the same way
as homeostatic functional relations explain the adaptive relations of
part to whole in maintaining a state of equilibrium in animal
organisms. The explanatory force of such functional explanations
rests on empirical generalizations which describe the state of
equilibrium to be found in particular species of organism and a
description of the mechanisms by which this state is maintained.
One homeostatic condition which Smith regards as holding for
human societies is the state of harmony,[2] defined in terms of the
absence of conflict and the presence of mutual friendliness. The
mechanism which maintains this state is that of sympathy, which
will be analysed in detail in later chapters.

Smith does not take the analogy between society and an organism
all the way since he realizes that harmony in society has, as its
purpose, the happiness of individuals within society. This gives us a
clue as to how the mechanism of sympathy can establish harmony in
society. Just as protozoa will move randomly round a tank of water
until they reach water of the right temperature, so human beings
rest content only when they have achieved a state of happiness. We
have seen that Smith regards this as a state of tranquillity, or the
absence of irritation; not necessarily a state of inactivity but of
smooth operation. Those actions which tend to produce such a
state are reinforced while others are left behind or not repeated.
This does not imply any conscious forethought on men's part any
more than in the random behaviour of animals. For although men
are able to reflect on this functional utility and admire it, Smith
never admits that this is the explanation for its operation and
maintenance.

Functional explanations in terms of a homeostatic state of
happiness not essential to survival are not so rigorous as those which
state the necessary conditions for the operation of a system, since we
cannot appeal to the theory of natural selection to explain the
presence of such functional relationships; but they can be incor-
porated into a causal theory of human behaviour of the mechanistic

[1] T.M.S., IV.2 (I.476).   [2] T.M.S., I.i.4 (I.40).

type which explains goal-seeking behaviour by reference to states of discomfort which precede and provoke the behaviour which eventually results in tranquillity and an end to the discomfort. While it is somewhat artificial to interpret Smith's teleological explanations in terms of the concept of homeostasis, it does help us to see similarities between eighteenth- and twentieth-century social science and to show that, despite the decline in theological telecism, it is possible to see some continuity between Smith's approach and more radically secular post-Darwinian social science.

In partial justification of applying the concepts of equilibrium and homeostasis to the analysis of the *Moral Sentiments* we can point to the many examples in the *Wealth of Nations* of the idea that the economy tends to establish a natural or normal level of wages or prices or interest and so on.[1] For instance there is the tendency of the natural price of a commodity to establish itself after it has been artificially disturbed,[2] or, more strikingly, the way in which the profitability of different trades, professions and employments tend to become equalized: all this is described and explained by showing how the functional inter-relations of prices, wages, rents, profits, interest rates and so on are maintained by the persistence of men's economic motivations which prompt them to employ their labour and capital where they offer the greatest reward for the least effort.[3] The economic system is likened to a human body which is normally able to recover from sickness and return to its usual healthy state of its own accord.[4] Although it may be hindered by bad laws, the natural system of liberty 'establishes itself'.[5] Of Quesnay, Smith argues that 'he does not seem to have considered that in the political body, the natural effort which every man is continually making to better his own condition, is a principle of preservation capable of preventing and correcting, in many respects, the bad effects of a political economy, in some degree both partial and oppressive'. And again: 'In the political body, however, the wisdom of nature has fortunately made ample provision for remedying many of the bad effects of the folly and injustice of man; in the same manner as it has done in the natural body, for remedying his sloth and intemperance!'[6] The use

[1] Cf. p. 65f. This is admirably discussed by Andrew Skinner in his introduction to *The Wealth of Nations* (Penguin Books, 1970), pp. 52-75.

[2] W.N., I.iv (I.33).

[3] W.N., I.vii (I.64f.); cf. I.x (I.111): 'The whole advantages and disadvantages of the different employments of labour and stock must, in the same neighbourhood, be either perfectly equal or continually tending to equality.'

[4] W.N., IV.v (II.49) and W.N., II.iii (I.364).

[5] W.N., IV.ix (II.208).   [6] W.N., IV.ix (II.194f.).

of this analogy shows that the idea of a state of equilibrium maintained by a homeostatic mechanism was part of his way of thinking and inseparable from his conception of an economic and social system. It is not, therefore, unrealistic to see it as affecting his approach to the study of morality.

III. THE HISTORICAL DIMENSION

Functionalism is sometimes considered to imply a static view of society, but this is not true in Smith's case; in fact this method may properly be called genetic or historical.[1] However he is not concerned to trace the development of *particular* historical events; his interest is, in his own terminology, with didactic writing rather than with narrative history.[2] The 'origins' which he has in mind are not dateable events but the raw materials of human nature and the basic types of social situation within which human behaviour is formed, partly in each individual and partly in the development of society itself. In general, Smith's method is historical, first, in the broad sense that it is empirical, and secondly, because he stresses that the laws of social science include many laws of social development. These provide a necessary link between his analysis of the constituent elements of human behaviour and the explanation of specific patterns of activity. Thus, for instance, he indicates how man's 'original' desire to please his fellows leads, by a process of mutual adjustment and social learning, to the emergence of detailed patterns of behaviour which find favour in specific types of social group. Similarly the general desire to attain the respect of mankind through the accumulation of wealth comes to manifest itself in the pursuit of those particular material objects which are considered to be desirable in specific types of society.

Smith's main historical aim is, therefore, to establish and illustrate his general laws of individual and social development. It is wrong to say, as Dugald Stewart does, that Smith indulges to any considerable extent in what, after Stewart, has come to be called 'conjectural' or 'theoretical' history, at least not in so far as the essence of this type of history is taken to be the attempt to reconstruct the probable course of unrecorded history on the basis of 'the known principles of human nature'.[3] The sample of such conjectural history which Stewart had in mind was Smith's 'Considerations concerning the first Formation of Languages', in which there is a speculative

---

[1] For a useful summary of Smith's 'History of Civil Society', see Andrew Skinner (ed.), *The Wealth of Nations* (Penguin Books, 1970), pp. 29-43.
[2] Cf. L.R.B.L., p. 85f.   [3] E.P.S. ('Account'), p. xlii ff.

account of the stages through which language may have developed in the earliest periods of society.

This sort of investigation clearly interested Smith, but his feeling for historical fact is even stronger than his curiosity about unknown historical origins. The *Wealth of Nations* contains some discussion of the earliest stages of societal development and the origins of some aspects of economic life, such as the use of money, just as the *Essays* contain conjectures about the unrecorded first steps in the emergence of science and religion. But this approach is abandoned as soon as Smith can lay his hands on any hard facts, or even travellers' tales. To the extent that conjectural history is important for Smith's general theory this is due to its ability to fill in some of the 'gaps' in the factual material which Smith uses to outline social development. But it features little in the *Moral Sentiments* although Smith does speculate on the effect which entry into a social group would have on a person who had hitherto lived outside society.[1] This device is important for the distinction which he draws between the original passions which men, as it were, bring with them into society, and the secondary passions, which arise out of social interaction. Yet Smith does not place importance on the historical likelihood of such a series of events; it is, rather, that he is attempting, by reference to such a model, to analyse the effects of processes which are going on all the time in society, and which do not need to be tested against some long past and unrecorded events.

However, Smith is certainly an exponent of conjectural history if that is identified with the practice of regarding history as a process of social development which comes about through the operation of diffuse social causes rather than as a consequence of particular individual acts or events.[2] The development of societies from barbarism to civilization is an integral part of the *Essays*, the *Lectures on Jurisprudence* and the *Wealth of Nations*. By 'civilization' Smith means settled agricultural and commercial society, and 'progress' is measured in terms of economic development. This is not an ultimate moral assessment on Smith's part. He knows that economic development can bring unfortunate consequences for human character and individual development which have to be balanced against the advance in material welfare. His concern over the bad effect of the division of labour on the 'intellectual, social and

---

[1] T.M.S., IV.1 (I.277f.).

[2] Cf. Duncan Forbes, ' "Scientific" Whiggism: Adam Smith and John Millar', *Cambridge Journal*, VIII (1955), pp. 643-70. Forbes attempts to show that the idea of progress is *the* central and unifying theme of all Smith's work, but this is inadequately demonstrated with respect to the *Moral Sentiments*.

martial virtues' of the labouring classes has led some commentators to argue that Smith anticipated Marx's concept of alienation.[1] But Smith deplores the lack of moral and intellectual development rather than the exploitation or estrangement of the labouring poor, and he considers that these side effects of the divison of labour can be mitigated by education.

It is somewhat more convincing to think of Smith as a forerunner of Marx's historical materialism. Smith defines each type of society according to its basic method of production, starting with the society of hunters, then pastoral society, followed by the society of farmers which gradually develops into commercial society, dominated by artificers and merchants. Economic change is a consequence of the 'propensity to truck and barter' in conjunction with man's desire for material wealth, and reaches whatever level is made possible by 'material' factors such as the extent of the market, the development of communications, the use of money, and so forth. Moreover, Smith describes, especially in the *Lectures on Jurisprudence*, how changes in the means of production give rise to new social ranks or classes which in turn affect the method of government.[2] For instance, commercial society has three 'great constituent orders', landlords, capitalists and wage labourers. The development of religion is likewise affected by economic change,[3] and, as we shall see, morality also changes from age to age and varies between the different orders within each society. There is also evidence that Smith saw that intellectual systems and economic doctrines were the result of economic class interest, mercantilism being the class morality of the merchants.[4]

But to think of Smith as an economic determinist ignores the fact that he did not consider even economic progress to be inevitable or irreversible; it also oversimplifies his theory of social change. For instance, there are elements within men's ideas about justice which limit economic development and are not affected by it. The proper administration of justice, which is a precondition of the develop-

---

[1] W.N., V.i.3.art. 2 (II.302ff.). Cf. E. G. West, 'The Political Economy of Alienation: Karl Marx and Adam Smith', *Oxford Economic Papers*, vol XXI (1969), pp. 1-23. West points out significant differences between Marx's and Smith's concepts of 'alienation', but even he goes too far in suggesting that there is an element of 'self-estrangement' in Smith's diagnosis of the ailments of the labouring poor in an industrial society.

[2] Cf. Chapter 10.

[3] W.N., V.i.3.art.3 (II.309ff.).

[4] W.N., IV.iii.2 (I.519). On this whole theme see R. L. Meek, 'The Scottish Contribution to Marxist Sociology', in *Economics and Ideology* (London, 1967), p.34.

ment of commerce,[1] does depend on a sufficient economic basis for its finance, but the central prohibition of justice against harming others is not an economic imperative. Religion also affects the content of the law.[2] But of more importance than this is the complex inter-relationship between the economic basis of society and the governmental function of defence. It is not simply a case of the wealthiest group in society holding political power, since political power is to some extent dependent on the ability to become wealthy by extra-economic methods, such as raising taxes. This ability depends in part on the citizen's sense of the utility of government in maintaining peace and security, and partly on the 'principle of authority'[3] which refers to the fact that age, long possession of power, and physical and mental abilities, as well as wealth, are qualities which receive respect and obedience. Wealth alone is not sufficient, especially if it is not spent in maintaining dependants who are willing to form an army when necessary. The actual course of societal development is therefore a matter of the complex inter-relationships of economic, military, political, religious, moral and legal factors; social institutions grow up and change in response to a wide variety of factors, even although the economic one is perhaps the most decisive. But this is not a process which occurs without resistance; custom and habit as well as the vested interests of the declining economic and political groups can maintain institutions after the causes which produced them have ceased to operate. This enables Smith to hold both that institutions are the natural result of man's interaction with his environment, and that the particular institutions at a particular time are a hindrance to natural liberty, for natural liberty is not an absence of institutional restraints but presupposes the operation of those institutions which allow spontaneous human behaviour to manifest itself in a manner appropriate to each stage of societal development.

Many points in this outline of Smith's social theory will become clearer once we have examined those important elements of the theory which are contained in the *Moral Sentiments*. For the moment it is enough to note that Smith had a theory of social change which was primarily but not entirely based on his economics. But it must always be remembered that the economic motive is more a desire for rank and reputation than for the accumulation of material wealth for its own sake. It is within this context that we have to see Smith's explanation of the more static forces of morality and

[1] W.N., IV.vii.2 (II.76) and V.i.2 (II.232).
[2] W.N., IV.v (II.48).
[3] L.J., p. 9.

justice which provide the framework within which economic change takes place. On the other hand, this economic background does affect the form and content of moral and legal rules, and it is part of Smith's achievement, which will be illustrated throughout the coming chapters, that he was able not only to allow for this, but to offer explanations for it.

PART II
ADAM SMITH'S MORAL THEORY

CHAPTER 4

APPROVAL AND SYMPATHY

The terms 'moral' and 'morality' may be used to refer to certain types of conduct which are judged to be good or bad, right or wrong, or to the processes of forming, making, or being disposed to make moral judgments; to describe a person's 'morals' may thus involve giving a report either on his conduct or on his beliefs about what is morally good and bad. A theory of morality may, likewise, be a theory about moral conduct or about moral judgments. Smith's theory is mainly of the latter sort: the 'moral sentiments' to which he refers are those involved in making moral judgments rather than the sentiments embodied in the behaviour which these moral judgments assess. Since moral judgments are judgments on conduct, and since conduct is affected by moral judgments, there can be no sharp distinction between a theory of moral behaviour and a theory of moral judgment, but Smith's primary interest is in the latter phenomenon, the sentiments involved in moral evaluations, or, in the words of the explanatory sub-title introduced in the fourth edition of the *Moral Sentiments*, 'the Principles by which Men naturally judge concerning the Conduct and Character, first of their Neighbours, and afterwards of themselves'.[1]

I. THE DEFINITION OF 'MORAL'

Any study of morality, whether it be scientific or philosophical, requires to be clear about what is to count as 'morality', if only to delimit the area to be investigated. For a theory of moral *judgment* this means indicating what is to count as a 'moral' judgment. On this point Smith would agree with those modern philosophers who describe moral judgments as expressions of approval and disapproval concerning human conduct. However, while approval or disapproval may feature in all moral judgments, they are also present or implied in non-moral evaluations and prescriptions. Smith

[1] T.M.S., sub-title (I.iii). Cf. J. A. Schumpeter, *History of Economic Analysis*, p. 129.

himself mentions that we approve and disapprove of men's literary and mathematical ability and of their aesthetic taste and good judgment.[1] Nor is it sufficient to say, as Smith does, that moral approval and disapproval are directed towards 'conduct and character',[2] since this includes the assessment of behaviour according to standards of skill, usefulness and beauty, which are not, in themselves, moral standards. And we are not greatly helped by being told that moral judgments concern virtue and vice since Smith counts intellectual abilities as a type of virtue,[1] and in any case this merely transfers the burden of definition to these terms.

However Smith does provide us with sufficient synonyms for judgments concerning virtue and vice, in their moral connotations, to enable us to see what sort of judgments of approval and disapproval he has in mind. Virtue and vice are qualities ascribed to 'the sentiment or affection of the heart from which any action proceeds'[3] and in assessing virtue 'the mind prefers one tenour of conduct to another, denominates the one right and the other wrong; considers the one as the object of approbation, honour, and reward, and the other of blame, censure, and punishment'.[4] Or, again, 'what is agreeable to our moral faculties, is fit, and right, and proper to be done; the contrary wrong, unfit, and improper'.[5]

As we shall see, Smith divides moral judgments into judgments of propriety and judgments of merit. 'Propriety' is his term for rightness or fitness and is the quality of deserving approval or praise while impropriety deserves disapproval or blame. An action has merit if it is proper to reward it and demerit if it is proper to punish it. This is exceedingly general, particularly in the case of propriety, which is a standard he sometimes applies to what would normally be considered non-moral conduct; for instance, he writes that 'we may often approve of a jest, and think the laughter of the company quite just and proper'.[6] The use of the words 'just' and 'proper' in this context raises doubts about the adequacy of Smith's definition of morality, and it is often said that he failed to distinguish between morality proper and non-moral judgments such as those concerning social convention or expressing admiration for human skills. Smith certainly did not set out, as many present-day philosophers do, with a narrow definition of morality, singling out, for instance, a particular type of over-riding obligation or universalizable imperative, or the self-conscious choice of ultimate goals. On the contrary, he tends to take in a wide variety of inter-personal attitudes in so far as they

---

[1] T.M.S., I.i.4 (I.32 and 34). [2] T.M.S., sub-title (I.iii).
[3] T.M.S., I.i.3 (I.28). [4] T.M.S., VII.i (II.197).
[5] T.M.S., III.5 (I.412). [6] T.M.S., I.i.3 (I.26).

express preferences for one type of conduct over another; indeed, he concentrates as much on what is sometimes called customary morality, and on unthinking assessments of conduct, as on the types of judgments which are usually said to be characteristically moral ones.

There is, perhaps, no such thing as a 'correct' definition of morality, and suggested definitions ought to be assessed by their appropriateness to the purpose which they are intended to serve. Smith's broad interpretation of the term is suited to his purpose of explaining as wide as possible a variety of social phenomena using the minimum number of explanatory principles. The unity of the *Moral Sentiments*, therefore, does not lie in an initial definition of morality but springs from the fundamental scientific generalizations on the basis of which Smith builds up his 'moral' theory. It is, in fact, the concept of sympathy which provides the unifying theme that gives the work its coherence. Smith believed that he could explain all the judgments which we should normally call moral ones by reference to the various operations of sympathy, but his interest in this latter phenomenon leads him to attempt explanations of many social attitudes which, on most definitions of 'morality', would not be considered as instances of moral judgments. In this chapter we shall analyse Smith's concept of sympathy, indicate why he considered it to be such an important factor in society, and outline the main generalizations which he makes about its operation.

II. AGREEMENT AND APPROVAL

Whatever difficulty there may be in determining exactly what Smith considered to be the defining characteristics of a moral judgment, there is no doubt about the broad category to which he assigns it: a moral judgment is a judgment of approval or disapproval. His entire moral theory is built on certain assumptions about the conditions under which men approve and disapprove, not only of the behaviour, but also of the perceptions, reasonings, feelings, opinions and beliefs of their fellows. He argues, firstly, that men judge the opinions, perceptions or sentiments of each other by comparing them with their own; if they 'agree', that is, if one man perceives that he shares the opinion, perception or feeling of another, then he judges it to be correct:

'Every faculty in one man is the measure by which he judges of the like faculty in another. I judge of your sight by my sight, of your ear by my ear, of your reason by my reason, of your resentment by my resentment, of your love by my love. I neither have, nor can have, any other way of judging about them.'[1]

Not only is judgment based on the 'perception of this coincidence',[2] or the lack of it, but approval and disapproval are claimed to be necessary consequences of perceiving that one shares or does not share the opinions or sentiments of another:

'To approve of another man's opinions is to adopt those opinions, and to adopt them is to approve of them. If the same arguments which convince you convince me likewise, I necessarily approve of your conviction; and if they do not, I necessarily disapprove of it: neither can I possibly conceive that I should do the one without the other. To approve or disapprove therefore, of the opinions of others is acknowledged, by every body, to mean no more than to observe their agreement or disagreement with our own. But this is equally the case with regard to our approbation or disapprobation of the sentiments or passions of others.'[3]

This seems to assert that there is some sort of necessary connection between the perception of agreement, in the sense of seeing that one shares the opinion or sentiment of another, and the approval of that opinion or sentiment. 'Approval' here, for Smith, means not only judging an opinion or sentiment to be correct, but also commending the person for having this opinion or sentiment. The quotation I have given concentrates on the agreement and disagreement of opinions, but Smith makes the same point about admiring the same picture or poem, laughing at the same joke, feeling the same emotions, and perceiving the same objects.[4]

The multiplicity of examples which he gives are all designed to support the argument, which is crucial for the *Moral Sentiments*, that one man approves of the sentiments of another when he shares these sentiments, and disapproves of his sentiments if he does not share them. He wants to argue that approbation simply *is* the perception of the coincidence of sentiments, and talks of 'that perfect harmony and correspondence of sentiments which constitutes approbation'.[5] This point, which seemed so evident to Smith, has been disputed by others. Jouffroy points out that 'I share a thousand emotions, without morally approving or disapproving them; I condemn many emotions which I share; and, on the other hand, I approve many things which are neither emotions nor the result of

---

[1] T.M.S., I.i.3 (I.30f.).   [2] T.M.S., I.i.3 (I.26).
[3] T.M.S., I.i.3 (I.25).   [4] T.M.S., I.i.3 (I.24).
[5] T.M.S., I.iii.1 (I.103).

emotions; . . . and I even approve of emotions . . . which are absolutely displeasing to me.'[1] Here Jouffroy is wide of the mark in thinking that Smith did not allow that men approve of things other than emotions, or that there is any difficulty about approving of displeasing emotions, since it is just as possible to share displeasing emotions as pleasing ones. But the assertion that it is possible to share emotions without approving of them and to approve of emotions without sharing them is more to the point. It is an argument which has been repeated by those who say that Smith consistently confuses 'fellow-feeling', or sharing emotions, with approval or praise.[2]

We shall see later how Smith's theory of the impartial spectator takes into account the fact that approval and agreement do not in every instance coincide, but it must be allowed that Smith has been, to some extent, misled by failing to see that 'approval' can mean either 'judging to be correct' or 'expressing favourable attitudes', and also by thinking of 'agreement' both as 'the perception of coincidence' and as 'the expression of favourable attitudes'. These confusions led him to say, on occasions, that to share a sentiment is the same thing as to approve of it, and this must surely be a mistake. But it is not a simple linguistic error: he does have arguments to back up his identification of agreement and approval.

The first argument is an epistemological one: it is only possible, he says, to judge one person's 'faculty' by comparing it with one's own. The second argument, which he states as if it were a logical one, asserts that it is impossible to share an opinion or sentiment without approving of that opinion or sentiment. The first or epistemological argument is most convincing when it is the accuracy of a perception or the correctness of an argument that is being assessed, for while it is true that there are many external tests by which perceptions and arguments can be examined, in the end these do involve some reference to one's own perceptual or intellectual faculties to check the processes of perception or the arguments

---

[1] *Jouffroy's Ethics,* translated by W. H. Channing (Boston, 1841), vol. 2. p. 146.

[2] Cf. Thomas Brown, *Lectures on Ethics* (Edinburgh, 1846), p. 165: 'It [sympathy] is generally employed, indeed, to signify a mere participation of the feelings of others; but it is also frequently used as significant of approbation itself.' Also J. A. Farrer, *Adam Smith* (London, 1881), pp. 196f.: 'It is difficult to read Adam Smith's account of the identification of sympathy and approbation, without feeling that throughout his argument there is an unconscious play upon words, and that an equivocal use of the word "sympathy" lends all its speciousness to the theory he expounds . . . The first meaning is fellow-feeling, the second praise or approval.'

which are being assessed. But, unfortunately for Smith, the parallel with sentiments does not seem to hold: there is no immediate equivalent, in the case of sentiment, to checking the accuracy of a perception or the validity of an argument: sentiments, in themselves, are not judged by this sort of standard; they cannot be said to be accurate or valid; it is not, therefore, clear what is being assessed when I compare my sentiments with those of another person. If Smith is intending to say that the assessment must be one of moral approbation or disapprobation, then the parallel seems a weak one, for there seems to be no reason why, just because I usually judge the accuracy of a perception by reference to my own perceptions, I must make moral judgments by comparing the sentiments of others with my own; and similarly, in the case of reasoning, the standards of correctness which apply to arguments do not apply to sentiments, and therefore there is no reason why the method of testing which is suitable for the one should apply to the other.

It may be more plausible to say that I assess the moral judgments of another by comparing them with my own, but Smith cannot be said to have established anything about the assessment of sentiments in general by the epistemological parallels he draws between the judgment of perceptions and reasonings on the one hand and the 'judgment' of sentiments on the other. Perhaps, in this instance, he had not entirely freed himself from the analogy he thought to be implied in Hutcheson's phrase, the 'moral sense'.[1]

The analogy between opinions and sentiments is also misleading in the form in which it occurs in the second part of Smith's argument; there he states it to be a necessary fact that a person approves of opinions and therefore also of sentiments with which he agrees. It does seem odd to say that I approve of an opinion with which I disagree, but this is because, in this context, approve usually means 'agree with' or 'think to be correct'. But if by 'approval' and 'disapproval' we mean holding 'pro' or 'con' attitudes then it is often the case that we agree or disagree with the opinions of others without approving or disapproving of them. Such attitudes are not always appropriate. Indeed we may disapprove of someone's expressing an opinion with which we agree in the sense that we think it to be true, since that opinion may not be favourable to our interests. Smith is, therefore, mistaken in making the logical point that, where adopting an opinion and approving of it is concerned, 'I cannot possibly conceive that I should do the one without the other'.[2]

However, if his logical argument is reinterpreted as a psychological

---

[1] Cf. p. 222.   [2] T.M.S., I.i.3 (I.25).

one, then it becomes more plausible. There may be grounds for saying, as an empirical generalization, that men do approve of opinions which they share; in so far as men hold opinions which they believe to be true and approve of other's believing what is true, this generalization will be valid. In the same way we may interpret Smith as saying, in the case of sentiments, that it is a contingent fact that men approve of sentiments which they share and disapprove of sentiments which they do not share. But this is not as plausible in the case of sentiments as in the case of opinions, since men would appear to disapprove of their own sentiments in a way in which they do not disapprove of their own opinions. This point is underlined by pointing out that it is logically necessary for men to 'approve' of their own opinions in the restricted sense of 'think them to be correct', but there is no equivalent logical necessity in the case of sentiments, since sentiments *per se* cannot be said to be correct or incorrect, true or false.[1]

In depriving Smith of the support of these two arguments by denying the parallels he suggests between opinions and perceptions on the one hand, and sentiments on the other, we have not necessarily destroyed the basis of his theory, since it might still be true to say that, even in the case of sentiments, approval and disapproval are normally consequent upon the perception of agreement or disagreement. It becomes apparent that Smith *is* making an empirical claim when he comes to argue his case against the utilitarians, for he then admits that, while we *can* judge a sentiment by its utility, this is not the *usual* method. In fact, throughout the *Moral Sentiments* he takes pains to explain many of the apparent exceptions to the constant conjunction of agreement and approval of sentiments. His theory of the impartial spectator is designed to show that, if we wish to understand the origins and causes of moral judgments, then we must start from the assumption that the fundamental causes of approval and disapproval are perceptions of the agreement and disagreement of sentiments. This does not, however, mean, as we shall see, that every moral judgment must be accompanied by such a perception. To deny that there is a necessary epistemological relationship between agreement and approval does make Smith's theory more open to question. His explanatory system can only have as much validity as the suggested causal relationship between agreement and approval, and it may, therefore, be more limited in its scope than Smith thought it to be.

[1] A similar point is made in A. N. Prior, *Logic and the Basis of Ethics*, pp. 66f.

III. SYMPATHY

'Sympathy' is Smith's word for agreement, coincidence or harmony of sentiments, or 'our fellow-feeling with any passion whatever'.[1] This fellow-feeling involves *awareness*, on the part of the person sympathizing, that he shares the feelings of another; 'mutual' sympathy exists when both persons are aware that their sentiments coincide. Smith uses the term as a 'success' word, that is, he says that two people sympathize when they are aware that their sentiments are in harmony, or at least when one person thinks that his sentiments coincide with those of another person. But he is just as concerned with men's awareness of the absence of sympathy, or the lack of coincidence between their sentiments, since, although sympathy explains judgments of approbation, it is the lack of sympathy which is required to account for judgments of disapprobation, and much of the *Moral Sentiments* is taken up with explaining why men fail to sympathize with each other. Sympathy, or the agreement of sentiments, is fundamental to Smith's theory, simply because it is that particular form of agreement on which approval of sentiments is founded.

It cannot be said that Smith's concept of sympathy accords with the normal meaning of the term, even in his own day, and, as a result, it is not uncommon to find it misrepresented and his theory consequently distorted. Despite the opening paragraph of the *Moral Sentiments*, which points out the obvious fact that men feel pity and compassion for each other, sympathy is not to be identified with these sentiments.[2] It may give rise to sentiments like pity and benevolence, but it is not itself a sentiment; it is a correspondence between sentiments. For Smith fellow-feeling is a matter of sharing feelings and is essentially feeling *with* someone, although it does give rise to fellow-feeling in the sense of feeling *for* another; but, in order to understand this theory correctly, it is necessary to realise that this latter feeling is a consequence of the former; sympathy should not be identified with the feelings to which it gives rise.

Smith's concept of sympathy must not, therefore, be confused with that used by philosophers like Shaftesbury, who regarded it as one of the natural affections.[3] It is this confusion which leads

---

[1] T.M.S., I.i.1 (I.6f.).
[2] Cf. E. Westermarck, *Ethical Relativity*, p. 97. Westermarck thought Smith's sympathy was 'a conative influence to promote the welfare of others'.
[3] Cf. *Characteristics*, edition of 1723, vol. II, p. 99.

some interpreters to say, as Lange does, that 'sympathy and interest were with him [Smith] the two great springs of human action,'[1] as if sympathy were equivalent to benevolence. The *desire* for sympathy, as we have seen, is an important motive in Smith's theory of action, but sympathy is not itself a sentiment and it is certainly not to be equated with benevolence or pity.[2]

Another erroneous exposition of Smith's concept of sympathy presents it as being something similar to empathy or any process by which the feelings of one person are transferred to another: what Scheler calls 'emotional infection'.[3] This is Hume's meaning of the term, and Smith's originality is often obscured by those who equate their concepts of sympathy.[4] Hume held that to sympathize was to 'receive by communication their [other people's] inclinations and sentiments, however different from or contrary to our own',[5] and Hutcheson, Smith's teacher, said that sympathy was 'a sort of contagion or infection';[6] Smith does not deny that such transference of emotion does take place and that it can result in sympathy, but it is unusual, and even when it does occur it is not to be equated with sympathy. As we will often have to emphasize in expounding Smith's theory, 'sympathy . . . does not arise so much from the view of the passion, as from that of the situation which excites it'.[7] Smith wants to make the sympathetic feelings in one person the standard by which he judges the feelings of another. If sympathetic feelings were feelings communicated from that other person, then they would invariably coincide with the feelings being assessed and

---

[1] F. A. Lange, *History of Materialism* (London, 1881), p. 234.

[2] Cf. A. L. Macfie, *The Individual in Society*, p. 63. Macfie is doubly mistaken in saying that Smith regarded sympathy as 'an emotion, and an unselfish emotion'.

[3] M. Scheler, *The Nature of Sympathy* (1913), translated by P. Heath (London, 1954), p. 14.

[4] Cf. W. C. Swabey, *Ethical Theory from Hobbes to Kant*, p. 180: Swabey describes Smith's idea of sympathy as 'a passing of any sort of feeling or desire from one person to another'; and G. R. Morrow, 'The Significance of the Doctrine of Sympathy in Hume and Adam Smith', *The Philosophical Review*, vol. XXXII (1923), p. 69, footnote: 'Adam Smith's statement of the principle of sympathy differed but little from that of Hume in the *Treatise*'. The same mistake is made by J. Cropsey, *Polity and Economy* (The Hague, 1957), p. 16.

[5] *Treatise of Human Nature*, edited by Selby-Bigge, book II, part I, section XI, p. 316.

[6] *A Short Introduction to Moral Philosophy* (4th edn, 1772), vol. 1, p. 15. Smith's concept of sympathy can be traced to Hutcheson's 'public sense'. Cf. *British Moralists*, edited by Selby-Bigge, §433; and T.M.S., VII.iii.3 (II.345).

[7] T.M.S., I.i.1 (I.10). Selby-Bigge is near the mark in saying that Smith 'established sympathy on the basis of thought', *British Moralists*, p. lix.

there would be no absence of sympathy on which to base judgments of disapproval.

Smith is particularly interested in that type of sympathy in which the coincidence of sentiments is brought about by one or both of the persons concerned undergoing an imaginary change of situation. I will call the process by which this comes about, imaginative sympathy; it is the cause of what Smith calls sympathetic feelings: the feelings which arise within us when we conceive of ourselves in a situation other than our present one.[1] If two people are in the same situation there is no need for this imaginary change of position in order for them to sympathize with each other, but when two people are in different situations and therefore feel different emotions, one cannot sympathize with the other unless he imagines himself as being in the other's place.

The two different situations which Smith has chiefly in mind are those of the spectator on the one hand and the agent, or 'the person who is principally interested in any event',[2] on the other. The spectator is the person who tries to sympathize with the agent by conceiving himself to be in the agent's position and comparing his own sympathetic feelings with the real feelings of the agent. It is this process which Smith considers crucial for the understanding of the moral sentiments, and he even tends to write as if the ability to feel sympathetic emotions is the meaning of the term 'sympathy'.[3] We may say that Smith has a general meaning for 'sympathy', namely the perception of the coincidence of sentiments, and a specific meaning, the capacity to achieve such coincidence through the imaginary change of one's point of view; I have called this latter imaginative sympathy. In this specific meaning sympathy is not a success word in that the sympathetic feelings need not coincide with the actual feelings of another person for it to be said to have taken place; thus it is possible to 'sympathize even with the dead'[4] by conceiving what it would be like to be in their position, even although they have no feelings which we can share, and, even with respect to the living. 'we sometimes feel for another, a passion of which he himself seems altogether incapable.'[5]

[1] T.M.S., I.i.3 (I.21); cf. L.R.B.L., p. 85. They are what M. Scheler calls 'vicariously visualized feelings', *The Nature of Sympathy*, p. 14.
[2] T.M.S., I.i.3 (I.21).
[3] T.M.S., VII.iii (II.342) and I.i.4 (I.32).
[4] T.M.S., I.i.1 (I.12).
[5] T.M.S., I.i.1. (10).

Smith begins his discussion of the place of imaginative sympathy in moral judgments by asserting the essential privacy of individual experience: 'we have no immediate experience of what other men feel', for our senses 'never did, and never can, carry us beyond our own person', and, in consequence, 'we can form no idea of the manner in which they are affected, but by conceiving what we ourselves should feel in the like situation'.[1] This is the work of the imagination which uses copies of our own sense impressions to build up a picture of what we should feel were we in another's place; he cites as an example the situation of one person watching another on the rack:

'By the imagination we place ourselves in his situation, we conceive ourselves enduring all the same torments, we enter as it were into his body, and become in some measure the same person with him, and thence form some idea of his sensations, and even feel something which, though weaker in degree, is not altogether unlike them.'[2]

Without these operations of the imagination men would be unable to judge whether they 'agree' with the sentiments of those in situations different from their own, and moral judgments could not be made on the conduct of such persons.

The activity of comparing sympathetic and real sentiments does presuppose that we can have some awareness of the sentiments of others, for, if this were not the case, we could never know the actual feelings of others and so we could not compare them with our own feelings. Smith says little about how we can discover the real feelings of others, but we must simply assume that it is possible to get some idea of the sentiments of others by drawing inferences from their overt behaviour and verbal reports without imagining ourselves in their position. He does go into this to some extent in the *Lectures on Rhetoric* where it is suggested that knowledge of 'internal [facts] . . . to wit, the thoughts and sentiments or designs of men which pass in their minds'[3] can be 'well described only by their effects'.[4] If this implies that they can only be *known* by their effects, then it would seem that the spectator infers what must be the sentiments of the agent from the latter's observable behaviour, relying on experience of his own sentiments and their manifestations to know the sort of external effects that are associated with the various sorts of 'internal' facts.

---

[1] T.M.S., I.i.1 (I.2). [2] T.M.S., I.i.1 (I.3).
[3] L.R.B.L., p. 59. [4] L.R.B.L., p. 71; cf. T.M.S., VII.iv (II.363).

IV. THE 'LAWS OF SYMPATHY'

Although the sentiments of the spectator and the agent may, on occasions, be said to 'correspond', Smith does not think that it is ever possible for the spectator to feel sympathetic sentiments as strongly as the agent feels his 'real' sentiments; sympathetic emotions are only 'similar to' the sentiments of the agent.[1] All sympathetic feelings are 'weaker in degree' than the originals, but some feelings are much more difficult to imagine than others. The spectator's ability to sympathize with an agent therefore varies with the situation and the feelings of the agent. Smith presents a series of empirical generalizations about the extent to which the imagination can reproduce different types of feeling, and therefore the degree to which the spectator can 'enter into' the sentiments of the agent. It is by means of these generalizations, which I shall call the laws of sympathy, that he attempts to explain the large variety of social, and, in particular, moral phenomena described in the *Moral Sentiments*. A brief summary of the laws of sympathy will be helpful at this stage:

(1) *Passions which take their origin from the body are less easy to enter into than those which take their origin from the imagination.* Although some of the passions, like hunger and sex, which 'arise from a certain situation or disposition of the body'[2] are among the strongest that occur, they are amongst the most difficult passions with which to sympathize, for, when our bodily state is of one sort, it is extremely difficult to imagine what it is like for it to be otherwise. The man with a full stomach finds it hard to imagine himself hungry; in the absence of bodily pain it is difficult to imagine anything approaching an actual pain. The imagination is, Smith argues by means of many examples, severely limited in relation to bodily feelings; for instance,

'Nothing is so soon forgot as pain. The moment it is gone the whole agony of it is over, and the thought of it can no longer give us any sort of disturbance.'[3]

He notes that our difficulty in feeling imaginative sympathy with bodily passions is modified slightly when the passion is connected with an injury which has visible manifestations, although we soon get used to the sight of bodily suffering; on the other hand internal injuries like 'gout and the toothach (sic), though exquisitely painful, excite very little sympathy'.[4] This accounts for the fact that tragedies

---

[1] T.M.S., I.i.4 (I.40).　　[2] T.M.S., I.ii.1 (I.55).
[3] T.M.S., I.ii.1 (I.61).　　[4] T.M.S., I.ii.1 (I.62).

are rarely about physical injuries: 'What a tragedy would that be of which the distress consisted in a colic!'[1]

In contrast 'those passions which take their origin from the imagination', by which he means from the agent's view of his own situation in its psychological and social aspects, are easily reproduced by the imagination:

> 'The frame of my body can be but little affected by the alterations which are brought about upon that of my companion: but my imagination is more ductile, and more readily assumes, if I may say so, the shape and configuration of the imaginations of those with whom I am familiar. A disappointment in love, or ambition, will, upon this account, call forth more sympathy than the greatest bodily evil.'[2]

These psychological facts about the operations of sympathy are used by Smith to explain why it is necessary for the bodily passions of the agent to be held strictly in check if they are to be shared by the spectator: such control of bodily passions is the virtue of temperance. The approved standard for bodily passions is not, therefore, a matter of their normal felt strength but of the level with which a spectator, who does not feel such a passion, can 'go along with': thus 'The little sympathy which we feel with bodily pain is the foundation of the propriety of constancy and patience in enduring it.'[3]

(2) *It is difficult to sympathize with those 'passions which take their origin from a particular turn or habit of the imagination'*.[4] By this Smith means that a person who has developed some particular interest, or experiences a passion which is not shared by other people, cannot expect to find that they readily sympathize with him. The chief example cited by Smith to illustrate this limitation on the scope of imaginative feeling is that of love between the sexes in so far as this love has a particular person as its object; a lover feels a passion for his love which is not shared by others and they cannot enter into it by conceiving themselves in his situation, for, unless they are in love with the same person, it will always be the case that 'The passion appears to every body, but the man who feels it, entirely disproportioned to the value of the object; and love, though it is pardoned in a certain age because we know it is natural, is always laughed at, because we cannot enter into it.'[5] What we *can* sympathize with are the 'secondary passions', which arise out of

---

[1] T.M.S., I.ii.1 (I.64).   [2] T.M.S., I.ii.1 (I.59f.).
[3] T.M.S., I.ii.1 (I.64).   [4] T.M.S., I.ii.2 (I.66).
[5] T.M.S., I.ii.2 (I.67).

being in love: the fear for the lover's safety, hope for a happy future, and it is these, rather than love itself, which are, therefore, portrayed in the theatre.[1]

This is not perhaps the best illustration of Smith's general point, since love is a passion closely associated with a bodily appetite, but he adds a second example:

'It is for a reason of the same kind, that a certain reserve is necessary when we talk of our own friends, our own studies, our own professions. All these are objects which we cannot expect should interest our companions in the same degree in which they interest us. And it is for want of this reserve, that the one half of mankind make bad company to the other. A philosopher is company to a philosopher only; the member of a club, to his own little knot of companions.'[2]

Smith is making a rather wider point here than is strictly relevant to his observations on the operation of sympathy, but it does serve to illustrate the generalization that men sympathize more easily with interests and emotions which they share with the agent because they have experience of the same interests and emotions in their own lives; other things being equal, this means that the more common or widespread a sentiment may be, the more likely it is to find sympathy and, therefore, approbation. Moreover, it has important repercussions in comparing the moral judgments of different social groups: those that have similar experiences are more likely to approve of each other's conduct than those that have not: there will, therefore, be a general tendency to approve more of those who are similar to oneself than those who are different. It is this law of sympathy which explains such a tendency.

(3) *It is easy to sympathize with pleasant emotions, difficult to sympathize with unpleasant ones.* This is the most important law of sympathy. It follows from the general principle that men choose pleasure rather than pain. Sympathy with agreeable emotions like joy, comes easily, while sympathy with painful ones, like grief, does not:

'. . . our propensity to sympathize with joy is much stronger than our propensity to sympathize with sorrow; and . . . our fellow-feeling for the agreeable emotion approaches much more nearly to the vivacity of what is naturally felt by the persons principally concerned, than that which we conceive for the painful one.'[3]

---

[1] T.M.S., I.ii.2 (I.71). [2] T.M.S., I.ii.2 (I.73). [3] T.M.S., I.iii.1 (I.105f.).

The fact that agreeable sympathetic emotions approach much closer to the original than disagreeable ones is true, in Smith's opinion, despite the fact that pain is 'a more pungent sensation than pleasure, and our sympathy with pain, though it falls greatly short of what is naturally felt by the sufferer, is generally a more lively and distinct perception than our sympathy with pleasure'.[1] This is one of a series of arguments Smith uses to show that pleasure and pain are not simple opposites; he has to account for the fact that men are more indulgent to excessive manifestations of pain than of pleasure; in addition to saying that this is due to the differences between pleasure and pain in their nature as sensations, Smith adds that we make allowances for the fact that it is more difficult to control joy than grief.

(4) *Passions which are closer to the natural, that is to the normal state of the person sympathizing, are easier to enter into than those which are far removed from it.* Smith might have argued that our tendency to have a livelier sympathy with pain than with pleasure despite the unpleasantness of sympathetic pain follows from the fact that men are normally unhappy. But, in fact, it is one of his optimistic beliefs that happiness 'is the normal condition of most men', and, in conjunction with his fourth law of sympathy, he concludes that 'The greater part of men, therefore, cannot find any great difficulty in elevating themselves to all the joy which any accession to this situation can well excite in their companion.'[2] Misery is disapproved of not only because it is unpleasant but also because it is unusual.

It is important to stress that all these laws should be interpreted in the context of Smith's assumption that, by and large, the spectator accurately imagines the kind of sentiments he would feel in the agent's situation, although he does not feel them so intensely as he would were he actually to experience them. This means that he judges the sentiments of an agent by comparing them to a mild reproduction of the sentiments he would feel were he in the agent's place. The laws simply modify this basic fact. But the modifications are given more emphasis than they might seem to merit because they are used to explain 'irregularities' amongst moral judgments, that is those moral judgments which seem out of line with the normal run of moral evaluations. It is because he thinks he can account for these quirks of the moral life that Smith is confident of the superiority of his scientific explanation of morality in terms of sympathetic feelings and intentions.

[1] T.M.S., I.iii.1 (I.104).   [2] T.M.S., I.iii.1 (I.107).

For some judgments of the sentiments of others no imaginary change of situation is necessary; if two people are affected in the same way by an event, or are both observing some object which has 'no peculiar relationship to either', then they can make an immediate comparison of their sentiments. Smith does not consider this to be the most important sort of sympathy for explaining moral judgments and he does not pay a great deal of attention to it in the *Moral Sentiments*, but it features in his account of the appraisals which we make of the *judgments* of others, as when we attribute to them 'qualities of taste and good judgment':

'The beauty of a plain, the greatness of a mountain, the ornaments of a building, the expression of a picture, the composition of a discourse, the conduct of a third person, the proportions of different quantities and numbers, the various appearances which the great machine of the universe is perpetually exhibiting, with the secret wheels and springs which produce them; all the general subjects of science and taste, are what we and our companions regard as having no peculiar relation to either of us. We both look at them from the same point of view, and we have no occasion for sympathy, or for that imaginary change of situations from which it arises, in order to produce with regard to these, the most perfect harmony of sentiments and affections.'[1]

Smith then goes on to point out similarities between judging the aesthetic taste of other people and assessing their intellectual capacities. It is not clear whether by mentioning 'the conduct of a third person' as one of the objects which can affect both the judge and the person judged in the same way he is thinking of their aesthetic or their moral appreciation of the conduct of this person; if it is the latter then Smith is classifying the approval or disapproval of the moral judgments of others as one of the instances which does not require an imaginary change of situation.

The phenomenon of imaginative sympathy is of much wider significance. All judgments of the actions, and most judgments of the feeling of others, involve imaginative sympathy. He says that to achieve mutual sympathy in this way is at once more difficult and 'vastly more important'.[2] It is more difficult because the exercise of the imagination requires a certain amount of effort and, in any case, it is never completely successful in reproducing the sentiments men actually feel in various situations. It is more important because men's feelings are more intimately and deeply involved when they

---

[1] T.M.S., I.i.4 (I.32).   [2] T.M.S., I.i.4 (I.35).

are either the actors in a situation or the persons particularly affected by any object or event. Smith relies on imaginative sympathy to explain how members of a society, who occupy different positions and have conflicting interests, are able to evolve agreed standards of conduct. Imaginative sympathy is the only possible means whereby people in different situations can make any judgments whatever on each other's behaviour; it is, moreover, the key activity which Smith attributes to the spectator; indeed, the spectator, who is, by definition, someone who is not acting, is the only person who is able to feel sympathetic emotions. In the moment of action it is not possible for anyone to exercise imaginative sympathy. The spectator, therefore, represents the social position which Smith believes to be fundamental to the understanding and explanation of moral judgments. The spectator, or every man in his moments of reflection on the conduct of others, occupies the vantage point from which men are able to reach some sort of agreement in their attitudes towards different types of conduct; as agents men tend to disagree because their aims conflict with each other and their attitudes are determined by their immediate discordant interests. As spectators they have no conflicting interests and their attitudes tend to coincide. Virtue and vice are therefore terms which, according to Smith, get their significance from the attitudes of spectators towards the conduct of agents. Imaginative sympathy derives its importance, for Smith's theory, from the fact that it is the only method whereby the spectator can assess the conduct of agents. He therefore considers it to be the social phenomenon which has the most important part to play in the explanation of moral judgments. The entire *Moral Sentiments* is an attempt to justify this view.

V. THE PLEASURE OF MUTUAL SYMPATHY

The laws of sympathy explain the extent to which men are *able* to sympathize with the feelings of others, but Smith requires to demonstrate why they should wish to sympathize with each other at all. What is the motive for comparing our own sentiments with those of others, especially when this involves the effort of an imaginary change of situation? Smith's answer is to say that mutual sympathy, the awareness of sharing sentiments with others, is one of the chief pleasures of human life, whereas to be aware of a lack of sympathy with our own feelings is extremely unpleasant:

'. . . nothing pleases us more than to observe in other men a fellow-feeling with all the emotions of our own breast; nor

103

are we ever so much shocked as by the appearance of the contrary.'[1]

This provides the motive for adopting the standpoint of the observer and seeking to establish harmony of sentiments on the basis of an imaginary change of place. When Smith calls sympathy an unselfish principle he means that the pleasure of mutual sympathy is spontaneous and does not depend on one person's calculation that he will obtain the assistance of those who share his feelings. He also denies that this pleasure arises from the additional vivacity which mutual sympathy imparts to the emotions;[2] he points out that although sympathy increases our pleasure, it also alleviates our griefs. This is illustrated by his disagreement with Hume, who, in a letter to Smith, written when the latter was working on the second edition of the *Moral Sentiments*, picks on the alleged pleasure of mutual sympathy as the dubious point of the whole system:

'I wish that you had more particularly and fully prov'd, that all kinds of Sympathy are necessarily Agreeable. This is the Hinge of your System, & yet you only mention the Matter cursorily in p. 20. Now it would appear that there is a disagreeable Sympathy as well as an agreeable: And indeed, as the Sympathetic Passion is a reflex Image of the principal, it must partake of its Qualities, & be painful where that is so. Indeed, *when we converse with a man with whom we can entirely sympathize*, that is, where there is a warm & intimate Friendship, the cordial openness of such a Commerce overpowers the Pain of a disagreeable Sympathy, and renders the whole Movement agreeable. But in ordinary Cases this cannot have place; a man tir'd & disgusted with every thing, always *ennuié;* sickly, complaining, embarrass'd; such a one throws an evident Damp on Company, which I suppose wou'd be accounted for by Sympathy; and yet it is disagreeable.

'It is always thought a difficult Problem to account for the Pleasure, receivd from the Tears & Grief & Sympathy of Tragedy; which wou'd not be the Case if all Sympathy were agreeable. An Hospital would be a more entertaining Place than a Ball. I am afraid that in p. 99 and 111 this Proposition has escaped you, or rather is interwove with your Reasonings in that place. You say expressly, *it is painful to go along with Grief & we always enter into it with Reluctance.* It will probably be requisite for you to modify or explain this sentiment, & reconcile it to your System.'[3]

[1] T.M.S., I.i.2 (I.15).
[2] Cf. Hume's *Treatise,* ed. by Selby-Bigge, II.i.11, p. 317.
[3] *The Letters of David Hume,* ed. by J. Y. T. Greig (Oxford, 1932), vol. I, p. 313.

Smith did take this objection seriously enough to add, in the second and subsequent editions, the following footnote to one of the passages which Hume had mentioned in his letter:

'It has been objected to me that as I found the sentiment of approbation, which is always agreeable, upon sympathy. it is inconsistent with my system to admit any disagreeable sympathy. I answer, that in the sentiment of approbation there are two things to be taken notice of; first, the sympathetic passion of the spectator; and, secondly, the emotion which arises from his observing the perfect coincidence between this sympathetic passion in himself, and the original passion in the person principally concerned. This last emotion, in which the sentiment of approbation properly consists, is always agreeable and delightful. The other may either be agreeable or disagreeable, according to the nature of the original passion, whose features it must always, in some measure, retain.'[1]

This passage does not add anything new to what can be found in the first edition but it does bring out quite clearly that Smith and Hume mean different things by the term 'sympathy', the former using it for the agreement of sentiments and the latter for the communication of sentiments.

However, Hume was justified in writing to Smith that the alleged pleasures of mutual sympathy are 'the hinge of your system'. For even if it is true that the spectator standpoint represents the situation from which men are best able to reach agreement concerning their judgments on conduct, it still has to be shown why they make the effort to adopt this standpoint and exercise their imaginative faculties in order to see if they can sympathize with the sentiments and feelings of those in quite different situations from their own.[2] Smith thinks that the pleasures of mutual sympathy are sufficient to account for the fact that they do so. The points made in Hume's letter count against this view, but, on the other hand, Smith allows for the fact that the pleasure of mutual sympathy may be outweighed by the unpleasantness of the sympathetic emotions. In such cases it is the agent who, seeking relief for his painful emotions, has a stronger desire for mutual sympathy than the spectator. To prove the theory that moral judgments are based on the comparison of the real sentiments men have as agents and the imagined sentiments

---

[1] T.M.S., I.iii.1 (I.109).
[2] Hume himself had a similar problem in explaining why men adopt the general point of view represented by moral language; cf. *An Enquiry Concerning the Principles of Morals*, ed. by Selby-Bigge, §186.

which they have as spectators, Smith attempts to show that the nature and content of these judgments can be deduced from men's desire for mutual sympathy and the laws of imaginative sympathy. To see how he attempts to do this it will be necessary for us to look further at his analysis of the 'principle of approbation'.

CHAPTER 5

THE PRINCIPLE OF APPROBATION

Smith's theory 'concerning the nature and origin of our moral sentiments'[1] is an attempt to show that all moral judgments can be
explained by demonstrating that they are the consequences of one or
other, or some combination, of the laws of sympathy. The development of moral rules involves a definite social context and the exercise
of other human faculties, such as reason, but imaginative sympathy
is the key to the whole process. For Smith this has the attraction of
using a familiar phenomenon to account for a wide variety of
apparently dissimilar social facts, and thus conforming to one of his
requirements for a good scientific theory[2]:

'Nature . . . acts here, as in all other cases, with the strictest economy, and produces a multitude of effects from one and the same
cause; and sympathy, a power which has always been taken notice
of, and with which the mind is manifestly endowed, is . . . sufficient
to account for all the effects ascribed to this peculiar faculty.[3]

The theory he propounds is not one which is primarily intended to
analyse the moral sentiments as they are actually felt, but attempts to
trace the origin of these sentiments to their *sources* in the operation
of sympathy. He assumes, however, that these sources or origins are
not simply left behind as the moral sentiments develop, for he
considers that they exercise a continuing influence in the maintenance
and development of moral codes.

I. PROPRIETY

Smith separates out four distinct elements as representing the four
sources of moral judgment:

'When we approve of any character or action, the sentiments which
we feel, are, according to the foregoing system, derived from four

---

[1] T.M.S., VII.i (II.195).   [2] Cf. p. 40f.
[3] T.M.S., VII.iii.3 (II.342). By 'peculiar faculty' Smith means a 'moral sense'.

sources, which are in some respects different from one another. First, we sympathize with the motives of the agent; secondly, we enter into the gratitude of those who receive the benefit of his actions; thirdly, we observe that his conduct has been agreeable to the general rules by which those two sympathies generally act; and, last of all, when we consider such actions as making a part of a system of behaviour which tends to promote the happiness either of the individual or of the society, they appear to derive a beauty from this utility, not unlike that which we ascribe to any well-contrived machine.'[1]

Since the last source is an 'after-thought' and not really a part of the *origin* of moral judgments, and the third source is derived from the first two sources, the basic distinction is between the first two sources, one being connected with judgments of propriety and the other with judgments of merit. So far it has been shown that, for Smith, a moral judgment is an expression of approval or disapproval based on the perception of the agreement or disagreement of sympathetic and real sentiments; however:

'The sentiment or affection of the heart from which any action proceeds, and upon which its whole virtue or vice must ultimately depend, may be considered under two different aspects, or on two different relations; first, in relation to the cause which excites it, or the motive which gives occasion to it; and secondly, in relation to the end which it proposes, or the effect which it tends to produce'.[2]

It is this distinction between the backward look to the origin of the act and the forward look to its probable consequences, that Smith makes the basis of the distinction between judgments of propriety and judgments of merit:

'In the suitableness or unsuitableness, in the proportion or disproportion which the affection seems to bear to the cause or object which excites it, consists the propriety or impropriety, the decency or ungracefulness of the consequent action.

'In the beneficial or hurtful nature of the effects which the affection aims at, or tends to produce, consists the merit or demerit of the action, the qualities by which it is entitled to reward, or is deserving of punishment.'[3]

The test of propriety is the spectator's sympathy, or lack of sympathy, with the agent's motive when he conceives himself in the

[1] T.M.S., VII.iii.3 (II.355f.). [2] T.M.S., I.i.3 (I.28).
[3] T.M.S., I.i.3 (I.28f.).

agent's situation and regards the circumstances which led to the agent's act. Whether or not this sympathy is forthcoming depends on the laws of sympathy, so that to know these laws is to know why men judge some actions to be proper and others to be improper, for 'if we consider all the different passions of human nature, we shall find that they are regarded as decent, or indecent, just in proportion as mankind are more or less disposed to sympathize with them'.[1] For every passion there is a degree of 'mediocrity' which gains the sympathy of the spectator. For instance, on the basis of his observation that men tend to sympathize more readily with agreeable than with disagreeable sentiments,[2] Smith formulates a 'general rule', which 'admits not of a single exception':

'. . . the passions which the spectator is most disposed to sympathize with, and in which, upon that account, the point of propriety may be said to stand high, are those of which the immediate feeling or sensation is more or less agreeable to the person principally concerned: and that, on the contrary, the passions with which the spectator is least disposed to sympathize with, and in which, upon that account, the point of propriety may be said to stand low, are those of which the immediate feeling or sensation is more or less disagreeable, or even painful, to the person principally concerned.'[3]

Amongst the many examples he uses to 'demonstrate the truth' of this rule are some which point out that men are indulgent towards strong manifestations of 'affections which tend to unite men in society' but not towards those which tend to 'drive men from one another'.[4]

The least complex judgments of propriety concern the assessment of self-regarding behaviour: the agent must control his self-regarding passions so that they are reduced to the level at which the spectator can 'enter into' them. The bodily passions must be controlled more strictly than the imaginative ones, the painful ones more than the pleasant ones, the unusual and extreme ones more than the familiar and normal ones. But in the case of the unsocial and social passions, which are directed at the ill or good of persons other than the agent, there is an additional complicating factor. These passions prompt the spectator to consider the situation of the person who is affected by the action: the agent's resentment leads the spectator to sympathize with the fear of the person who is the object of this passion, while the benevolence of an agent prompts the spectator to share the pleasure of the recipient. The spectator is liable to sympathize with

---

[1] T.M.S., I.ii.Introd. (I.54).   [2] The third law of sympathy, cf. p. 100.
[3] T.M.S., VI.iii (II.134).   [4] T.M.S., VI.iii (II.135f.).

all persons involved in a situation. This results in what Smith calls a 'divided sympathy' which increases the spectator's difficulty in entering into the unpleasant emotion of resentment and a 'doubled sympathy' which increases his ability to sympathize with the pleasing emotion of benevolence, and so for all unsocial and social affections. With the unsocial passions,

> 'our sympathy is divided between the person who feels them, and the person who is the object of them. The interests of these two are directly opposite. What our sympathy with the person who feels them would prompt us to wish for, our fellow-feeling with the other would lead us to fear. As they are both men, we are concerned for both, and our fear for what the one may suffer, damps our resentment for what the other has suffered.'[1]

Smith assumes that the spectator, in sympathizing with any sentiment, shares the hopes and fears that are associated with that sentiment. Because he cannot, at the same time, both hope and fear that the same thing will happen, his ability to enter into unsocial sentiments is reduced. This would not be the case unless the spectator wished to attain mutual sympathy with all those involved in a situation which he is observing. For this reason, Smith talks of the 'impartial spectator', although he admits that actual spectators vary in the extent of their impartiality.[2]

The fact of divided sympathy makes men unwilling to sympathize with the unsocial passions until they have considered the situation which gave rise to the passion. If the spectator judges that he himself would have felt such a passion in this situation then he accepts that there has been provocation and enters into the passion, although only to a limited extent. If there has been no provocation then there is no sympathy and the act is judged to have been improper. This does not involve the calculation of the long-term consequences of the act (for frequently unsocial emotions have beneficial long-term consequences): it is based solely on the unpleasant nature of the passion and its immediate effects. For even if men are convinced, as were some Stoics, that evil eventually leads to good, 'No speculation of this kind, however, how deeply soever it might be rooted in the mind, could diminish our natural abhorrence for vice, whose immediate effects are so destructive, and whose remote ones are too distant to be traced by the imagination'.[3] The combined effect of these curbs on our general tendency to sympathize with all emotions is such that

---

[1] T.M.S., I.ii.3 (I.74f.).   [2] Cf. Chapter 6, p. 127ff.
[3] T.M.S., I.ii.3 (I.81).

the proper degree of the expression of unsocial emotions is much lower than the level to which they spontaneously spring up in the agent; strong control of these passions is therefore required if they are to gain approval. Yet it is possible for them to fall below the level of feeling which seems proper to the spectator:

'A person becomes contemptible who tamely sits still, and submits to insults, without attempting either to repel or to revenge them. We cannot enter into his indifference and insensibility: we call his behaviour mean-spiritedness, and are as really provoked by it as by the insolence of his adversary'.[1]

The social passions are also directed towards persons other than the agent. But in their case the spectator's sympathy is 'doubled' rather than divided:

'His [the spectator's] sympathy with the person who feels those passions, exactly coincides with his concern for the person who is the object of them. The interest, which, as a man, he is obliged to take in the happiness of this last, enlivens his fellow-feeling with the sentiments of the other.'[2]

As there is no obstacle to the spectator's full sympathy with the benevolent act it is rarely, if ever, that he feels the level of the social affections to be excessive.

II. MERIT

Smith's analysis of propriety constitutes the core of his moral theory, but it covers only one element of virtue, merit or desert being the other. Propriety depends on the suitableness of an act to its cause and judgments of propriety are based on the spectator's assessment of how he would behave in the circumstances which prompted the action; merit depends on the results which an action tends to produce and judgments of merit arise out of the spectator's assessment of how he would feel if he were *affected* by such an act, and in particular whether he would feel gratitude or resentment. We have just seen how, in assessing the propriety of unsocial passions, the spectator takes account of the feelings of those people who are affected by the actions which result from these passions. In the analysis of merit and demerit it is the emotions of such persons that come to the fore, and, in particular, it is their feelings of gratitude and resentment that are the basis of judgments of merit and demerit.

Gratitude and resentment, Smith argues, are the sentiments which

[1] T.M.S., I.ii.3 (I.76); cf. (I.85f.).   [2] T.M.S., I.ii.4 (I.88).

prompt men to give pleasure and pain to others, in the shape of rewards and punishments;[1] the proper degree of these retributive emotions is determined by the sympathetic gratitude and resentment of the spectator. He tends towards a rather narrow definition of merit and demerit as having to do only with the qualities of deserving reward and punishment, especially when he develops the relationship between demerit and justice,[2] but he also seems prepared, on many occasions, to include, as lesser degrees of merit and demerit, the qualities of deserving praise and blame.

The laws of sympathy affect the spectator's ability to sympathize with the emotions of resentment and gratitude: the latter is a pleasant feeling, the former unpleasant: men are therefore more ready to enter into the gratitude of others than into their resentment.[3] This effect is reinforced by the fact that gratitude is felt by those who have been benefited by an act and resentment by those who have been harmed:

'When we see one man assisted, protected, relieved by another, our sympathy with the joy of the person who receives the benefit serves only to animate our fellow-feeling with his gratitude towards him who bestows it'.[4]

On the other hand,

'as we sympathize with the sorrow of our fellow-creature whenever we see his distress, so we likewise enter into his abhorrence and aversion for whatever has given occasion to it.'[5]

Both these reactions are also affected by the spectator's general antipathy for unpleasant passions and his liking for agreeable ones. There is, in addition, a further complication regarding our sympathy with resentment and gratitude. We do not sympathize with these passions without first approving as proper the action which calls forth gratitude or disapproving as improper the action which calls forth resentment. Smith expresses this by saying that sympathetic gratitude and resentment are compounded sentiments which include but go beyond judgments of propriety:

'As we cannot indeed enter thoroughly into the gratitude of the person who receives the benefit, unless we beforehand approve of the motives of the benefactor, so, upon this account, the sense of merit seems to be compounded sentiment, and to be made up of two

1 T.M.S., II.i.1 (I.162f.).
2 Cf. p. 190.
3 This follows from the third law of sympathy, cf. p. 100.
4 T.M.S., II.i.2 (I.169).   5 T.M.S., II.i.2 (I.170).

distinct emotions; a direct sympathy with the sentiments of the agent, and an indirect sympathy with the gratitude of those who receive the benefit of his actions.'[1]

Thus the gifts of the prodigal and the spendthrift do not produce a sympathetic gratitude on a level with those of the more judicious gifts of worthier patrons.[2] And, similarly, there is no sympathy with resentment when the act is considered to be a perfectly proper infliction of injury. Both points Smith illustrates fully with examples drawn largely from classical history.[3]

Gratitude and resentment are themselves greatly dependent on the affected person's awareness of the agent's feelings and intentions. These retributive emotions arise spontaneously within the person who receives a benefit or injury, but they are not sustained unless he sees that the cause was a responsible agent who intended the benefit or harm,[4] and who can become aware that he is being made to feel pleasure or pain on account of his past actions.[5] Gratitude and resentment are therefore closely related to assessments of the agent's motive, and since Smith also declares that the spectator, in assessing merit and demerit, takes into consideration the propriety or impropriety of the agent's behaviour, there is a very close relationship between judgments of merit and judgments of propriety.[6] The former include but go beyond the latter. Smith does note an 'irregularity' in this respect, in that there is a tendency for people to feel a measure of gratitude and resentment towards anything which causes them pleasure or pain, including inanimate objects and animals; a particular form of this irregularity is the tendency for the merit of acts to be assessed by their actual and not their intended consequences.[7] He explains this by saying that the spontaneous gratitude and resentment felt towards the causes of pleasure and pain never entirely fade in the light of later reflection concerning the nature of the cause. If the effects of an action are such as are normally the consequence

---

[1] T.M.S., II.i.5 (I.182).

[2] T.M.S., II.i.3 (I.175).

[3] T.M.S., II.i.5 (I.183ff.).

[4] T.M.S., II.iii.1 (I.241): 'it must have produced them [pleasure or pain] from design, and from a design that is approved of in the one case and disapproved of in the other'.

[5] T.M.S., II.iii.1 (I.236): 'before anything can be the proper object of gratitude or resentment, it must not only be the cause of pleasure or pain, it must likewise be capable of feeling them'.

[6] T. Brown is quite wrong in attributing to Smith the view that we can 'conceive the demerit of the voluntary agent, without any notion of the impropriety of his action', *Lectures on Ethics*, p. 148.

[7] T.M.S., II.iii, *passim* (I.230-75).

of a particular type of behaviour, then the agent concerned is held responsible and rewarded or punished accordingly; but if, through good or ill fortune, abnormal and unintended benefits or injuries result from an action, then although the retributive emotions diminish, there remains a 'shadow' of gratitude or resentment which affects men's judgments of merit and demerit. Smith goes into some detail in showing the effect of this 'irregularity' on the laws of negligence.[1] It provides a good example of the sort of inconsistency in moral judgments that Smith is delighted to be able to account for, since he regards such 'irregularities' as a challenge and a test for his theory. However, these instances of irrational retributive emotions are exceptional, and it is Smith's view that judgments of merit usually presuppose, and are governed by, judgments of propriety, and, therefore, by the spectator's awareness of the agent's intentions.

III. MORAL RULES

Even if these laws concerning the operations of sympathy are accepted as rough approximations, and their influence on judgments of propriety and merit is accepted, there are immediate objections which spring to mind about this part of Smith's moral theory. In the first place, it might be said that, since to talk of propriety and merit is to speak of standards, rules, or norms of behaviour which are relatively fixed and invariable over a period of time in any particular society, it is implausible to explain these in terms of the capacity of one person to sympathize with another, since such sympathy is essentially fleeting, uncertain and unpredictable. Dependent, as it is, on every variation of mood and experience between person and person and even between different moments in the life of any single individual, sympathy might be regarded as too subjective and irregular a phenomenon from which to derive the relatively stable and enduring standards of moral propriety and merit.[2] To understand Smith's answer to this objection it is necessary to consider the third source of approbation which builds on, but modifies, the first two sources: the spectator's observation that an agent's 'conduct has been agreeable to the general rules by which those two sympathies generally act'.[3]

---

[1] T.M.S., II.iii.2 (I.243-63). This is discussed more fully in Chapter 9.
[2] Cf. the criticism of Thomas Brown, *Lectures on Ethics*, p. 146: 'our sympathy, is, in degree at least, one of the most irregular and seemingly capricious of principles in the constitution of the mind; and on this very account, therefore, not very likely to be the commensurable test or standard of feelings so regular, upon the whole, as our general estimates of right and wrong'.
[3] T.M.S., VII.iii.3 (II.356).

Smith accepts the fact that the spectator's feelings vary from time to time and that they may not always accord with the feelings of other spectators, but he argues that in every society moral rules are developed which reflect the normal feelings of most people. Thus each individual, through the exercise of his reason, is able to form generalizations about the sentiments with which he can normally sympathize and those with which he cannot sympathize:

'Our continual observations upon the conduct of others, insensibly lead us to form to ourselves certain general rules concerning what is fit and proper either to be done or to be avoided.'[1]

This explains how stable standards of propriety are developed in spite of variations in the individual's moods, and, because the individual usually makes his moral judgments by reference to these rules, it also explains why sympathy does not accompany most moral judgments. But Smith insists that the origin of these general rules is to be traced to sympathy and their content cannot be understood without seeing that this is so. This does not mean that Smith considered that each individual developed his own moral rules in isolation from his fellows: he accounts for the tendency to uniformity between men in their moral standards in much the same way as he shows how it develops within the life of a single individual. Most men do not themselves exercise their sympathy to any degree, indeed 'Many men behave very decently . . . who yet, perhaps, never felt the sentiment upon the propriety of which we found our approbation of their conduct, but acted merely from a regard to what they saw were the established rules of behaviour.'[2] Custom, the desire to win approval, the fear of punishment, whether human or divine, and the difficulty of sympathizing with unusual emotions, all combine to make the average person adopt the general rules current in his society.

This does not imply that different societies will adopt the same rules, but only that the same society and the same social group will tend to establish an agreed set of moral rules. Nor does Smith wish to deny that variations between individuals in the same society or social group will exist. On the contrary, he uses his general theory to explain why men differ in their moral judgments: some of these differences are explained by straightforward psychological differences, such as variations in imaginative powers, but other variations are more sociological in that they are due to the style of life of the person concerned: there are 'different degrees of attention, which our different habits of life allow us', as well as 'different degrees of natural

---

[1] T.M.S., III.4 (I.393).   [2] T.M.S., III.5 (I.402).

acuteness in the faculty of the mind to which they [the objects being viewed] are addressed'.[1]

IV. UTILITY

The fourth and final source of moral approbation is the consideration of utility. 'Utility' is a recurring theme throughout the *Moral Sentiments*; it crops up wherever Smith thinks that other theorists, and in particular David Hume, have given excessive importance to utility in the analysis and explanation of moral judgments. Right from the beginning, in his account of sympathy, Smith denies that considerations of utility have a fundamental effect on judgments of approval and disapproval, although they may be used to *justify* moral judgments arrived at on other grounds. In moral judgments as well as judgments of beauty and taste 'the idea of the utility of all qualities of this kind, is plainly an after-thought, and not what first recommends them to our approbation'.[2] To admit otherwise would be to allow that the perception of agreement and disagreement was not the primary and fundamental cause of all expressions of approval and disapproval. Smith devotes a whole part of the *Moral Sentiments* to considering 'the Effect of Utility upon the Sentiment of Approbation'.[3] In it he agrees that the perception of utility does have some influence on judgments of propriety, and accepts Hume's analysis that 'The utility of any object, according to him, pleases the master by perpetually suggesting to him the pleasure or conveniency which it is fitted to promote'.[4] His own contribution to this line of thought is to suggest that men also find pleasure in contemplating the fitness or suitability of means to ends quite independently of their feelings about the ends, and that this pleasure often supersedes the first so that we take more pleasure in seeing a machine or system which exhibits a nice adjustment of means to ends than in the thought of the ends themselves. Smith is rightly proud of this observation and considers it something of a discovery:

'. . . that this fitness, this happy contrivance of any production of art, should often be more valued, than the very end for which it was intended; and that the exact adjustment of the means for attaining any conveniency or pleasure, should frequently be more regarded, than that very conveniency or pleasure, in the attainment of which their whole merit would seem to consist, has not, so far as I know, been yet taken notice of by any body. That this however is frequently

[1] T.M.S., I.i.4 (I.32f.); cf. W.N., I.ii (I.19f.).   [2] T.M.S., I.i.4 (I.35).
[3] T.M.S., IV, *passim* (I.451-88).   [4] T.M.S., IV.1 (I.452).

the case, may be observed in a thousand instances, both in the most frivolous and in the most important concerns of human life.'[1]

The frivolous instances he cites to illustrate this 'love of system' include the passion which some men have to acquire a device, such as a watch, which is accurate far beyond their requirements, and the important illustrations consist of examples of men's preoccupations with the mechanics of gaining wealth and prestige, the great households and estates which take up the labour of a life time to erect and maintain, so that their organization takes precedence over the actual enjoyment of the conveniences they promote:

'The pleasures of wealth and greatness, when considered in this complex view, strike the imagination as something grand and beautiful and noble, of which the attainment is well worth all the toil and anxiety which we are so apt to bestow upon it.'[2]

Utility, so viewed, Smith allows to be a most powerful motive of human action, and, allied to the other causes which he gives for men's admiration for wealth and greatness,[3] he counts it as a 'deception which rouses and keeps in continual motion the industry of mankind'.[4] It is therefore central to the understanding of Smith's economic theory, for it explains why men erect vast productive systems which yield results far beyond that which they need for themselves and so provide support for others who receive the benefits of this over-production.[5]

In the case of judgments of propriety Smith considers that the same principles hold, but to a much smaller extent: when we see that a particular type of character is well suited to promote or hinder the happiness of a man or his fellows, then we are pleased by the appropriateness of the means to the end. But he firmly denies that this is an important consideration for any but a few abstract thinkers, and therefore disagrees with the quoted views of Hume that 'no qualities of mind . . . are approved of as virtuous, but such as are useful or agreeable either to the person himself or to others',[6] if this is taken to imply that this is *why* men approve of them. Using his parallel between the approval of utility in the case of machines on the one hand and of character on the other, he argues:

1 T.M.S., IV.1 (I.453f.).
2 T.M.S., IV.1 (I.464).
3 T.M.S., I.iii.2 (I.120ff.); cf. W.N., I.xi.2 (I.192).
4 T.M.S., IV.1 (I.464), cf. p. 171.
5 T.M.S., IV.1 (I.466). This is the context in which Smith talks of the 'invisible hand'.
6 T.M.S., IV.2 (I.476).

'. . . it seems impossible that the approbation of virtue should be a sentiment of the same kind with that by which we approve of a convenient and well-contrived building; or that we should have no other reason for praising a man than that for which we commend a chest of drawers'.[1]

In this way he points to the very different 'feel' which moral judgments have from everyday judgments of utility, a difference he is willing to explain in terms of the complex of sympathetic emotions that are involved in the one but not the other.

This attack is rather unfair on Hume who does not rely on the perception of the nice adjustment of means to end to provide *his* explanation of the appeal which utility has for the sentiments of mankind. In fact Smith is somewhat misleading in the way in which he draws a sharp contrast between his own views and those of Hume. For although Smith denies that calculation of long-term effects features in the formation and reinforcement of moral judgments, he does include the *immediate* effects of action in the assessment of propriety and merit; this may be regarded as the observation or imagination of effects rather than as a process of rational calculation, but it does show that, whenever an act affects persons other than the agent, the immediate utility of the act has a very substantial influence on the moral sentiments, even on Smith's own view. Moreover, Smith agrees with Hume that no aspect of conduct and character is considered virtuous unless it is in fact 'useful or agreeable either to the person himself or to others'.[1] The only difference between them is that Smith considers this to be the result of nature's plan and not man's calculation. 'Abstract and philosophical study' will show how 'that system which places virtue in utility, coincides too with that which makes it consist in propriety' since 'every affection is useful when it is confined to a certain degree of moderation; and every affection is disadvantageous when it exceeds the proper bounds'.[2] But although utility is the principle used by God it is immediate sense and feeling that are the causes of moral approbation in man.

Smith uses two different and somewhat conflicting arguments to show that strong sentiments of approval and disapproval are not based on utility. For the first he draws on examples of judgments made about acts which are useful but whose utility has never been present to the minds of those making the judgments; for the second he points to instances when men approve of what is not useful and disapprove of what is useful, as when they disapprove less of the wickedness of great persons than of ordinary people, although it is

[1] T.M.S., IV.2 (I.476f.).   [2] T.M.S., VII.ii.1 (II.299f.).

the great who cause most harm by their actions.[1] The latter instances seem to conflict with his view that propriety and utility coincide, while the former can be countered by drawing on Smith's own belief that the factors which are decisive in the origin of moral judgments may not be operative in habitual moral judgments. A Humean could use many of Smith's own arguments to show that custom, habit and the use of general rules may account for the average moral judgment but that the origin of moral rules must be traced back to considerations of utility. The main argument on Smith's side is that there is no evidence that in the past men were more rational in their judgments than they are now, and that utility plays so small a part in moral reflection in everyday life as to make it implausible to suggest that some men in the past have established general rules on the basis of calculations of utility. Moreover, even if the origin of moral rules can be explained in this way, it is still necessary to show how they persist, and Smith is certainly able to present a more convincing picture of how moral rules are reinforced and re-established from generation to generation, since the operations of sympathy he describes are more pervasive elements in the average moral judgment than the calculations of utility on which Hume relies. Nevertheless Smith himself seems to have been in two minds over the place which the assessment of utility has in some moral judgments, as we shall see when we come to consider his views on justice.[2]

V. THE MORAL NEUTRALITY OF SYMPATHY

A common objection to Smith's moral theory is that its plausibility comes from the fact that he is able to smuggle covert moral evaluations into the very factor, namely sympathy, which is meant to explain the moral sentiments. For example, it is said that the spectator, in deciding whether or not to sympathize with the behaviour of the agent, draws upon his own moral ideas as to what is right and proper in such a situation. His approval is based, therefore, not on what he considers he *would* feel in this situation, but on what he considers he *ought* to feel. Again the objection is lucidly put by Thomas Brown who writes that the essential error of Smith's system is 'no less than the assumption, in every case, of those very moral feelings which are supposed to flow from sympathy, the assumption of them as necessarily existing before that very sympathy in which they are said to originate'.[3]

[1] T.M.S., VI.i (II.64); this passage is not in the first five editions and perhaps reflects Smith's declining optimism.   [2] Cf. pp. 199.

[3] *Lectures on Ethics*, p. 147; cf. A. Small, *Adam Smith and Modern Sociology*, p. 48, and W. C. Swabey, *Ethical Theory from Hobbes to Kant*, p. 185.

This objection holds most forcibly if we are considering the analysis of sympathy as it actually occurs in moral judgments. An individual modifies his conduct according to his own standards of right and wrong and his moral feelings will therefore affect his judgment when he is considering how he would act in a certain situation, for he will only sympathize with an agent who acts in accordance with the moral rules by which he, the spectator, usually governs his conduct. On such grounds as these Sidgwick says that Smith's analysis of the moral sentiments errs 'in underrating the complexity of the moral sentiments, and in not recognising that, however these sentiments may have originated, they are now, as introspectively examined, different from mere sympathy with the feelings and impulses of others; they are compounds that cannot be directly analysed into the simple element of sympathy, however complicated and combined'.[1]

The short answer to this criticism is to say that it rests, as do so many similar criticisms, on a mistaken idea of the nature of Smith's theory. He is not concerned to analyse moral judgments as they actually occur in order to present an accurate phenomenological description of them. He aims to explain their existence and content by presenting an analytical model from which the facts to be explained can be deduced; in this it partakes of the nature of a genetic explanation, outlining the various features of human nature so far as is necessary to explain how men could have developed a system of moral judgments. Smith's appeal to sympathy is to a series of generalizations by means of which we can understand how the moral sentiments have been historically derived; he does not claim that, as actually experienced, moral judgments can be analysed without remainder into the operations of sympathy. The process he describes is a cumulative one in which the continual functioning of sympathy modifies the moral rules which its previous operations have established. Smith goes along with his objectors in saying that most actual cases of sympathy are influenced by moral presuppositions, but he concentrates on what may be called non-moral cases of sympathy, where this influence is not present, to establish his generalizations about the workings of sympathy. Having formulated the laws of sympathy by reference to these non-moral cases he can then go on to show how they can be used to explain moral judgments, even although the element of sympathy in such judgments is not free from the influence of the prior moral assumptions of the spectator.

[1] H. Sidgwick, *Outlines of the History of Ethics* (1886), 6th edn, 1931, p. 218.

The plausibility of this theory depends on his ability to outline a convincing analysis of how 'non-moral' sympathy develops into the complex moral judgments which occur in fully socialized human beings. The test of the theory is not whether moral judgments, as experienced, can be dissected into various strands of sympathy, but whether the model he erects can be used to provide developmental explanations of the form and content of moral codes. Even if his theory is, in the end, rejected or drastically modified, it is wrong to prejudge this issue and dismiss the theory out of hand simply because most instances of sympathetic feelings are affected by the moral assumptions of the person in question: it might be the case that such moral assumptions are the effect of previous workings of sympathy in the development of that individual and his society.

The obverse of this objection is the criticism that sympathy is inadequate to explain moral judgments because it lacks moral relevance. On this view, approval based on sympathy alone is not moral approval. In part this is the old objection that I may agree without approving, in which case it amounts to saying that I may sympathize without approving, but the variation of this criticism with which we are here concerned is the one which argues that, when approval is based on sympathy *alone*, then my approval and disapproval are not moral. Thus Laurie says that 'an appeal to what ought to be, rather than what is, forces us beyond the facts of sympathetic feeling'; and 'it must be objected that the imperative command of duty cannot be resolved into sympathetic feeling. My sympathy with the feelings of another contains in itself no moral approbation; and his sympathy with me, real or supposed, entails no moral obligation'.[1] A more specific form of this criticism is to say that the variations in the operation of sympathy to which Smith points have no moral relevance: for instance, it may be true that I sympathize less with painful emotions than with pleasurable ones, but does this constitute a justifiable moral reason for approving of the latter more readily than of the former?

This objection brings together several lines of thought which cause us some disquiet at Smith's easy transition from sympathy to propriety. For one thing, many of the examples which he gives, such as sympathizing with grief, do not seem to be about the sort of behaviour which we regard in moral terms. How then can the fact that imaginative sympathy is operative in a judgment be sufficient to make it a moral judgment? Our doubts on this score are partly a matter of the correct definition of morality, and this has already

[1] H. Laurie, *Scottish Philosophy*, (1902), p. 120.

been discussed.[1] Smith chooses to bracket approval and disapproval of conduct which we might want to regard as being solely the business of the agent himself, with approval and disapproval of conduct which takes place in an interpersonal context and affects the interests of persons other than the agent. His justification for this is a scientific one, since he wishes to demonstrate that sympathy is casually operative in the assessment of both types of behaviour. Others may wish to delimit the sphere of moral judgments so as to exclude the assessment of what Smith calls selfish passions. Nothing fundamental to the theory is at stake here. If we like to argue that the exercise of imaginative sympathy can result in non-moral as well as moral judgments this at least has the advantage of showing that Smith wishes to explain moral judgments by reference to a conjunction of generalizations about human behaviour, few of which are unique to moral phenomena.

But this may be thought to admit too much. It might be said that, if *some* judgments involving imaginative sympathy are non-moral, how can we explain the distinctive nature of moral judgments by means of sympathy? At one level the answer to this question requires the complete exposition of Smith's theory, especially his explanation of conscience, which has yet to come.[2] But two points can be made at this stage. The first is that Smith is not arguing that men appeal to the laws of sympathy in order to justify their moral judgments. He is not saying that, in the assessment of the moral sentiments, sympathy features as an ultimate criterion. In fact, no claims about the logic of moral argument are involved. The laws of sympathy are introduced as the basis for causal explanations, not as principles of moral discrimination.

Secondly, in so far as the criticism implies that the theory is attempting to perform an impossible task, it can also be dealt with immediately. For instance, it can be argued that, even if Smith does show that sympathy affects some moral judgments, he has done nothing to show that it *ought* to. This is to accuse him of committing the naturalistic fallacy by arguing that something ought to be the case simply because it is the case. But, again, such a criticism mistakes the nature of Smith's theory; it presupposes that he is seeking to provide a normative theory which is able to select and justify true or correct moral judgments. This is not so, and the objection, therefore, fails; Smith is presenting a scientific theory and if he can show that the moral judgments which are observed to occur in different societies can be deduced from the laws of sympathy, then this theory is successful in its own terms. It cannot be argued, *a priori*, that it is

[1] Cf. p. 87f.   [2] Cf. Chapter 7.

impossible for moral judgments to develop out of the operations of sympathy because the laws of sympathy do not appear to offer sufficient grounds for drawing evaluative conclusions. This is not their function; Smith uses them to explain the development of moral judgments, not to justify them.

VI. PROPRIETY AND ETIQUETTE

I have indicated that we have yet to bring into the discussion all those features of Smith's theory which are necessary for the assessment of its scientific worth, but it might be useful to deal now with another common criticism which is particularly relevant to his theory of propriety. This criticism, which draws much of its plausibility from the modern use of the term 'propriety' to denote etiquette or the petty conventional morality of polite society, is the argument that, while sympathy may explain the social conventions of a respectable eighteenth-century club, it cannot account for the morality of the individual conscience as exemplified in the Kantian categorical imperative.

Many of Smith's examples of sympathy do assume the context of an eighteenth-century drawing-room or meeting-place, where the sociable nature of the gathering puts a premium on agreeableness and concord. For instance, in expounding the pleasure of mutual sympathy Smith remarks:

'A man is mortified when, after having endeavoured to divert the company, he looks around and sees that nobody laughs at his jest but himself. On the contrary, the mirth of the company is highly agreeable to him, and he regards this correspondence of their sentiments with his own as the greatest applause.'[1]

When he goes on to say that such harmony of sentiments is the test of moral propriety it seems that he is setting up the conventions of the cocktail party as the touchstone of morality. Moreover he frequently stresses the need to control the strong expression of emotions if the approval of one's companions is to be obtained; for instance he holds that 'Such is our aversion for all the appetites which take their origin from the body: all strong expressions of them are loathsome and disagreeable'.[2] With such examples it is clearly the strong expression of such emotions *in company* rather than in private that he has in mind, and it would appear that what is important to him is how we conduct ourselves in public, by which he has in mind the polite society of his day. Again, in illustrating our greater sympathy

[1] T.M.S., I.i.2 (I.16).   [2] T.M.S., I.ii.1 (I.57).

with small joys which do not arouse envy than with greater ones, he writes:

'It is decent to be humble amidst great prosperity; but we can scarce express too much satisfaction in all the little occurrences of common life, in the company with which we spent the evening last night, in the entertainment that was set before us, in what was said and what was done, in all the little incidents of the present conversation, in all those frivolous nothings which fill up the void of human life. Nothing is more graceful than habitual cheerfulness, which is always founded upon a peculiar relish for all the little pleasures which common occurrences afford.'[1]

Not only does he sometimes make the sympathy of a convivial gathering the test of propriety, he also seems to indicate that the attainment of such social harmony is the *aim* of moral conduct, the goal of all acts which receive moral approval. This criticism is voiced in more general terms by one critic who says that Smith does not make it clear whether sympathy is the test or the aim of propriety.[2] In this particular context we might want to say that the propriety of the drawing-room and the pursuit of conviviality are hardly appropriate either as the standards or as the goals for conduct in other situations. It is then argued that Smith's theory may account for the virtues of respectability and conviviality but not those of morality proper.

It is perfectly true that Smith dwells on the moral significance both of the agent controlling his passions and maintaining them at a level with which the spectator can sympathize, and of the spectator making the effort to enter into the feelings of the agent; the former he calls self-control, the latter sensibility;[3] to this extent mutual sympathy is the aim of virtuous conduct:

'Upon these two different efforts, upon that of the spectator to enter into the sentiments of the person principally concerned, and upon that of the person principally concerned, to bring down his emotions to what the spectator can go along with, are founded two different sets of virtues. The soft, the gentle, the amiable virtues, the virtues of candid condescension and indulgent humanity, are founded upon the one: the great, the awful and respectable, the virtues of self-denial, of self-government, of that command of the passions which subjects all the movements of our nature to what

[1] T.M.S., I.ii.5 (I.96f.).   [2] W. C. Swabey, *op. cit.*, p. 182.
[3] T.M.S., I.i.v (I.48).

124

our own dignity and honour, and the propriety of our own conduct require, take their origin from the other'.[1]

These two efforts are not *identified* with the amiable and respectable virtues but are their 'foundation' or 'origin', by which Smith appears to mean that they are the means whereby men, desiring mutual sympathy, are able to feel that type and degree of sentiment which makes the spectator appear amiable and enables the agent to obtain approval. These virtues of sensibility and self-command have in common the fact that they have as their aim the attainment of mutual sympathy and in this way they are to be contrasted with other virtues, which, while they are *assessed* by whether or not they obtain sympathy, do not have this as their aim.

In this respect the virtues of sensibility and self-command, especially the latter, are similar to the virtue of moral goodness, that is the effort of doing what one believes to be right. Like moral goodness they are most valued when they involve a great deal of effort in the face of strong temptation, and, again like moral goodness, they are valued because of the contribution they make towards the attainment of other moral standards.[2] They are not therefore to be taken as typical of Smith's view of propriety. Other types of conduct are assessed by the spectator comparing the agent's conduct with how he, the spectator, imagines that he would behave in such a situation, not by the spectator observing whether the agent has made a strenuous effort to make himself pleasing company. The spectator does not judge by seeing if the agent's emotions harmonize with his own feelings at that moment, but with the emotions he considers that he would feel in the agent's situation. The mutual sympathy which is the test of propriety is not, therefore, to be equated with the conviviality of a social gathering where the stress is on amusement and decorum. It is true that the spectator wishes to sympathize, especially with agreeable emotions, but the prior requirement that the emotions concerned accord with his sympathetic feelings should not be lost sight of.

To say that the virtues of sensibility and self-command are untypical in this respect does not mean that they are unimportant; as Smith says, sensibility is the basis of the amiable emotions, presumably because sympathy with another person is the *source* of many social affections, and self-command is the usual means whereby the agent is able to conform to the standards of propriety. Moreover the

[1] T.M.S., I.i.v (I.44).
[2] Cf. T.M.S., VI.iii, *passim* (II.120-86): 'Of self-command'. This is discussed further in Chapter 8.

desire for mutual sympathy may often be the motive for the exercise of the virtues of sensibility and self-command, and it has, therefore, an important causal role in leading men to conform to moral rules; but this does not mean that these moral rules have the purpose of establishing conviviality. The impression that Smith is more concerned with good manners than with good conduct arises in part from his practice of using non-moral examples to illustrate his laws of sympathy, but a close analysis of what he says about the relationship between spectator and agent will show that the attainment of mutual sympathy is, typically, the test and not the aim of the moral virtues. This does not, of course, prove his analysis correct, but it clears him of the charge of thinking that he had explained moral judgments because he could explain the conventions of polite society. It still remains to be seen how he actually accounts for the categorical obligations associated with those moral judgments which feel more authoritative than the 'proprieties' of a social gathering.

CHAPTER 6

THE IMPARTIAL SPECTATOR

Smith's moral theory is best known for the concept of the 'impartial spectator'. The 'spectator' is a familiar figure in eighteenth-century moral philosophy; he appears, for instance, in the writings of Smith's teacher Hutcheson,[1] and also in those of his friend Hume.[2] In Smith's own theory the spectator is given a central place because he represents the point of view from which moral judgments are made: that is to say, it is not possible to understand how Smith derives moral judgments from sympathy unless the sympathetic sentiments concerned are taken to be those of a spectator. We have seen, in our analysis of Smith's account of moral approbation, that the spectator manifests the normal reactions of the ordinary person when he is in the position of observing other people's behaviour. He does not therefore embody the reactions of any particular person, but is an empirical ideal type who may be said to represent all those aspects of human nature which are brought into play in the development of moral judgments. The spectator is 'ideal' in the sense that he excludes all those features of actual spectators which relate to their special interests as particular individuals involved in the actual situation which they are observing; he is 'empirical' in the sense that, once this abstraction is made, the responses of the spectator are identified with the consensus towards which any actual group of persons can be observed to approximate in their attitudes to the behaviour of their fellows.

This interpretation of the impartial spectator conflicts with that put forward by those who see Smith as using the idea of a spectator who is ideal in that he represents certain normative standards which go beyond those to be found in the average spectator. Smith sometimes describes his spectator as impartial and well-informed, and, it is argued, ordinary spectators do not conform to these standards. The impartial spectator is therefore taken to embody the reactions of a normatively ideal observer of behaviour who stands above and

---

[1] D. D. Raphael, *British Moralists*, § 314.
[2] *Treatise* (edited by Selby-Bigge), III.iii.1, p. 576.

criticizes the moral judgments of ordinary men.[1] This is the understanding of Smith's theory which is found in modern proponents of what is called the 'Ideal Observer' theory of ethics, who claim to trace the origin of their theory back to Smith's impartial spectator.[2] It is interesting to compare these modern theories with Smith's own moral theory in order to see just how different they are. It is also important to distinguish them because there are some very cogent objections to the Ideal Observer theory which are assumed to apply to Smith's theory also. In the next two chapters I shall argue that this is not so, and that to present Smith's theory as a form of Ideal Observer theory is a mistake.

I. THE IDEAL OBSERVER THEORY

The Ideal Observer theory is an attempt to analyse the meaning of moral statements by reference to the dispositional reactions of an 'ideal observer'. I shall use as my example Roderick Firth's article 'Ethical Absolutism and the Ideal Observer'.[2] Firth writes:

'Using the term "ideal observer", then, the kind of analysis which I shall examine in this paper is the kind which would construe statements of the form "x is P", in which P is some particular ethical predicate, to be identical in meaning with statements of the form: "Any ideal observer would react to x in such and such a way under such and such conditions".'[3]

The reactions in question are those of approval and disapproval or the experience of 'apparent requiredness'. In this way Firth hopes to be able to translate ethical statements into non-ethical ones and so provide what is called a naturalistic definition. The description of the ideal observer must not, therefore, include any ethical characteristics. On the other hand he hopes to avoid the difficulty which naturalistic theories of ethics have in justifying 'absolutism', by

---

[1] Cf. *Jouffroy's Ethics*, p. 137: '... this abstract spectator, imagined by Smith, is nothing else than reason, judging, in the name of order, and of the immutable nature of things, the mutable and blind decisions of men'.

[2] Cf. Roderick Firth, 'Ethical Absolutism and the Ideal Observer', *Philosophy and Phenomenological Research*, vol. XII (1952), pp. 317-45; William Kneale, 'Objectivity in Morals', *Philosophy*, vol. XXV (1950), pp. 149-66; R. B. Brandt, *Ethical Theory* (Englewood Cliffs, 1959); Jonathan Harrison, 'Some Comments on Professor Firth's Ideal Observer Theory', *Philosophy and Phenomenological Research*, vol. XVII (1956-7), pp. 256-62, and Dorothy Emmet, 'Universalisability and Moral Judgment', *Philosophical Quarterly*, vol. XIII (1963), pp. 214-28.

[3] Ibid., p. 321.

which he means the view that moral statements are 'true or false and consistent or inconsistent with one another, without special reference to the people who happen to be asserting them'.[1] The attraction of such an analysis for Firth is that it makes practical moral problems empirically soluble since the ethically significant reactions of the ideal observer may, in principle, be observed, and it therefore avoids the epistemological problems of most absolutist theories.

A preliminary definition of the ideal observer describes him as a person characterized by the possession of certain non-moral characteristics to a certain, usually an extreme, degree. Firth reaches his conclusions as to what these characteristics are (or *would* be, since the adjective 'ideal' is used here 'in approximately the same sense in which we speak of a perfect vacuum or a frictionless machine'[2]) by asking what we consider to make one person a better moral judge than another. His method of argument is to present a series of assertions of the form: 'We sometimes disqualify ourselves as judges of particular ethical questions on the ground that we are not sufficiently *a*, *b* or *c*, and we regard one person as a better moral judge than another if, other things being equal, the one is more *a*, *b* or *c* than the other'.[3] On this basis he characterizes the ideal observer as:

(1) *Omniscient with respect to non-ethical facts.*[3] Lack of knowledge about the facts of a case disqualifies a person as a moral judge of that case, and since it is not possible to say that the ideal observer needs to know only the relevant moral facts without introducing moral presuppositions as to what is relevant, it is necessary, if he is to be defined in non-moral terms, to describe him as omniscient.

(2) *Omnipercipient:* that is, possessing such a vivid imagination that he is able 'simultaneously to visualize all actual facts, and the consequences of all possible acts in any given situation, just as vividly as he would if he were actually perceiving them all'.[4]

(3) *Disinterested, or impartial.* A perfect moral judge is not influenced by any particular interests, that is any interests 'directed toward a particular person or thing but not toward other persons or things of the same kind'.[5]

(4) *Dispassionate.* He must not be affected by any particular emotions, and perhaps not by any emotions at all, since emotions make a person less detached, and 'an impartial judge, as ordinarily conceived is . . . unaffected . . . by his emotions'.[6]

(5) In other respects the ideal observer must be '*normal*', by which

[1] Ibid., p. 319.   [2] Ibid., p. 321.
[3] Ibid., p. 333.   [4] Ibid., p. 335.
[5] Ibid., p. 337.   [6] Ibid., p. 340.

he means lacking 'none of the determinable properties of human beings',[1] about which, he admits, it is difficult to be precise.

If we are to know what to make of this theory it is imperative to bring out what Firth considers to be involved in the analysis. The appeal to our awareness of the criteria we employ for determining who is a well-qualified moral judge seems to indicate that he is involved in reporting the criteria actually used by ourselves and others when we engage in such an activity. In his reply to R. B. Brandt's discussion of his original paper he indicates that this is so: 'This analysis', he says, 'is intended to exhibit the meaning of ethical statements as they occur in ordinary language'.[2] This presupposes empirical knowledge of ordinary language and in particular of the criteria embodied in it when it is used to discriminate between potential moral judges. Firth's method is simply to appeal to our own experience of such matters rather than to do the empirical research which would be necessary to back up his impressions of normal linguistic behaviour. Such a method leaves the analysis open to objections based on empirical reports that criteria other than those he mentions are used in the actual discourse of particular persons or groups.

At this point it is open to him, as a *philosopher*, although not as a social scientist, to discount such instances because they involve the introduction of morally irrelevant criteria. This is presumably how he would deal with those who require that membership of a particular religious hierarchy or the attainment of a mature age is an important qualification for a moral judge. To reject such requirements out of hand, and not on empirical grounds, implies some sort of stipulation on his part, in which case some reason for the stipulation should be given. One possible reason is that such a meaning represents his own 'moral' choice, as would be the case if he endowed the observer with qualities he admires, or qualities which he thinks to be causally or logically related to the disposition to make the sort of moral judgments of which he approves. In this case he would not be defining the meaning of a moral statement in a morally neutral way, that is he would not be giving the meaning of 'moral' as opposed to 'non-moral' but of 'moral' as opposed to 'immoral'. It seems likely that he would wish to deny that this is his method of analysis, since he is aiming to produce a naturalistic definition of a moral judgment and stresses the importance of excluding moral predicates from his definition of the ideal observer.

[1] Ibid., p. 344.
[2] 'Reply to Professor Brandt', *Philosophy and Phenomenological Research*, vol. XV (1955), p. 416.

In the absence of any other justification for his exclusion of competitive analyses we are left with the assumption that he is attempting to report on the criteria which are actually employed by most persons in assessing the worth of a person as a moral judge. In this case it is inadmissible for him to extract from his theory any normative conclusions concerning the validity of certain types of moral argument or the acceptability of certain moral statements. And yet this is what he wishes to do, for, later on in the same discussion note, he concludes that 'If an ideal observer analysis is correct we shall be in a position to say that ethical beliefs (or attitudes) can be supported by arguments which are valid because of the very *meaning* of ethical statements',[1] and this is in line with his tendency in the original article to use the ideal observer not just as the concept by which to explicate the meaning of the new term 'moral' but to test moral statements and decide which are true and which false.[2] It would seem, therefore, that by deducing normative conclusions from what is alleged to be a morally neutral description of an 'ideal observer' Firth commits the naturalistic fallacy.

This criticism can be developed in several different ways. The characteristics of the ideal observer have been stated in such general terms that they might seem to be non-controversial. But this is not the case. There has been doubt over whether we should include the attribute of consistency[3]; Firth's only reply to this is that, given his other attributes, the ideal observer would be consistent as well.[4] Or there could be argument about identifying the moral point of view with impartiality, since it might be the case that one person ought to sacrifice his own interests to those of his family, or indeed any other person, and not accept the compromise balance of interests which an impartial observer might approve. However the particular quality that I shall discuss is that of the observer's dispassionate state. Might we not disqualify a moral judge as unfeeling who did not possess a benevolent and kind disposition towards those whom he judges? Even if omnipercipience includes the ability to know how other people feel (something approaching to Smith's sympathy) is this sufficient if the judge lacks a feeling *for* the persons concerned or does not exhibit an active concern for their welfare?

Firth is inclined to minimize the importance of points like these by saying that they are mere refinements of his theory and not an objection to it as such. He is quite willing to admit the emotional

---

1 Ibid., p. 421.
2 'Ethical Absolutism and the Ideal Observer', p. 329.
3 Brandt, *Ethical Theory*, p. 412.
4 'Ethical Absolutism and the Ideal Observer', pp. 341ff.

virtues such as love and compassion provided that we include them, not because they are virtues, but because of 'their relationship to certain ethically-significant reactions of an ideal observer'.[1] But, even if we accept this distinction, how can we say what are ethically significant reactions without intruding our own moral presuppositions about the content of true moral judgments as our only way of testing which ethically significant reactions are trustworthy? These difficulties reveal that it is not possible to specify the ethically significant emotions which an ideal observer must have without begging moral questions and thus involving the analysis in circularity. Contrary to what Firth says, it is not solely a psychological question to ask for a definition of 'ethically-significant reactions'.

Firth has a similar problem over the attempt to say what is ethically significant *knowledge*, but he is able to evade this issue by saying that the observer must be omniscient. This escape route is not open to him in the case of the emotional state of the ideal observer since, even if it were possible to conceive of a person who felt all possible human emotions, we would wish to say that certain emotions, such as boredom or envy, positively disqualify a moral judge. Harrison points out that 'if you allow an ideal observer to have passions, you are faced with the problem of specifying which of his passions may affect his moral reactions.'[2] Why love and not hate? There seems to be nothing in a non-moral ideal which allows one more than the other. If Firth retreats into his final qualification of 'normality' he might say that the ideal observer must feel only those emotions which are normal, but it is not at all clear that we should accept some sort of average emotional state as sufficient for a moral judge, since we might feel that, in this case, the more benevolence the better.

Relating this circularity criticism to the more general argument against the unspecific nature of Firth's type of analysis, we can say that, in reporting ordinary language, we can discover that many different criteria are used to disqualify and commend moral judges, and that it is not possible to make a selection between these without drawing on our own moral presuppositions, from which we may deduce the sort of person we should consider a well-qualified moral judge. That is, only by making it a normative analysis can we give any good reason to prefer one putative set of qualifications to another. I suggest, therefore, that Firth introduces his own moral standards into an analysis of meaning which he alleges to be normatively

[1] Firth, *op. cit.*, p. 341.
[2] Jonathan Harrison, 'Some Comments upon Professor Firth's Ideal Observer Theory', *Philosophy and Phenomenological Research*, vol. XVII (1956-7), p. 260.

neutral. This is an instance of the 'normative fallacy' which is the name I suggest for fallacious reasoning in which a person draws on his opinions as to what ought to be the case, in order to back up statements which assert that something actually is the case. One commits the naturalistic fallacy by arguing from 'is' to 'ought'. One commits the normative fallacy if one reasons from 'ought' to 'is'.[1]

In his attempts to avoid the criticism that he is arguing in a circle Firth is led to characterize the Ideal Observer in a way which renders him so different from any actual human being as to be more in the nature of a god than a man. No human being is dispassionate, omniscient, omnipercipient or even disinterested. These are all qualities they may approach to some degree but to extrapolate them to their logical limits and predicate them of a person is to describe a being of whom we have no experience. The difficulty of trying to reconcile normality with such characteristics is a problem concerning which much might be learned from an examination of most early and some modern attempts to formulate a Christology. Using the terms of Christian doctrine Firth is guilty of docetism, a heresy which gives Christ the appearance but not the real attributes of a man.[2] In other words Firth has landed us with at least some of the characteristics of the deity[3] and by so doing has removed the judge of human conduct from the comprehension of ordinary, normal persons. This is to make the reactions which we are told are the basis of moral statements into something too far removed from human experience for us to know what they would be like and whether we would accept their authority in the sphere of morality.

Heresy or not, Firth's docetism makes it impossible for him to answer certain key questions. How can we know that two different ideal observers would not disagree in their reactions? Brandt argues, I think rightly, that 'the facts of ethnology and psychological theory suggest that there could (causally) be two persons, both "Ideal Observers" in Firth's sense, who could have different or even opposed reactions of approval (or experience of apparent requiredness) with

[1] Cf. T. D. Campbell, 'The Normative Fallacy', *Philosophical Quarterly*, vol. XX (1970), pp. 368-77.
[2] Cf. J. N. D. Kelly, *Early Christian Doctrines*, 2nd edn (London, 1960), Chapter 6, pp. 141f.
[3] Cf. D. Emmet, 'Universalisability and Moral Judgment', *Philosophical Quarterly*, vol. XIII (1963), p. 223: 'It is easy to point out that an Ideal Observer who knew all the facts and the consequences of all possible alternatives and was completely impartial could only be God'; and W. K. Frankena, 'The Concept of Social Justice' in *Social Justice*, ed. by R. B. Brandt (Englewood Cliffs, 1962), p. 16.

respect to the same act, say on account of past conditioning, or different systems of desires, etc'.[1] Firth's only reply to this is to say that we cannot *know* that two ideal observers will disagree. But this means that we cannot know they *will* agree which is precisely the point.

Or, secondly, why should we accept the reactions of the ideal observer as morally relevant? The difficulty of knowing what such reactions would be like makes a decision on this point impossible. Firth does not feel that it is a matter of great importance to give an accurate preliminary phenomenological analysis of the feelings of approval and disapproval which are part of any moral judgment, but our almost total inability to characterize the reactions of his ideal observer make it impossible to know if reactions of such an observer would bear any resemblance to what we would recognize as a moral judgment. For a naturalistic analysis of moral judgments the lack of a convincing psychological analysis of moral judgments must always be a serious drawback; the strength of naturalistic theories usually lies in their ability to give a psychologically intelligible account of moral judgments which is often lacking in non-naturalistic theories. In this case the drawbacks are compounded since we are no longer sure that the reactions of an ideal observer would bear any phenomenological similarity to our own.

II. SMITH'S SPECTATOR

The most obvious ways in which Smith's impartial spectator differs from the ideal observer relate to the characteristics which are ascribed to the spectator. What Firth outlines is an abstraction distinguished by many superhuman qualities. It is an abstraction with which Smith's spectator has little in common. For Smith the spectator represents, in the first instance, the average, or normal or ordinary man. This can be seen from the many synonyms which Smith uses for the term: he speaks, interchangeably, of the 'spectator',[2] 'spectators',[3] 'bystander',[4] 'a third person',[5] 'every attentive spectator',[4] 'every impartial bystander',[6] 'every impartial spectator',[7] 'every indifferent person',[8] 'another man',[9] 'other men',[10] 'society',[11] and,

---

[1] 'Discussion of an "Ideal Observer" theory in ethics', *Philosophy and Phenomenological Research*, vol. XV (1955), p. 408.

[2] T.M.S., I.i.1 (I.11).	[3] T.M.S., I.i.4 (I.41).
[4] T.M.S., I.i.1 (I.6).	[5] T.M.S., I.ii.2 (I.67).
[6] T.M.S., IV.2 (I.484).	[7] T.M.S., II.i.2 (I.167).
[8] T.M.S., I.i.5 (I.47).	[9] T.M.S., III.1 (I.276).
[10] T.M.S., II.ii.2 (I.207).	[11] T.M.S., II.ii.2 (I.210).

most frequently of all, 'mankind'.[1] It seems a matter of indifference to him whether the singular or the plural forms are used; when he uses the plural it is usually to refer to what 'every' spectator would feel, but this sometimes becomes 'the bulk of mankind' or 'the greater part of mankind'. Add to this the fact that he often talks of what 'we' do, or do not, sympathize with in the same contexts as he refers to what the spectator feels, and it will be apparent that, in Smith's mind, the impartial spectator is very much a creature of flesh and blood whose characteristics are to be seen in the behaviour of each and every human person; there is no suggestion that he has any attributes not present 'in every human heart'.[2]

What distinguishes the impartial spectator from anyone else is not his special qualities but his particular viewpoint: he represents the reactions of the ordinary person when he is in the position of a non-involved spectator. We have already seen that the spectator is defined in contrast to the agent or 'the person principally concerned' as any person who is observing behaviour in a situation which does not affect him personally; the objects which excite the emotions of the agent have no particular reference to him and the effects of the agent's acts do not touch him.[3] This is the primary meaning of 'impartial' and 'indifferent' when applied by Smith to the spectator. The spectator is 'indifferent' relative to the sufferings of a person in pain because he does not feel this pain himself; this also makes him 'impartial' even when there is only one person principally concerned. To consider a situation in a 'candid and impartial light' is to regard it from the point of view of the spectator,[4] which is the position of 'every body, but the man who feels it'.[5]

In cases of social and unsocial acts, when the behaviour of an agent affects others, these persons are also 'principally concerned' and spectators are then often described as 'third persons'. The impartial spectator is in the position in which a juryman is intended to be: an ordinary person assessing a case the outcome of which is of no personal consequence to himself in that he stands to gain or lose nothing which any other person would not gain or lose. He is 'impartial' as between persons involved in the situation because he has no special reason for preferring the one to the other. He is indifferent because he himself is not affected either by the causes or the consequences of the agent's action. He is literally a bystander; observing

---

1 T.M.S., I.i.4 (I.38); I.ii.Intro. (I.54); I.ii.3 (I.75); II.ii.1 (I.197).
2 T.M.S., II.i.2 (I.167f.).
3 Cf. T.M.S., I.i.4 (I.31 and I.37), cf. p. 96f.
4 T.M.S., I.i.4 (I.41).
5 T.M.S., I.ii.2 (I.67).

but taking no part in the course of events. He represents the multitude of third persons in whose presence human actions take place.

He is not, however, 'indifferent' in the sense of being without emotions; he has all the normal feelings characteristic of human nature. If he is 'cool' it is only in the sense that he does not directly feel the passions of those involved in a particular situation, he does not possess the feelings of the persons principally concerned.[1] On the contrary he has the 'virtues of candid condescension and indulgent humanity' in so far as these are normal to persons in the place of a spectator,[2] and, most important of all, he has the same desires to obtain pleasure and avoid pain as any ordinary man, desires which, for someone in his situation, lead him to seek for harmony or concord of sentiment with those whom he is observing.[3]

Nor is the spectator omniscient, although he is, for the most part 'well-informed',[4] in that he knows the facts of the case and he does not make judgments in matters of which he has inadequate knowledge.[5] But he has no trouble in deciding whether or not he knows the relevant facts since these are those which would be important to him were he in the situation of the agent or that of the person affected by the agent's behaviour. Smith never attributes to the spectator knowledge beyond that which it is usually possible to obtain, and which is normally considered necessary before an observer can decide whether or not he sympathizes with the agent concerned. Limitations of his knowledge in regard to the outcome of acts and the remote causes of behaviour are taken for granted.

And he is certainly not omnipercipient, that is 'able to visualize all the alternative sets of acts and their consequences as vividly as if he were actually perceiving them',[6] although Smith sometimes talks of him as 'attentive'.[7] The laws of sympathy apply *in toto* to the ability of the impartial spectator to imagine the feelings of others. This means that he can never reproduce the original feelings of the agent in their full strength, and there are some feelings into which he can enter to a small degree only. In this he is at one with 'all mankind', the phrase which recurs most frequently in Smith's exposition of the laws of sympathy.

In consequence of his 'humanity' the impartial spectator is subject to all the failings or irregularities which alter the usual operations of the moral sentiments. He feels the 'irregularity' of sentiments due

---

[1] Cf. T.M.S., I.i.1 (I.2f.).   [2] T.M.S., I.i.5 (I.44).
[3] T.M.S., I.i.2 (I.21).   [4] T.M.S., I.iii.3 (I.151).
[5] T.M.S., I.ii.3 (I.81).   [6] Cf. p. 129.
[7] T.M.S., I.i.1 (I.6).

to the influence of fortune,[1] and enters into the 'fallacious sense of guilt'[2] associated with such cases. He too is 'blinded by success'[3] and shares in the admiration of the mass of mankind for wealth and greatness.[4] Far from always representing the judgments of 'cool reason'[5] he embodies the principles by which a 'weak and imperfect being' actually does approve and disapprove of actions.[6] There is, therefore, nothing docetic in Smith's image of the impartial spectator: all his characteristics are fully human, and he possesses these only to the degree which is common in the average person.[7] The contrast with Firth's ideal observer arises from the different method used to determine the spectator's characteristics. Smith is not enquiring into the qualities of a perfect moral judge; he certainly does not appeal to self-conscious and sophisticated moral arguments, which he considers camouflage the real sources of moral judgments which it is his purpose to discover.

Smith's impartial spectator does represent a relatively stable standard of moral judgment and this has misled commentators into assuming that this stability is due to some rational principle, beyond the workings of sympathy, which gives the impartial spectator a privileged position as a moral judge, able to stand above and assess the judgments of ordinary men. The spectator does embody a norm but it is a norm only in the sense of an average standard which emerges from the interplay of the reactions of ordinary spectators and agents; he personifies the results of a process of interaction whereby an agreed set of moral principles are evolved. The spectator is not an 'invention',[8] nor a 'fiction';[9] he is much nearer to what Small calls 'the ongoing social process'[10] in that he represents the judgments which result from the harmonizing of attitudes towards conduct.

[1] T.M.S., II.iii.2 (I.259): '. . . the indignation, even of the spectator, is apt to be animated by the actual consequences of the action'; and (I.263): '. . . did not even the impartial spectator feel some indulgence for what may be regarded as the unjust resentment of that other . . .?'; cf. (I.246).

[2] T.M.S., II.iii.3 (I.272f.).

[3] T.M.S., VI.iii (II.159f.).

[4] Cf. T.M.S., I.iii.2 (I.120) and T.M.S., I.iii.3 (I.148f.).

[5] T.M.S., II.iii.3 (I.266).

[6] Cf. T.M.S., II.i.5 footnote (I.189).

[7] He criticizes the Stoics for recommending men 'to enter into the views of the great Superintendant of the universe' in order to make moral judgments, T.M.S., VII.ii.1 (II.255-65).

[8] L. Stephen, *History of English Thought*, ix. 77.

[9] *Jouffroy's Ethics*, p. 137.

[10] A. Small, *Adam Smith and Modern Sociology*, p. 39.

Smith accounts for this process by which some sort of moral consensus is achieved, of a loose sort within each society and a somewhat tighter form in the case of each social group within a society, by showing how men's ability to generalize about their own and other people's morally relevant feelings, together with the universal desire of men to agree with their fellows and so obtain their approval, leads to an ironing out of moral disagreement. This is the sort of process with which modern students of small group behaviour have made us familiar.[1] The spectator standpoint is the common ground which unites men because it is when they are in the position of non-involved spectators that they tend to agree most readily. This process, which will be analysed in more detail in the next chapter, together with Smith's assumption that all human beings have basically similar emotional reactions, explains why he thinks he is justified in talking of *the* impartial spectator.

The attitudes of the spectator do not only represent the averaging out of differences between the reactions of spectators: they are also, as we have seen in Chapter 4, a compromise between the spontaneous feelings of man *qua* spectator and those of man *qua* agent, whereby each makes some accommodation to the sentiments of the other. In modern terms, we can say that the spectator's attitudes are a condition of equilibrium, in the sense of a balance of forces, held together, in this case, mainly by men's desires to maintain concord of sentiments. It is an unstable equilibrium in that, when environmental in-puts lead to alterations in the normal attitudes of spectators and agents, a new consensus, or balance of forces, emerges, rather than a re-establishment of the old attitudes.

On the other hand, by providing an agreed standard, the impartial spectator contributes to the order and harmony of society and so helps to maintain another sort of equilibrium. The feed-back mechanisms, as we may describe the interplay of spectator and agent feelings whereby social passions are reinforced and unsocial ones inhibited, help to maintain a state of dynamic stable equilibrium. Dynamic because it is a state of continuous interaction between members of a social group, and stable because the condition of harmony tends to re-establish itself whenever it is upset by unsocial behaviour. Smith's concept of the impartial spectator draws together these complex social processes and represents the means whereby

[1] Cf. Michael S. Olmsted, *The Small Group* (New York, 1959), chap. V, pp. 65ff.

the social consensus necessary for the harmony and therefore for the stability of society is achieved.[1]

The objectivity which attaches to such a spectator's moral judgments is the sort of objectivity which arises out of agreement and not that which implies an external standard known through the exercise of some rational faculty which transcends the normal sources of moral judgments. It is therefore wrong to say, as Bonar does, that 'every man *qua* reason is the impartial spectator',[2] or, as Swabey does, that the impartial spectator represents 'impersonal reason'.[3] Smith consistently denies that reason plays any part in moral judgments except in the formation of general moral rules by induction from particular moral judgments. He does not depart from this position when he introduces the term 'impartial spectator'. In his discussion of conscience, Smith does talk about the 'supposed impartial and well-informed spectator . . . the man within the breast'[4] in a way which appears to place him above the failings of the average spectator. But we shall see, in the next chapter, that the 'ideal man within'[5] is derived from the 'man without' and that his superiority in some directions is offset by his own particular failings.[6]

III. MORAL RELATIVITY

One way of demonstrating that Smith's spectator is an empirical concept, referring to the development of moral consensus in a society, is to show that he is prepared to allow for differences in moral attitudes between spectators in different societies and in different social groups. For although he does assume that similar societies will develop similar moral codes, he is perfectly prepared to allow for the diversity of codes between different types of society and social groups; he would not be concerned to uphold the 'absolutist' position of the Ideal Observer theories. Many examples of this will be given when we come to discuss Smith's explanation for the actual content

[1] The parallel here between the balance of social forces obtained by the operations of sympathy (the impartial spectator) and the 'natural' level of prices, wages etc. obtained through the operation of market forces (the invisible hand) is clear. Cf. E. G. West, *Adam Smith*, pp. 85 and 178.

[2] J. Bonar, *The Moral Sense*, p. 181.

[3] W. C. Swabey, *Ethical Theory from Hobbes to Kant*, p. 182. Cf. G. R. Morrow, 'The Significance of the Doctrine of Sympathy in Hume and Adam Smith', *Philosophical Review*, XXXII (1923), p. 72: '. . . the impartial spectator is the personification of that which is permanent, universal, rational, and natural in the phenomena of sympathy'.

[4] T.M.S., III.2 (I.321).   [5] T.M.S., III.3 (I.364).

[6] Cf. p. 155.

of moral codes, but the general point can be illustrated by reference to Smith's description of the part which custom plays in determining moral standards.

Custom is one of those influences Smith opposes to 'nature'. He describes its operation as follows:

> 'When two objects have frequently been seen together, the imagination acquires a habit of passing easily from the one to the other, If the first appear, we lay our account that the second is to follow. Of their own accord they put us in mind of one another, and the attention glides easily along them.'[1]

This is the Humean idea of the relation between our ideas of cause and effect: two objects or qualities which we are accustomed to seeing or experiencing together become so associated in the mind that their conjunction seems 'proper' and their separation 'improper'. The presence of the one leads us to expect the presence of the other and if this latter is absent then we feel unease and disappointment:

> 'The one we think is awkward when it appears without its usual companion. We miss something which we expect to find, and the habitual arrangement of our ideas is disturbed by the disappointment.'

This operation of the imagination, which unites two ideas for no other reason than that they constantly appear together, is contrasted with natural propriety, by which he means the propriety felt as a result of the more basic principles of the human mind such as reason and sympathy, as when, for instance, we approve of a mathematical solution or of an expression of grief.

Smith exhibits the influence of custom largely by reference to artistic and literary taste, going into considerable detail to show how our perception of beauty is influenced by what we are accustomed to see:

> 'Can any reason, for example, be assigned why the Doric capital should be appropriated to a pillar, whose height is equal to eight diameters; the Ionic volute to one of nine; and the Corinthian foliage to one of ten?'[2]

or, again

> 'According to the ancient rhetoricians, a certain measure of verse was by nature appropriated to each particular species of writing,

[1] T.M.S., V.1 (II.2). *Vide* Smith's explanation of the origins of science, cf. p. 32f.
[2] T.M.S., V.1 (II.7).

as being naturally expressive of that character, sentiment, or passion, which ought to predominate in it. One verse, they said, was fit for grave and another for gay works, which could not, they thought, be interchanged without the greatest impropriety. The experience of modern times, however, seems to contradict this principle, though in itself it would appear to be extremely probable. What is the burlesque verse in English, is the heroic verse in French.'[1]

He argues against the view that our ideas of beauty are *entirely* due to custom, that is, based on our experience of what is normal in nature, for, although this helps to explain how nations living in one part of the world develop different ideas of beauty from those living in dissimilar parts, it does not provide a sufficient explanation of our ideas of beauty:

'The utility of any form, its fitness for the useful purposes for which it was intended, evidently recommends it, and renders it more agreeable to us, independent of custom. Certain colours are more agreeable than others, and give more delight to the eye the first time it ever beholds them. A smooth surface is more pleasing than a rough one. Variety is more pleasing than a tedious undiversified uniformity.'[2]

This is the sort of thing he means by a natural sense of beauty. He considers that custom may emphasize or diminish it, but never entirely replace it. He then goes on to show that custom has the same sort of limited influence on the natural moral sentiments.

If we look at the way in which Smith uses the idea of custom to explain some of the diversities which exist between the moral sentiments of one group, nation, or age and another, we will see how he adapts the concept of the impartial spectator to these facts, and this will help to demonstrate the empirical character of the concept. The variations Smith considers are divided into those affecting 'the general style and character of behaviour' and those which are to do with 'particular usages or practices'. An example of the former includes 'the difference between the degrees of self-command which are required in civilized and in barbarous nations'[3] and, of the latter, the practice of exposing new-born infants in Ancient Greece.[4] Smith says that these examples show the influence of custom on moral sentiments and that custom can explain many of these 'irregularities', by which he means inconsistencies, within and between groups. This

---

[1] T.M.S., V.1 (II.9). [2] T.M.S., V.1 (II.16f.).
[3] T.M.S., V.2 (II.40f.). [4] T.M.S., V.2 (II.45ff.).

influence is not so pronounced as it is in matters of taste, since the moral sentiments are made up of some of 'the strongest and most vigorous passions of human nature'[1] and cannot, therefore, be changed very far from their natural state. The influence is least apparent with the general style and character of behaviour, although it can be seen in the tendency of those who have been brought up surrounded by examples of virtuous behaviour to be more shocked by vice than those who 'have been familiarized with it from their infancy'.[2]

This does not mean that Smith denies that fairly extensive variations in the approved style of life do not exist. He notes that different conduct is expected of those who are at different stages of life or are members of particular professions and ranks and that different general ideas of good and evil have been adhered to in different places and times:

> 'We expect in old age, that gravity and sedateness which its infirmities, its long experience, and its worn-out sensibility seem to render both natural and respectable; and we lay our account to find in youth that sensibility, that gaiety and sprightly vivacity which experience teaches us to expect.'[3]

Or:

> 'We cannot expect the same sensibility to the gay pleasures and amusements of life in a clergyman, which we lay our account with in an officer.'[4]

To some degree he puts these variations down to custom: in the past we have seen the old grave and the young vivacious, we have come to associate solemnity with the clergyman and gaiety with the soldier, but there is a deeper explanation for these variation which is uncovered by asking why these different types of person come to adopt different manners and styles of life. The explanation is that the general style and character of behaviour which is most suited to a particular type of person becomes the normal behaviour of such persons, and the impartial spectator therefore judges it to be appropriate to their circumstances:

> 'The propriety of a person's behaviour, depends not upon its suitableness to any one circumstance of his situation, but to all the circumstances, which, when we bring his case home to ourselves, we feel, should naturally call upon his attention'.[5]

---

[1] T.M.S., V.2 (II.19). [2] T.M.S., V.2 (II.20); cf. VI.ii.1 (II. 84-5).
[3] T.M.S., V.2 (II.22f.). [4] T.M.S., V.2 (II.25f.).
[5] T.M.S., V.2 (II.24).

The spectator thus judges behaviour to be proper in one category of person which would not be proper in another; propriety consists in the suitability of an action to its situation, and one important feature of the situation is the age, rank and profession of the person who is the agent; the spectator approves if the behaviour is in accord with the way in which he imagines he would behave if he were a person of this type in the same situation, and his ideas about this will be affected by his knowledge about what is normal behaviour for this type of person; this is a matter of custom if he judges simply on the basis of the association of ideas, but it is a matter of natural propriety if his judgment is based on an imaginary change of situation in which he visualizes himself as being a person of this type.

For instance, we judge that the task of a clergyman, which Smith takes to be a matter of keeping 'the world in mind of that awful futurity which awaits them, who is to announce what may be the fatal consequences of every deviation from the rules of duty'[1] is suited to a grave, austere and abstracted severity. We know that we would be solemn if this was our job and therefore approve of solemnity in those whose task it is. The gaiety normally associated with an army officer is, on the other hand, more a case of custom. Gaiety does not seem appropriate to a man about to face danger in battle; the explanation for such behaviour is to be found in the need for men in this situation to avoid thinking of the risks they incur, and so they develop the carefree attitudes which we associate with a soldier without having any sense of their natural propriety.[2]

Because men are influenced by the constant associations presented to them in their past experience, a spectator brought up in one group or nation will be marginally different from one brought up in another group or nation. But of more importance in explaining general variations in moral values is the fact that the spectator takes into account the different situations of those whose behaviour he is assessing. Smith illustrates this by contrasting barbaric and civilized moralities; this he does, not by arguing that one is superior to the other, but by showing that each is suited to the circumstances of barbarous and civilized ages:

'Among civilized nations, the virtues which are founded upon humanity, are more cultivated than those which are founded upon self-denial and the command of the passions. Among rude and barbarous nations, it is quite otherwise, the virtues of self-denial are more cultivated than those of humanity.'[3]

[1] T.M.S., V.2 (II.26).   [2] T.M.S., V.2 (II.27f.).
[3] T.M.S., V.2 (II.31).

This is not on account of differences in their nature, nor is it due to inconsistency between the impartial spectators in one society and those in another, but it is explained solely by the difference between the situations of the spectators. It is because of 'the necessity of his situation'[1] that the savage is inured to every hardship and must control the expression of his many distresses. The effects of this hard and dangerous life are felt by the spectator as well as by the agent, and this is why self-control is expected and admired in such societies. Smith observes that 'before we can feel much for others, we must in some measure be at ease ourselves'. Since the spectator in savage society does not enjoy such ease, a member of the society 'expects no sympathy from those about him'.[2]

This may be accounted for by 'natural' (pre-customary) moral sentiments, but an admiration for strict self-control may outlast the situation which gave rise to it; this is due to the influence of custom. Similarly the exposure of infants in Sparta may have been necessary at one time for the survival of the group, but familiarity with the practice means that it persists long after this necessity has gone.[3] This is a tendency which Smith frequently notes in his study of the relationship between economics and law.[4]

These examples show that Smith was not only prepared to admit that there are many impartial spectators but considered that he could explain why this should be so. Each spectator is the product of a particular society, in which, through his training and experience, he has come to regard as normal the behaviour which is, or, in some cases, which was, suited to the circumstances, usually the economic circumstances, of that society. This is only to some extent explained by custom; recourse has to be had to the deeper causes of behaviour, which have been discussed in Chapter 3, to explain why a form of behaviour is normal in a certain type of society. The many different spectators are basically similar in that the laws of sympathy apply to them all, but these laws are such as to allow for the effects of their different situations on their moral judgments. Some laws apply only when spectators have sufficient leisure. Others have written into them variables which are a function of the past experience of the spectator. For instance, law three, which deals with the difficulty or ease of entering into unpleasant and pleasant emotions, allows for

---

[1] T.M.S., V.2 (II.32f.).   [2] T.M.S., V.2 (II.33).
[3] T.M.S., V.2 (II.47).
[4] W.N., III.ii (I.408): 'Laws frequently continue in force long after the circumstances, which first gave occasion to them, and which could alone render them reasonable, are no more'; cf. W.N., V.i.3.art.2 (II.289).

variations in the things which minister to men's pleasures, or cause them pain, in different societies. And law four, which states that men sympathize most easily with feelings which are closest to their normal state, obviously leaves open the possibility that what is normal in one society will not be in another.

There are, therefore, many impartial spectators, similar in their main characteristics, but different in many respects. The impartial spectator takes on a variety of guises in different societies and in different groups within the same society. To talk of *the* impartial spectator is simply a short-hand way of referring to the normal reaction of a member of a particular social group, or of a whole society, when he is in the position of observing the conduct of his fellows. This is a sociological concept far removed from the abstract speculations of the Ideal Observer theory.

CHAPTER 7

CONSCIENCE

Smith's account of the moral sentiments concentrates on the spectator standpoint because he considers that it is by examining the nature of the spectator's reactions that we can best understand and explain these sentiments; in his view, they simply *are* the sentiments of the spectator; to understand these is to understand morality. An approach of this sort is open to the objection that the fundamental function of morality is to guide conduct and not to pass judgments on the behaviour of others. Such judgments, it is true, may affect the actions of agents in so far as they value the approval of the spectator, but a moral judgment, it may be said, commits the spectator himself to pursue that which he conceives to be good and avoid that which he regards as evil, and therefore imposes on the judge himself clear moral obligations. So far Smith has shown how the spectator might be prompted to reward the persons whom he considers meritorious and punish those who have caused justified resentment to others, but he has not explained how the spectator judges his own behaviour and comes to regard himself as being obliged to adopt the standards which he sets for others. A crucial part of the theory, therefore, consists in the explanation of how the detached approval of the spectator becomes the authoritative imperative to which the individual feels he ought to conform.

I. 'AS OTHERS SEE US'

Smith takes all this into his theory with deceptive ease. He argues that there is no difference in principle between judging our own and other people's conduct: both types of judgment are a matter of comparing one set of sentiments with another, and approving if they agree or disapproving if they disagree. When I, as spectator, judge the behaviour of another I compare his sentiments with those I imagine I would feel were I in his place, but when I judge my own behaviour I compare the sentiments I actually feel with

146

those I imagine I would feel were I a spectator judging my own behaviour:

'We can never survey our own sentiments and motives, we can never form any judgment concerning them; unless we remove ourselves, as it were, from our own natural station, and endeavour to view them as at a certain distance from us. But we can do this in no other way than by endeavouring to view them with the eyes of other people, or as other people are likely to view them. Whatever judgment we can form concerning them, accordingly, must always bear some secret reference, either to what are, or to what, upon a certain condition, would be, or to what, we imagine, ought to be the judgment of others. We endeavour to examine our own conduct as we imagine any other fair and impartial spectator would examine it.'[1]

This general idea has been introduced already in the explanation of how an agent modifies his passions so as to reduce them to a level with which a spectator can sympathize, the virtue of self-command. Self-command presupposes the ability of the agent to regard his own behaviour from the standpoint of others. This ability also explains 'our Judgments concerning our own Sentiments and Conduct, and . . . the Sense of Duty'.[2] All the elements of this aspect of his theory are present in the first edition of the *Moral Sentiments*,[3] but they are developed further both in the second and, more extensively, in the sixth editions; in this last edition there is to be found a detailed theory of the origins and operations of conscience. There Smith describes how each individual comes to guide his own conduct by internalizing the judgments which he knows, or imagines, that other people pass on his conduct, and fitting these in with his own judgments on the conduct of others which he learns to apply to his own behaviour.

Conscience, then, is the mechanism whereby the individual comes to adopt the standpoint of the spectator in order to assess and guide his own conduct, and so gain the approbation of actual spectators, including his own approbation in those moments when he is reflecting on his own conduct. In this way conscience opposes the 'natural' (spontaneous and pre-moral) preference which each man has for his own pleasure, and encourages the

[1] T.M.S., III.1 (I.276f.); cf. (1st edn) III.ii (p. 257) and III.i (pp. 248f.).
[2] T.M.S., III.title (I.275).
[3] Cf. T.M.S., (1st edn) III. *passim* (pp. 245-316), especially pp. 283 and 296, and VI.ii (p. 478).

practice of such mild forms of altruism as exist in unsocialized man:

'Independent of any regard either to what are, or to what ought to be, or to what upon a certain condition would be, the sentiments of other people, the first of those three virtues (prudence) is originally recommended to us by our selfish, the other two (justice and benevolence) by our benevolent affections. Regard to the sentiments of other people, however, comes afterwards both to enforce and direct the practice of all those virtues; and no man . . . ever trod steadily and uniformly in the paths of prudence, of justice, or of proper beneficence, whose conduct was not principally directed by a regard to the sentiments of the supposed impartial spectator, of the great inmate of the breast, the great judge and arbiter of conduct.'[1]

The most important task of conscience is to curb the natural preference which each man has for his own happiness,[2] for without the growth of conscience men would pay little regard to the happiness of others. By saying that man is naturally selfish Smith means that, if the controls of conscience and public opinion were removed, men would unthinkingly harm others in order to gain their own ends; since conscience is a social product, this amounts to saying that pre-social man, that is man considered in abstraction from the social relationships which produce conscience, would normally act with partiality towards himself. However, since men do grow up within society, it becomes a matter of habit to regard their own conduct from the point of view of the spectator, and moral conduct becomes natural (spontaneous, pre-reflective) to them:

'Here, too, habit and experience have taught us to do this so easily and so readily, that we are scarce sensible that we do it; and it requires, in this case too, some degree of reflection, and even of philosophy, to convince us, how little interest we should take in the greatest concerns of our neighbour, how little we should be affected by whatever relates to him, if the sense of propriety and justice did not correct the otherwise natural inequality of our sentiments.'[3]

Smith argues his case by offering the outline of a developmental hypothesis of a type which is familiar in present-day social psychology.

---

[1] T.M.S., VI. Conclusion (II.187f.).
[2] T.M.S., II.ii.2 (I.205f.): 'Every man is, no doubt, by nature, first and principally recommended to his own care'; cf. T.M.S., III.4 (I.393).
[3] T.M.S., III.3 (I.333-4).

He imagines what life would be like outside society, and the transformation which would take place in a solitary unsocialized individual were he to be brought into society:

'Were it possible that a human creature could grow up to manhood in some solitary place, without any communication with his own species, he could no more think of his own character, of the propriety or demerit of his own sentiments and conduct, of the beauty or deformity or his own mind, than of the beauty or deformity of his own face. All these are objects which he cannot easily see, which naturally he does not look at, and with regard to which he is provided with no mirror which can present them to his view. Bring him into society, and he is immediately provided with the mirror which he wanted before. It is placed in the countenance and behaviour of those he lives with, which always mark when they enter into, and when they disapprove of his sentiments; and it is here that he first views the propriety and impropriety of his own passions, the beauty and deformity of his own mind.'[1]

This account is easily transposed into a description of the means whereby an infant learns to guide his behaviour in such a way as to gain the approval of those who care for it. In Smith's words:

'Bring him into society, and all his own passions will immediately become the causes of new passions. He will observe that mankind approve of some of them, and are disgusted by others. He will be elevated in the one case, and cast down in the other.'[2]

Smith's basic theory of conscience is, therefore, that because men desire the approval and dread the disapproval of others they learn to judge their own conduct and model their behaviour according to the patterns which gain approval and avoid disapproval. This is of a piece with modern psychological and sociological theories of the development of the super-ego, of self-consciousness, and the whole process of socialization. He himself has his own view on the various stages in this process:

'A very young child has no self-command; but, whatever are its emotions, whether fear, or grief, or anger, it endeavours always, by the violence of its outcries, to alarm, as much as it can, the attention of its nurse, or of its parents. While it remains under the

---

[1] T.M.S., III.1 (I.277f.). This might appear to be an example of conjectural history, but there is no suggestion that he is representing an actual or even a possible sequence of events. He is really building up a model of those forces at work in society which create and maintain individual consciences.

[2] T.M.S., III.1 (I.279).

149

custody of such partial protectors, its anger is the first, and, perhaps the only passion which it is taught to moderate. By noise and threatening, they are, for their own ease, often obliged to frighten it into good temper; and the passion which incites it to attack, is restrained by that which teaches it to attend to its own safety. When it is old enough to go to school, or to mix with its equals, it soon finds that they have no such indulgent partiality. It naturally wishes to gain their favour, and to avoid their hatred or contempt. Regard even to its own safety teaches it to do so; and it soon finds that it can do so in no other way than by moderating, not only its anger, but all its other passions, to the degree which its play-fellows and companions are likely to be pleased with.'[1]

Because he wishes to insist that self-judgments are impossible unless they are preceded by judgments on the conduct of others, Smith sometimes puts his theory of the development of conscience in a temporal sequence which may seem to conflict with modern developmental theories:

'. . . our first moral criticisms are exercised upon the characters and conduct of other people; and we are all very forward to observe how each of these affects us. But we soon learn, that other people are equally frank with regard to our own. We become anxious to know how far we deserve their censure or applause. . . . We begin, upon this account, to examine our own passions and conduct. . . .'[2]

This may well be a fair picture of a certain stage of adolescent self-awareness, but it is clear that children learn to control their own behaviour in the light of their parents' attitudes as soon as, if not before, they make criticisms of others. However, Smith is well aware of this,[3] and he would probably not attribute this early form of self-control to conscience, which requires the child to make the imaginative leap of regarding his own behaviour through the eyes of others. In any case it is not a major problem for Smith's theory, since he can preserve the causal primacy of the spectator's judgments over judgments of self-criticism by saying that the judgments in question need not be made by the same person, and that it is on account of the approval and disapproval of other people that small children learn to approve and disapprove of their own conduct. There is thus no necessity for Smith to insist on a rigid temporal

---

[1] T.M.S., III.3 (I.355).   [2] T.M.S., III.1 (I.281).
[3] L.J., p. 74: '. . . children have so long a dependence upon their parents, to bring down their passions to theirs, and thus be trained up at length to become useful members of society'.

priority, in each individual, of judgments passed on the conduct of others over judgments passed on his own behaviour.

II. THE AUTONOMY OF CONSCIENCE

To understand the workings of Smith's conscience it is important to note that, in the development of conscience, the individual is split into two distinct halves: the self as agent and the self as spectator of the self as agent:

'When I endeavour to examine my own conduct, when I endeavour to pass sentence upon it, and either to approve or condemn it, it is evident that, in all such cases, I divide myself as it were, into two persons: and that I, the examiner and judge, represent a different character from that other I, the person whose conduct is examined into and judged of. The first is the spectator, whose sentiments with regard to my own conduct I endeavour to enter into, by placing myself in his situation, and by considering how it would appear to me, when seen from that particular point of view. The second is the agent, the person whom I properly call myself, and of whose conduct, under the character of a spectator, I was endeavouring to form some opinion.'[1]

The 'proper' self is the agent, the spectator is in some sense the artificial presence of society within the individual. The conflict between desire and conscience is interpreted by Smith in terms of a conflict between the unsocialized impulses of the individual and the constraining influence of an internalized social imperative.

This internal voice, representing the attitudes of the impartial spectator, achieves, in its developed form, a certain autonomy and independence of the real spectators without. It comes to possess an authority which makes it natural to speak of it as being a 'higher tribunal'[2] than the opinions of mankind, and to regard its dictates as the 'vicegerents of God within us'.[3] Smith attains his pinnacle of rhetoric in describing its character:

'It is reason, principle, conscience, the inhabitant of the breast, the man within, the great judge and arbiter of our conduct. It is he who, whenever we are about to act so as to affect the happiness of others, calls to us, with a voice capable of astonishing the most presumptuous of our passions, that we are but one of the multitude, in no respect better than any other in it; and that when we prefer

[1] T.M.S., III.1 (I.282-3). [2] T.M.S., III.2 (I.321f.).
[3] T.M.S., III.5 (I.413).

ourselves so shamefully and so blindly to others, we become the proper objects of resentment, abhorrence, and execration.'[1]

To understand how Smith accounts for this phenomenon it is necessary to distinguish different stages in the development of conscience.

The origin of conscience is traced back to the effect which the approbation and disapprobation of other people have upon the individual. In the first place, every man wishes to be liked and fears to be disliked. He therefore takes heed of the views of the spectators; he learns to see his conduct from their point of view, and so to feel something of the emotions they manifest towards himself; as spectator of his own actions he feels sympathetic approval and disapproval, gratitude and resentment, and it becomes impossible for him to act on selfish principles and continue 'to look mankind in the face'.[2] In the beginning this involves a straightforward dislike of being the object of disapproval and a wish to enjoy the approval of his fellows, but as he succeeds in actually looking at his own conduct from their point of view he begins to feel something of the same emotions which they feel towards him, the agent. And when he shares, for instance, their disapproval, he 'feels all the agonies of shame, or horror, and consternation'.[3] Remorse and shame are the consequences of the self-condemnation which follows from the agent imaginatively adopting the standpoint of the spectator. When a person has committed a grave injustice, not only is he unable to 'look mankind in the face', he cannot, in his role as spectator, look himself in the face; this is the feeling of guilt, which Smith describes in vivid detail.[4]

But although he insists that the approval and disapproval of actual spectators is the origin of conscience,[5] Smith notes that the latter develops an autonomy which enables the individual to think that he acts with moral propriety even when the real spectators condemn his behaviour. The supposed impartial spectator within begins to take on a higher authority than the actual spectator without:

'Man naturally desires, not only to be loved, but to be lovely; or to

---

[1] T.M.S., III.3 (I.336-7). This echoes Butler's view of conscience (*Fifteen Sermons* (1726), Preface), and shows that Findlay is wrong in saying that Smith's concept of conscience lacks authority; cf. J. N. Findlay, *Values and Intentions* (London, 1961), p. 210. [2] T.M.S., II.ii.2 (I.206).
[3] T.M.S., II.ii.2 (I.209). [4] T.M.S., II.ii.2 (I.211).
[5] This theory is echoed by Edward Westermarck, *Ethical Relativity*, p. 111: 'Public disapproval is the prototype of moral disapproval'.

be that thing which is the natural and proper object of love. He naturally dreads, not only to be hated, but to be hateful; or to be that thing which is the natural and proper object of hatred. He desires, not only praise, but praise-worthiness; or to be that thing which, though it should be praised by nobody, is, however, the natural and proper object of praise. He dreads, not only blame, but blame-worthiness; or to be that thing which, though it should be blamed by nobody, is, however, the natural and proper object of blame.'[1]

There are therefore two distinct passions of human nature, which are 'original' in the sense that they cannot be reduced to a combination of other passions,[2] a desire to be loved, and a desire to be worthy of love; conscience, originating in man's accommodation to the former desire, comes to serve the latter, and instructs men as to how they may become worthy of praise rather than simply how they may obtain it.[3]

This element of Smith's theory has been thought by most critics to destroy its whole basis, since it seems to indicate that Smith thought that, via conscience, the individual has the ability to know what is good and evil, right and wrong, independently of the empirically determinable judgments of the impartial spectator, an unaccountable new factor having entered into the analysis. It is said that, through the 'love of praise-worthiness', Smith is able to smuggle in a normative standard which he uses to pass moral judgment upon the sort of impartial spectator with whom he started, a spectator who represents the attitudes of the normal person.[4] Thus Stephen says that the appeal to the 'demi-god' within, as Smith calls the voice of conscience, is 'ultimately to an inaccessible tribunal' which reveals the incompleteness of his analysis built up on the basis of the approval of actual spectators and the effects of sympathy.[5] Swabey agrees that the appeal to the ideal spectator within concedes the moral inadequacy of the praise of actual spectators and 'comes close to admitting that praise-worthiness and blame-worthiness are indefinable terms', and he backs up this criticism by pointing out Smith's description of some moral sentiments as 'corrupt' which shows that he 'claims an ability to distinguish between authentic and unauthentic moral judgments'.[6] This is the sort of consideration that leads Cropsey to say that, for

[1] T.M.S., III.2 (I.284). [2] Cf. T.M.S., III.2 (I.292); cf. p. 67.
[3] T.M.S., III.2 (I.295ff.).
[4] Cf. A. Small, *Adam Smith and Modern Sociology*, p. 48.
[5] L. Stephen, *History of English Thought in the Eighteenth Century*, ix, 78.
[6] W. C. Swabey, *Ethical Theory from Hobbes to Kant*, pp. 182f.

Smith, 'conscience is the innate means by which every human being, as human, has direct, if imperfect knowledge, of the natural rights of all others',[1] and it is the main argument in favour of those who attribute a supra-empirical character to Smith's impartial spectator.

It is certainly true that, in discussing conscience and the love of praise-worthiness, Smith does talk of the spectator in apparently non-empirical terms which are similar to some of the adjectives applied to the ideal observer. He refers, for instance, to 'the supposed impartial and well-informed spectator . . . the man within the breast, the great judge and arbiter of their conduct',[2] 'the ideal man within the breast'[3] and 'the abstract and ideal spectator of our sentiments and conduct',[4] but these terms all get their meaning either from man's ability to build up a picture of the conduct he approves and disapproves of from his experience of the attitudes of normal spectators, which he can then, on occasions, use to oppose the judgments of particular spectators, or from his ability to become the (supposed) spectator of his own conduct. Many critics misconceive the distinction which Smith is making between the desire for praise and the desire for praise-worthiness. It is true that he regards these two desires as 'distinct and independent of one another'[5] in that they are different desires, and to this extent we can accept that Smith is introducing a new factor into the analysis. But it is not true that this new factor is some rational, innate or non-sensory awareness of good and evil not derived from the attitudes of actual spectators. The contrast he is making is between the praise of actual spectators and the praise which the self as spectator gives to the self as agent and to other people. These may not coincide, for when the individual imagines how we would regard his behaviour were he observing it, he may come to adopt an attitude towards himself which is different from that which he perceives the actual spectators to adopt. If his 'sympathetic spectator emotions', if I may call them that, disagree with those of the real spectator, then he will judge the emotions of the real spectator to be wrong. If his sympathetic spectator emotions agree with his emotions as agent, then he will approve of his own behaviour, and, Smith insists, he desires this self-approval as well as the approval of others. In the mature adult, conscience, or the 'man within', becomes the mechanism whereby the individual as spectator judges himself as agent, something he is only able to do because of his past experience of being the object of the approval and disapproval of other men.

---

[1] J. Cropsey, *Polity and Economy*, p. 20.   [2] T.M.S., III.2 (I.321).
[3] T.M.S., III.3 (I.364).   [4] T.M.S., III.3 (I.380).
[5] T.M.S., III.2 (I.285).

This 'man within' usually agrees with the judgments of the actual spectator, but on occasions he may not. Sometimes this is because the 'man within' does not take an impartial enough viewpoint and is too far removed from the position of the real spectator, so that:

'The man within the breast, the abstract and ideal spectator of our sentiments and conduct, requires often to be awakened and put in mind of his duty, by the preference of the real spectator.'[1]

Men are apt to be too kind to themselves when they observe their own conduct. For although they are able to scrutinize their own conduct,

'Unfortunately this moral looking-glass is not always a very good one. Common looking-glasses, it is said, are extremely deceitful, and by the glare which they throw over the face, conceal from the partial eyes of the person many deformities which are obvious to every body besides.'[2]

On other occasions the 'man without' may be partial and, therefore, unrepresentative of the normal response of non-involved third persons, or he may be ill-informed; in these cases the individual may give more importance to the internal approbation of conscience than the approval of the real spectators:

'If the man without should applaud us, either for actions which we have not performed, or for motives which had no influence upon us; the man within can immediately humble all that pride and elevation of mind which such groundless acclamations might otherwise occasion, by telling us, that as we know that we do not deserve them, we render ourselves despicable by accepting them.'[3]

In such instances the man within, being better informed as to the nature of the act in question, knows that if the real spectators had similar information they would withdraw their praise. And very often the man within *has* superior information to the real spectators and this enables the individual to regard him as a higher tribunal, but this higher tribunal is no more nor less than an appeal to the attitudes which the real spectators would adopt did they have the information which is available to the agent, for he knows that such an attitude is the 'natural and ordinary effect of such conduct'.[4] This is what he means by saying that we sometimes judge ourselves by 'what ought'[5] to be the judgments of others.

[1] T.M.S., III.3 (I.380).   [2] T.M.S. (1st edn), III.ii (pp. 260f.).
[3] T.M.S., III.2 (I.322); cf. T.M.S. (1st edn), III.i (pp. 248f.).
[4] T.M.S., III.2 (I.291).   [5] T.M.S., III.2 (I.277).

155

This degree of independence Smith is willing to grant to the individual conscience, but he leaves us in no doubt that there are very strict limits to the extent to which the man within can break free from the 'clamour of the man without':

'Very few men can be satisfied with their own private consciousness that they have attained those qualities, or performed those actions, which they admire and think praise-worthy in other people; unless it is, at the same time, generally acknowledged that they possess the one, or have performed the other; or, in other words, unless they have actually obtained that praise which they think due both to the one and the other.'[1]

Not only is a man not satisfied with praise-worthiness without actual praise, but his judgment as to what it is that is praise-worthy cannot stand against the constant opposition of the real spectators, even if he judges that they are 'ignorant and weak' and therefore wrong:

'He may think himself very confident that their unfavourable judgment is wrong: but this confidence can seldom be so great as to hinder that judgment from making some impression upon him'[2]

The degree to which individuals and groups have confidence in their own judgments is an empirical variable which Smith notes and makes some attempt to explain. Some men are more readily satisfied than others with actual praise in the absence of deserved or self-praise. Those, he says, 'are the most frivolous and superficial of mankind only who can be much delighted with that praise which they themselves know to be altogether unmerited',[3] that is praise which they know would be withdrawn if other men knew as much as the agents concerned. On the other hand, a man of 'sensibility' is more inclined to pay attention to praise-worthiness.[4]

Smith leaves this variation between men largely unaccounted for, but he does indicate a few general tendencies. In the first place, the less certain and clear-cut the spectator's judgments of self-assessment, the more he is swayed by the judgment of others:

'The agreement or disagreement both of the sentiments and judgments of other people with our own, is, in all cases, it must be observed, of more or less importance to us, exactly in proportion as we ourselves are more or less uncertain about the propriety of our own sentiments, about the accuracy of our own judgments.'[5]

---

[1] T.M.S., III.2 (I.318f.).   [2] T.M.S., III.2 (I.308).
[3] T.M.S., III.2 (I.299).   [4] T.M.S., III.2 (I.305).
[5] T.M.S., III.2 (I.308). This is a typical example of Smith's attempts to formulate his generalizations in quasi-mathematical terms.

Secondly, the stronger the feelings of the agent the less he is able to worry about the opinions of the spectators.[1] Some differences relate to the style of life of the persons involved. Royalty, and others who are perpetually surrounded by those who stand to gain by flattery and who come across relatively few impartial spectators of their behaviour, tend to be more susceptible than most to the 'man without'.[2] Persons who are habituated to evil-doing are not so troubled by false accusations as those who are innocent not only in this particular case but in the general tenor of their behaviour.[3] Men who are attached to warring factions in any walk of life tend to reduce their susceptibility to the mass of impartial spectators around them.[4] Those whose professions have to do with matters on which it is difficult to be certain, such as literature and art, have a particular tendency to form cabals and to seek for actual praise rather than praise-worthiness, while those who are more accustomed to dealing in matters which are amenable to rational solution such as mathematics, tend, in morals as well, to be more independent in judgment and therefore attach less importance to the clamour of the 'man without'.[5] Men of 'rank and fortune' who live in the public eye and depend on public respect pay greater attention to the opinions of others than men of 'low condition', especially when these latter leave their small village communities and enter the anonymity of a great city.[6] These tentative hypotheses illustrate the potential sociological fruitfulness of Smith's theory of conscience in suggesting possible explanations of individual and group variations with respect to the dependence of the individual conscience on the opinions of actual spectators.

III. THE SENSE OF DUTY

Whatever degree of autonomy Smith allows to the individual conscience, it must be stressed that the independence of the 'man within' may express itself by being either more or less impartial or well-informed than the actual spectators. On the whole, the main tendency of the internal spectator is towards selfishness, and it is the 'man without' who provides the necessary social pressure to counteract the partiality of inward conscience:

'Such, it seems, is the natural insolence of man, that he almost always disdains to use the good instrument, except when he cannot or dare not use the bad one.'[7]

[1] T.M.S., III.3 (I.364). [2] T.M.S., III.2 (I.327f.).
[3] T.M.S., III.2 (I.304). [4] T.M.S., III.3 (I.384ff.).
[5] T.M.S., III.2 (I.310ff.). [6] W.N., V.i.3.art.3 (II.317).
[7] W.N., V.i.3.art.3 (ii.321).

It is particularly in the moment of action, when he is unable to reflect on his own conduct, that the agent is indulgent towards himself. The distinction between the self as agent and the self as spectator of the self as agent is often a temporal one. In reflective moments the spectator dominates and the individual is relatively impartial in the assessment of his own behaviour, but:

'When we are about to act, the eagerness of passion will seldom allow us to consider what we are doing, with the candour of an indifferent person. The violent emotions which at that time agitate us, discolour our views of things, even when we are endeavouring to place ourselves in the situation of another, and to regard the objects that interest us in the light in which they will naturally appear to him. The fury of our own passions constantly calls us back to our own place, where everything appears magnified and misrepresented by self-love.'[1]

In order to counter this 'self-deceit' which is 'the source of half the disorders of human life'[2] men learn to use moral rules to guide their actions in the knowledge that, if they depart from these rules, they will condemn themselves in their moments of reflection. We have noted how Smith explains the origin of general rules by arguing that they result from inductive reasoning based on the experience of particular moral judgments; this explanation is completed by showing that these rules are needed, not only to render moral assessments habitual, but to fulfil the vital function of enabling men to follow the line of duty when they least desire to do so. Smith defines the sense of duty as obedience to these general moral rules and says that:

'Those general rules of conduct, when they have been fixed in our mind by habitual reflection, are of great use in correcting the misrepresentations of self-love concerning what is fit and proper to be done in our particular situation.'[3]

Because of their function in the moral life these rules become endowed with something of the authority of individual moral judgments; this is enhanced by the fact that they represent the agreed standards of a particular society, so that they appear to have an even greater authority than the judgments from which they originate; in consequence the ordinary person comes to accept that they 'are to be regarded as the commands and laws of the Deity, promulgated

---

[1] T.M.S., III.4 (I.389).   [2] T.M.S., III.4 (I.393).
[3] T.M.S., III.4 (I.398).

by those vicegerents which he has thus set up within us,'[1] thereby adding even further to their *de facto* authority:

'It is in this manner that religion enforces the natural sense of duty: and hence it is, that mankind are generally disposed to place great confidence in the probity of those who seem deeply impressed with religious sentiments.'[2]

In this way the individual's partiality towards himself is controlled by his sense of duty which, by enabling him to adhere to the moral rules of his community, corrects the natural selfishness of the 'man within'.

However, the supposed internal spectator, who is usually more partial than the 'man without', may, on occasions, be less partial and better informed than the actual spectators. We have already noted the tension, in Smith's theory of the impartial spectator, between the average external spectator and the more 'ideal' impartial and well-informed spectator.[3] The tension is partly between the impartial spectator as representing the general moral rules which emerge in every society on the one hand, and, on the other hand, individual spectators who may be partial, inattentive and ill-informed; but it is also a contrast between the average spectator who embodies the ordinary rules of propriety, and the supposed spectator within each man who may often be better informed and more attentive, and occasionally more impartial, than the average spectator. Smith points out that the internal spectator is able to go beyond the established moral rules of his society and build up, through observing his own and other people's behaviour, an abstract picture of a more 'perfect' standard of virtue. Each individual is capable, not only of internalizing the general rules of morality, but of transcending these rules by asking himself what sort of behaviour he, as a spectator, approves most strongly:

'The wise and virtuous man directs his principal attention to the first standard; the idea of exact propriety and perfection. There exists in the mind of every man, an idea of this kind, gradually formed from his observations upon the character and conduct both of himself and of other people. It is the slow, gradual, progressive work of the great demigod within the breast, the great judge and arbiter of conduct.'[4]

This ability of the internal spectator to erect a picture of a 'perfect' man which contrasts with the average standards of his society does not present a peculiar difficulty for Smith's theory in that he attributes

---

[1] T.M.S., III.5 (I.412).   [2] T.M.S., III.5 (I.426).
[3] Cf. pp. 154-7.   [4] T.M.S., VI.iii (II.147).

to every individual the capacity for inductive reasoning, so that there is no problem in regarding each spectator as being able to generalize about his feelings concerning the behaviour of others, and, once society has forced him to observe his own behaviour, concerning this as well.

But what motive has the individual for forming this more 'ideal' set of behavioural norms? Smith's answer to such a question is partly to say that the desire for self-approbation is an irreducible fact about human nature. Just as men get pleasure from sharing the sentiments of others, so they get a similar enjoyment from experiencing a harmony between their own sentiments as agents and those they feel as spectators of their own behaviour. Once society has led the individual into the role of observing his own actions, then he cannot help but seek to attain the pleasure of his own approbation and avoid the pains of self-condemnation. And, in so far as he is a reflective and sensitive person, the individual may set himself standards which are more difficult to attain and therefore may be said to be 'higher' than those which society expects him to achieve.

Yet this is not the whole story, for Smith goes some way towards presenting a picture of the social forces which impel the individual towards this higher form of conscience. Especially in its more ideal forms, Smith's conscience acts as a court of appeal against the moral judgments of partial and ill-informed spectators:

'In order to defend ourselves from such partial judgments, we soon learn to set up in our own minds a judge between ourselves and those we live with. We conceive ourselves as acting in the presence of a person quite candid and equitable, of one who has no particular relation either to ourselves, or to those to whose interests are affected by our conduct, who is neither father, nor brother, nor friend either to them or to us, but is merely a man in general, an impartial spectator, who considers our conduct with the same indifference with which we regard that of other people.'[1]

If we develop this line of thought and consider the dynamic process of moral argument in which each person tries to get the other to adopt what he considers to be the impartial view-point in order to reach some form of agreement, then we will see one way in which the individual's sense of duty can be related to the normal attitudes of the average spectator.[2]

[1] T.M.S. (2nd edn), III.2 (pp. 207f.).
[2] The relationship between impartiality and argumentation is briefly discussed by J. D. Bailiff 'Some Comments on the "Ideal Observer" ', *Philosophy and Phenomenological Research*, vol. XXIV (1963-4), pp. 423-8.

IV. MORAL ARGUMENT

The idea that moral argument is, at least in part, an effort to reach a common attitude of approval or disapproval towards particular instances of different types of behaviour fits in easily with Smith's belief that the desire for mutual sympathy is a powerful human motive. Adopting this interpretation of moral argument and taking it to be an essential part of the development of moral consensus in any society, it is possible to regard the impartial spectator, in his more ideal form, as being identified not only with individuals' moral reflections on their own conduct, but also as an indication of the point of view to which appeal is made in those moral arguments which succeed in bringing some measure of agreement into moral disputes. Given the situation that Smith imagines: an agent with a tendency to selfish behaviour seeking to obtain the approval of a spectator, and a spectator who cannot enter into the selfish motives of the agent and yet who wishes to approve of his behaviour, if this is possible, then we can see how both might appeal to what I will call the 'ideal impartial spectator viewpoint', as the best means to reach a compromise agreement. For instance a child who is suffering the disapproval of its mother for hitting his little sister might argue that the mother was unaware of the provocation he had received and so hope to change the mother's attitude by making her better informed, and similarly he would hope to change the attitude of any third person who was not aware of all the facts of the case as he saw them; the mother, in reply, might say that the child did not take into account the suffering of his little sister and argue that, if the son looked at the matter from the sister's point of view he would see how wrong he was, and that this would be the judgment of anyone else to whom she told the facts of the case. The son could counter this by saying that the daughter was the mother's favourite, and that other people would therefore not agree but would accept that he had received sufficient provocation to justify his action. If either can be shown to be partial in this way then he must give way or else forfeit the approval of all those third persons whom they also wish to please. Moreover, this gives both disputants a reason for modifying their attitudes when they are shown to be partial or ill-informed, and thus the standpoint of the impartial well-informed spectator emerges as the court of appeal. Since the agent is usually better informed about his act than anyone else, this means that conscience is a court of appeal beyond the opinions of the actual spectators; it is 'higher' in the sense that appeal is made to it after and against the views of real spectators, and because it is usually better informed.

On the other hand, its weakness is partiality, and although the immediate spectator will often be partial as well, both will have a tendency to appeal to third persons who are less likely to be partial as they are not immediately involved in the same situation. Thus the innumerable third persons to whom appeal may be made will correct the partiality of agent and immediate spectator, and in so far as the agent realizes this, his conscience may help him as a guide to the feelings of these third persons which can be used to counter the immediate spectators of his behaviour.

There are many loose ends to this model of a typical moral argument, but, if it has any validity, it may help us to see how Smith's impartial spectator, at first identified in his mind with the average spectator, comes to take on certain 'ideal' qualities such as being 'well-informed' and completely 'impartial' which may not correctly characterize the average spectator. My suggestion is that this latter concept of the ideal impartial spectator represents both the inner tribunal of conscience and the point of view towards which moral argument leads in its attempt to achieve harmony of sentiments, and as such it is to be identified with the point of view to which any ordinary person may be led by a process of argument, in contrast to the point of view which a casual observer naturally adopts. This fits with Smith's statement that, while nature has made mankind the immediate judge of human behaviour, conscience is a court of appeal against the actual opinions of mankind; we can take this to mean that the agent's knowledge of his own actions and his accumulated knowledge about the usual reactions of spectators enable him to present arguments to justify his behaviour which not only satisfy himself but also permit him to make some headway in convincing partial and ill-informed spectators of the rightness of his conduct.

Smith presents us with an analogy which may help us to see why it is that the impartial viewpoint gives most chance of reaching agreement, and is therefore the point towards which moral argument tends. The analogy is between the moral judgment and visual judgments in so far as these take account of perspective:

'As to the eye of the body, objects appear great or small, not so much according to their real dimensions, as according to the nearness or distance of their situation; so do they likewise to what may be called the natural eye of the mind: and we remedy the defects of both these organs pretty much in the same manner.'[1]

He indicates that we naturally build up in our mind an image of the

---

[1] T.M.S., III.3 (I.331f.).

world which abstracts from the fact that we, as individuals, are located in any one place, and in this way we judge of the size of objects relative to each other, and ignore the effect which the fact of nearness or distance to our particular position has on our perception of their size. In this way men come to agree on a picture or map of the world and so reach agreement on its dimensions. They do so by ignoring the perceptual effects of their own particular position at a particular time. Smith then applies this analogy to moral judgment and indicates that conscience enables us to make a similar abstraction from our individual viewpoint and see ourselves and the things near to us 'in proportion' which means looking on ourselves as but one of a multitude and no more significant than any other. The suggestion is that such a picture of the world, which corresponds to no actual person's vision, is nevertheless the only one which can make for agreement amongst men.

Similarly, the moral point of view, which discounts the individual's own self-regarding desires according to which the most trifling discomfort of our own appears of more significance than the death of thousands of persons whom we do not know, is to be identified with that view of human conduct which emphasizes the respect in which the world of conduct and character seems the same to us as to everyone else.[1] Thus, although individual spectators, as well as individual agents, may be partial, their partial views do not coincide with the partial views of others; but, if all imagine the situation in the absence of those factors which relate particularly to themselves, then they reach an image of the situation which coincides with that of everyone else. The impartial spectator thus represents what is common to the reaction of actual spectators rather than that which divides them. It will therefore not be identical with their average reaction, since some will be partial and others will be ill-informed, but these factors will tend to produce disagreement and will therefore cancel each other out.

In so far as men wish to obtain the agreement and so the approval of their fellows they will tend towards an impartial and well-informed viewpoint which will be productive of such agreement. It is not a viewpoint which will correspond to the actual outlook of a spectator who is particularly partial or ignorant, but it will represent what is *common* to most actual spectators and it can therefore serve as a basis of agreement between them. It does not, however, represent an ideal viewpoint in the sense of one to which no one can readily

---

[1] Cf. T.M.S., II.ii.2 (I.206): 'Though every man may, according to the proverb, be the whole world to himself, to the rest of mankind he is a most insignificant part of it.'

attain. There may be situations in which all the spectators are partial and ill-informed,[1] but in normal instances most spectators participate, to some extent, in the impartial and informed attitude. Men are least inclined to adopt the impartial standpoint when they are judging the conduct of their own family, friends or country, since, in these cases, all those whose agreement one seeks are as partial as oneself towards one's own country; the absence of real impartial spectators leads us to approve of conduct, on the part of our country to other countries, which we would never approve in the conduct of one individual in our society to another.[2] This is presumably because Smith believes that, *within* a society, in any particular case which is up for moral assessment, the majority of persons are in a relatively impartial position, in that they have no reason to prefer the interests of one involved person to those of another.

While this is to move some way in the direction of granting that Smith's impartial spectator is an 'ideal' being with no real existence, it is a long way yet from attributing to the spectator attributes of omniscience, omnipercipience and emotional indifference. If the function of the ideal spectator is to facilitate agreement about standards of behaviour, then the characteristics he possesses cannot exceed the sum of those which the real agents and spectators can bring into the process. 'Well-informed' means possessing such knowledge as agent and spectator together can contribute; percipience is limited to the degree of imaginative insight to which the average person can be led by his more sensitive fellows, which is strictly limited by the laws of sympathy; finally 'emotional indifference' means no more than the absence of those particular emotions which affect the immediate participants in any situation.

Smith's discussion of conscience shows that he was far from underestimating the fact that one important function of moral standards is to guide the choices of the person whose standards they are. Despite his concentration on the spectator standpoint, it is in many ways the agent's situation and the agent's moral decisions which are at the centre of his theory. After all, the spectator, in making his judgments, imagines himself as being in the place of an agent, and when the agent adopts the spectator standpoint it is in order to reflect on his own conduct *as an agent*. The importance of the spectator lies in the fact that he is the person whom the agent is trying to please. In the first instance this spectator is the man without, the multitude of third persons in whose presence men's everyday activities are performed, but, in time, the agent is able to

[1] Cf. L.J., p. 94. Smith suggests that this is the position with domestic servants.
[2] T.M.S., VI.ii (II.96ff.).

substitute his own reflective approval for the approval of other persons.

Far from minimizing this aspect of conscience, Smith lays great stress upon it. He certainly did not feel that to emphasize the relative independence of the mature conscience contradicted his theory of its social origin. The final answer to those who, like Scheler, argue that on Smith's view 'a man unjustly condemned and universally considered to be guilty should also acknowledge his guilt himself'[1] must be to say that this ignores the genetic nature of Smith's theory: his view that, from the judgments of the 'man without', the 'man within' can build up his own picture of virtue and vice which comes to have its own authority. The possibility of this happening should not be so difficult to accept in post-Freudian times. As far as Smith is concerned, the evidence for such a theory consists of pointing to the effect which the opinions of a man's peers have on his own attitudes, and showing that the actual content of the moral rules which are dictated to a man by his conscience can be shown to exemplify either the 'natural', that is the normal attitudes of the non-involved spectators of his conduct, or the attitudes of especially careful and sensitive observers of human behaviour. This takes us on to consider Smith's answer to his 'first' question in moral philosophy: 'wherein does virtue consist?'.[2]

[1] M. Scheler, *The Nature of Sympathy*, p. 6.
[2] T.M.S., VII.i (II.196).

CHAPTER 8

VIRTUES AND VICES

While the main interest of Smith's moral theory lies in his attempt to erect a causal theory of moral approbation and disapprobation around the concept of 'the impartial and well-informed spectator',[1] he himself regarded this as constituting only one part of moral philosophy, the other part being to answer the question: 'wherein does virtue consist?'[2] His own reply to this question is clear enough: virtue is that which is approved of by the self-same spectator. And the attempt to show that this is compatible with the content of moral judgments is one of the main tests of his theory. For if, by systematic deduction from the behavioural laws which are embodied in the concept of the impartial spectator, he is able to determine, and in principle to predict, the nature and content of the moral principles which exist in different types of society, then this is the firmest possible confirmation of his theory.

Unfortunately there are so many variables involved in his theory, and some of its laws are so open-ended, that any decisive test of his principles is exceptionally difficult, if not impossible to conduct. However, it remains true that the persuasiveness of his theory must depend to a large extent on how far he can explain the manner and content of actual systems of morality by means of the empirical model of an impartial spectator. He must be able to provide a convincing relationship between his answer to the question 'wherein does virtue consist?' and his answer to the question 'by what power or faculty in the mind is it, that this character, whatever it be, is recommended to us?'[3]

I. ORDINARY AND EXCEPTIONAL VIRTUE

In accordance with the idea that morality is a social phenomenon, originating in and being sustained by social interaction, Smith defines virtue and vice by reference to the reactions of persons other

---

[1] T.M.S., VII.ii.1 (II.266).   [2] T.M.S., VII.i (II.196).
[3] T.M.S., VII.i (II.197).

than the agent, or, in other words, of the impartial spectator. Virtue is what the spectator loves and rewards, vice that which he finds odious and feels impelled to punish:

'Virtue is not said to be amiable, or to be meritorious, because it is the object of its own love, or of its own gratitude; but because it excites those sentiments in other men'.[1]

There are two basic types of variable which Smith explores in his considerations of virtue and vice: the first is the precise type and intensity of attitude felt by the spectator, what may be called the quality and degree of the moral judgment, and the second relates to the sort of behaviour which is the object of this attitude: the content of the moral judgment. The latter is his main concern, but he does go into some detail concerning the former; moral approval may amount to no more than the absence of disapproval, it may be a mild 'pro' attitude, or it can be strong enough to express itself in praise and, in cases where merit is involved, in reward; similarly with disapproval, there are variations in the degree of disapproval from the simple absence of approval to strong antipathy, the latter being associated with the desire to blame and, in cases of demerit, to punish.[2] These differences are explained by saying that they follow from the extent to which the agent's motives do or do not coincide with the spectator's sympathetic feelings, the intensity of these feelings, and whether or not they are pleasant or painful. In addition there is a considerable difference between sharing retributive emotions and sharing non-retributive emotions.

These basic determinants of the quality and intensity of the spectator's attitudes have already been discussed and are largely unproblematical. But Smith introduces another factor into his analysis of moral judgment by saying that some virtuous conduct obtains admiration which goes beyond mere approval. In fact he uses the contrast between approval and admiration in order to distinguish two different moral standards. He argues that:

'Virtue is excellence, something uncommonly great and beautiful, which rises far above what is vulgar and ordinary,'

and concludes:

'There is, in this respect, a considerable difference between virtue and mere propriety; between those qualities and actions which deserve to be admired and celebrated, and those which simply deserve to be approved of.'[3]

[1] T.M.S., III.1 (I.283).   [2] Cf. p. 108.   [3] T.M.S., I.i.5 (I.48f.).

167

This difference is not between the moral rules of society and the higher tribunal of the individual conscience, but between two socially acknowledged standards of virtue, that which is normally expected and that which is unusually virtuous.[1] Approved conduct which is normally expected is that which is easy to perform; that which is particularly difficult, and consequently rare, gains admiration as well as approval.

In his general discussion of virtue and vice Smith is mainly concerned with the ordinary standards of propriety, but with respect to the virtues of sensibility and self-command[2] he indicates that it is only when these qualities are manifested in an extreme degree that they are called virtues at all; in particular, the virtue of self-command 'astonishes by its amazing superiority over the most ungovernable passions of human nature'.[3] Smith's appreciation of the Stoics shows itself in the attention which he devotes to the virtue of self-command; its importance lies in enabling men to act in accordance with other moral standards;[4] it is therefore closely allied to the sense of duty.[5] He gives many examples of men's admiration for self-command, either over transient passions such as fear and anger (the virtue of fortitude) or over less fierce but more persistent emotions such as the love of pleasure (the virtue of temperance). These virtues come into play only when there is some form of temptation, and Smith goes so far as to say that:

'To act according to the dictates of prudence, of justice, and of proper beneficence, seems to have no great merit where there is no temptation to do otherwise.'[6]

Because self-command is the virtue which enables men to achieve the other standards of virtue it is almost denominated *the* virtue, since 'from it all the other virtues seem to derive their principal lustre'.[7] Yet, for all this, there is a sense in which self-command is not a moral virtue at all, since men may exercise it in the pursuit of evil ends.[7] Admiration for self-command is more a species of wonder than of moral approbation; it is of a kind with man's awe of unusual physical phenomena which, Smith argues, is a stimulus to scientific endeavour[8]; it is also akin to admiration of the intellectual virtues:

'The man who directs and conducts our own sentiments, the extent and superior justness of whose talents astonish us with wonder and

---

1 Cf. T.M.S., VII.iii (II.146). 2 Cf. pp. 124.
3 T.M.S., I.i.5 (I.48f.). 4 T.M.S., VI.iii (II.120).
5 T.M.S., VI.Conclusion (II.189). 6 T.M.S., VI.iii (II.129).
7 T.M.S., VI.iii (II.130). 8 Cf. p. 32f.

surprise, who excites our admiration, and seems to deserve our applause.'[1]

Another similar non-moral attitude is admiration of the ostentatious ways adopted by men of wealth and rank.[2] Self-command is not therefore a uniquely moral virtue, but it is closely connected with moral virtues since, without it, men would not be able to conform to the standards of propriety.

Smith relates the 'virtue' of self-command to his general outline of virtues and vices by saying that the degree of self-command which is necessary to gain the admiration of the spectator varies according to the effort which is required to bring down the different types of passion to the proper level. This proper level is that which, irrespective of the agent's efforts to attain it, gains the approval rather than the admiration of the spectator. He believed that the point of propriety which 'is different in different passions'[3] could be precisely determined by the sympathetic emotions of the spectator; this is the main contention which Smith wishes to prove concerning the content of moral standards.

On the whole it is the ordinary standard of virtue rather than the exceptional one which Smith uses to test his theory; he believed that the content of the ordinary moral rules in each society is the outcome of the interplay of the laws of sympathy, on the one hand, and, on the other hand, the patterns of behaviour which would be normal for men if sympathy were not a factor in the situation; the judgments of the spectator reflect his knowledge of the normal behaviour of the average person in his society modified by the effects of the law of sympathy. To predict the content of moral judgments it is necessary to know, therefore, not only the laws of sympathy, but also the behaviour which would normally occur in abstraction from the operations of sympathy. Unfortunately it is very hard to discover what this 'normal' behaviour is, since, in all actual societies, behaviour is modified by the moral standards which result from the interaction of sympathetic and real sentiments. To test Smith's theories properly it would be necessary to know what *would* be usual behaviour in the absence of sympathetic emotions, to combine this with generalizations about the variability of sympathy with the different passions, and so to deduce the content of moral standards in actual societies. This almost puts Smith's theory in the category of untestable hypotheses, but a clue to 'normal' behaviour can probably be found in observing what men *wish* to do but feel they ought not to do: the impulses which they continually modify in the light of the reactions

[1] T.M.S., I.i.4 (I.34).   [2] Cf. p. 173.
[3] T.M.S., I.ii.Intro. (I.54); cf. T.M.S., VI.iii (II.134).

of the impartial spectator and which are never entirely eradicated by the socialization and internalization processes. Whatever difficulties there are in determining what 'normal' behaviour would be, the fact that this features as an element within the general theory from which Smith attempts to deduce particular moral judgments means that he is, in principle, able to account for variations between the moral standards of different societies, since what is 'normal' will vary according to the circumstances of the group or nation in question:

'The different situations of different ages and countries are apt . . . to give different characters to the generality of those who live in them, and their sentiments concerning the particular degree of each quality, that is either blamable or praise-worthy, vary, according to that degree which is usual in their own country and in their own times.'[1]

In practice it is very difficult to complete detailed explanations of such variations and Smith is rarely able to do more than indicate ways in which the different circumstances of each society can affect the way in which men's spontaneous impulses work themselves out. Moreover, we have already referred to the oblique way in which Smith has to approach the phenomena from which he builds up his laws of sympathy.[2] This is necessary because most actual cases of sympathetic emotions are affected by prior moral standards, which means that it is difficult to assess the empirical justification of these laws. The combination of these drawbacks, together with the grand scale on which Smith operates, makes it difficult to relate, with precision, his general moral theory to the assertions he makes concerning the content of moral standards. It is, therefore, unlikely that we can share Smith's certainty that his theory is a great advance on those of his contemporaries because of its greater precision:

'None of those systems either give, or even pretend to give, any precise or distinct measure by which this fitness or propriety of affection can be ascertained or judged of. That precise and distinct measure can be found nowhere but in the sympathetic feelings of the impartial and well-informed spectator'.[3]

Yet it is important to note that it is Smith's intention to achieve this precision. It is, of course, an intention which arose out of his admiration for the scientific ideal of providing detailed explanations for a variety of apparently unconnected phenomena by reference to a few

[1] T.M.S., V.2 (II.30).   [2] Cf. p. 120.
[3] T.M.S., VII.ii.1 (II.266).

familiar principles. If he fails in his aim it is largely because the principles he propounds are too vague and open-ended. But even the effort to achieve precision is interesting, and many of Smith's hypotheses prove suggestive even if they can rarely be tested with sufficient rigour.

II. RESPECT FOR WEALTH AND GREATNESS

Before going on to consider some examples of the manner in which he accounts for the content of moral judgments, it will be useful to prepare the way by considering some of the other phenomena which Smith explains by way of the laws of sympathy. This will help us to see the *width* of his explanatory endeavours and so illustrate another aspect of his desire to conform to the Newtonian ideal. It is also a necessary preliminary if we are to understand how he develops his theory of class morality. The particular law of sympathy in question, law three, states that 'it is easy to sympathize with pleasant emotions, difficult to sympathize with unpleasant ones',[1] and the specific pleasant and unpleasant emotions concerned are those connected with the situation of the rich and powerful in contrast to that of the poor and the weak. Smith writes that:

'When we consider the condition of the great, in those delusive colours in which the imagination is apt to paint it, it seems to be almost the abstract idea of a perfect and happy state.'[2]

He does not believe that the great are in fact happier than the lowly, but it is enough that men consider them to be so for law three to apply and for Smith to be able to use it to explain the tendency to sympathize eagerly with all the passions of those who enjoy wealth and power.

On the basis of these generalizations about men's sympathy with the supposed happiness of the wealthy and great, and the consequent pleasure of mutual sympathy enjoyed by them in their role as agents, Smith proceeds to explain three distinct but related social phenomena. The first is the nature of the ambition which leads men to strive to improve their material situation:

'. . . it is chiefly from this regard to the sentiments of mankind, that we pursue riches and avoid poverty. For to what purpose is all the toil and bustle of this world? What is the end of avarice and ambition, of the pursuit of wealth, of power, and pre-eminence? . . . To be observed, to be attended to, to be taken notice of with sympathy,

---

[1] Cf. p. 100.   [2] T.M.S., I.iii.2 (I.125).

complacency, and approbation, are all the advantages which we can propose to derive from it. It is the vanity, not the ease, or the pleasure, which interests us.'[1]

To back up this hypothesis Smith provides many vivid illustrations of the way in which men focus their attention on every detail in the lives of rich and powerful men, share their supposed enjoyments, and grieve with them when their fortunes decline. For instance, he notes how it appears to the ordinary person that 'To disturb, or to put an end to such perfect enjoyment, seems to be the most atrocious of all injuries'.[2] Although those excluded from the pleasures of wealth and power may be mistaken about the enjoyments of these advantages, the very attention they pay to these 'fortunate' persons constitutes the real enjoyment which they bring to their possessors. Riches and power together with 'rank, distinction, pre-eminence' are all valued by men because they enable them to 'stand in that situation which sets them most in the view of general sympathy and attention', and this 'is the end of half the labours of human life'.[3] It is this theory of human ambition and avarice which lies behind Smith's belief that each man constantly strives to improve his own material circumstances and underpins the entire doctrine of the *Wealth of Nations*.[4] To realize this is to see how mistaken it is to identify sympathy with benevolence and oppose it to self-interest,[5] for in this explanation of worldly ambition it is made clear that sympathy can give rise to selfish as well as unselfish forms of behaviour.

The second social phenomenon which Smith explains by means of the same set of observations is the obedience and deference shown by the lower ranks of society to those above them. It has often been pointed out that Smith frequently assumes the essential equality of man. In the *Wealth of Nations*, for instance, everyone is considered to have an equal right to participate in economic life and a certain measure of equality in the distribution of wealth is regarded as just and desirable;[6] this seems to stem from Smith's belief that all men have roughly the same potential; a belief which is manifested in his well-known remark that it is only because of the difference between their occupations that a philosopher comes to possess more abilities than a porter.[7] And in the *Moral Sentiments* Smith expounds on the nature of sympathy as something which operates between all men; it will be remembered that in accounting for the divided sympathy which men feel with unsocial passions he argued that '*As they are*

---

[1] T.M.S., I.iii.2 (I.120 and 122).   [2] T.M.S., I.iii.2 (I.126).
[3] T.M.S., I.iii.2 (I.140f.); and (I.122).
[4] Cf. W.N., I.x.1 (I.119) and I.xi.2 (I.192).   [5] Cf. p. 95f.
[6] Cf. W.N., IV.ix (II.183) and I.viii (I.88).   [7] W.N., I.ii (I.19).

both men, we are concerned for both'.[1] Yet, despite the fundamental equality implied in the idea of sympathy, it is the same sympathy which is the basis of the stability of unequal social divisions:

'Upon this disposition of mankind, to go along with all the passions of the rich and the powerful, is founded the distinction of ranks, and the order of society'.[2]

Although reasoning may lead us to the conclusion that kings are the servants of the people, the natural instincts associated with sympathy 'teach us to submit to them for their own sake, to tremble and bow down before their exalted station, to regard their smile as a reward sufficient to compensate any services, and to dread their displeasure, though no other evil were to follow from it, as the severest of all mortifications'.[3]

Smith, as we shall see, does not assume that this motive is always sufficient to ensure obedience to governmental authority, since he also recognizes that the envy and indignation felt by the poor against the rich may overcome men's deference; but the existence of inequalities of wealth is, in the *Moral Sentiments*, stressed as a cause of obedience and not of rebellion.[4]

The third social phenomenon Smith explains by means of men's sympathy with the great and the wealthy is that of fashion. Of such men he writes:

'Their dress is the fashionable dress; the language of their conversation, the fashionable style; their air and deportment, the fashionable behaviour. Even their vices and follies are fashionable; and the greater part of men are proud to imitate and resemble them in the very qualities which dishonour and degrade them'.[5]

This is hardly a complete explanation of fashion, but it does contribute an interesting hypothesis concerning the causes which make a particular social group the leaders of fashion, and it should be seen alongside the explanations Smith gives concerning the reasons why the rich and the powerful adopt an ostentatious style of life.[6]

These examples indicate how Smith uses the laws of sympathy to account for some judgments of approval and disapproval which we might not consider to be moral ones. In the case of respect for the rich and the powerful he himself admits that we are not dealing with moral approbation but with something that is, in large measure, opposed to it. In the sixth edition of the *Moral Sentiments* a chapter

---

[1] T.M.S., I.ii.3 (I.74). My italics. Cf. p. 110.   [2] T.M.S., I.iii.2 (I.127).
[3] T.M.S., I.iii.2 (I.128).   [4] Cf. p. 208.
[5] T.M.S., I.iii.3 (I.153).   [6] Cf. p. 175.

is devoted to 'the corruption of our moral sentiments, which is occasioned by this disposition to admire the rich and the great, and to despise or neglect persons of poor and mean condition'.[1] In it he displays an interesting uncertainty about whether or not to regard respect for the rich as in some way 'natural' and therefore proper. Approval of wealth and approval of virtue are both based on the comparisons of real and sympathetic emotions; the distinction between them seems to depend only on the fact that the pleasure to be found in sympathizing with the rich and the powerful is due, in large measure, to an erroneous assessment of their happiness. Trying to have it both ways he writes that:

'It is scarce agreeable to good morals, or even to good language, perhaps, to say, that mere wealth and greatness, abstracted from merit and virtue, deserve our respect. We must acknowledge, however, that they almost constantly obtain it; and that they may, therefore, be considered as, in some respects, the natural objects of it.'[2]

Whether, on his principles, he is able to draw this distinction between respect for virtue and respect for wealth, and so between the proper and the corrupt form of our moral sentiments, we shall discuss later. Here we should simply note his remark that:

'The respect which we feel for wisdom and virtue is, no doubt, different from that which we conceive for wealth and greatness; and it requires no very nice discernment to distinguish the difference.'[3]

This indicates that we must look for some phenomenological difference between moral and non-moral approbation. It is not clear how he can account for this, especially as he complicates the matter by linking respect for wisdom with respect for virtue.

III. MORALITY AND SOCIAL CLASS

Of great interest, from the sociological point of view, is the way in which he uses the distinction between the two types of respect to build up a picture of two different sets of 'virtues' or moralities, the first of which is connected with men's admiration for the rich and the powerful, and the second with the ordinary man's admiration for outstanding men of his own rank. What emerges is a theory of class morality in which he contrasts the moral qualities associated with

[1] T.M.S., I.iii.3 (I.146).   [2] T.M.S., I.iii.3 (I.149).
[3] T.M.S., I.iii.3 (I.148f.).

persons of 'middling and inferior stations of life'[1] on the one hand, with those associated with men of rank and fashion on the other. Since the latter have an 'easy empire over the affections of mankind'[2] they cultivate 'proud ambition and ostentatious avidity'.[3] Because they have everybody's attention their behaviour is 'gaudy and glittering in its colouring', marked by meticulous attention to small proprieties; describing a young nobleman, Smith writes:

'As he is conscious how much he is observed, and how much mankind are disposed to favour all his inclinations, he acts, upon the most indifferent occasions, with that freedom and elevation which the thought of this naturally inspires. His air, his manner, his deportment, all mark that elegant and graceful sense of his own superiority, which those who are born to inferior stations can hardly ever arrive at. These are the arts by which he proposes to make mankind more easily submit to his authority, and to govern their inclinations according to his own pleasure: and in this he is seldom disappointed.'[4]

In order to obtain the approval and respect of the lower strata of society the man of rank develops such behaviour as his way 'to deserve, to acquire, and to enjoy the respect and admiration of mankind'.[5] Nor is this simply a matter of obtaining the approval of those beneath him, for even his equals are prepared to tolerate and even admire behaviour which, in the common people, would be considered immoral:

'In every civilized society, in every society where the distinction of ranks has once been completely established, there have been always two different schemes or systems of morality current at the same time; of which the one may be called the strict or austere; the other the liberal, or, if you will, the loose system. The former is generally admired and revered by the common people: the latter is commonly more esteemed and adopted by what are called people of fashion. The degree of disapprobation with which we ought to mark the vices of levity, the vices which are apt to arise from great prosperity, and from the excess of gaiety and good humour, seems to constitute the principal distinction between those two opposite schemes or systems'.[6]

This tendency for persons of the same class to develop their own standards of behaviour follows, in part, from the different ways

[1] T.M.S., I.iii.3 (I.150). [2] T.M.S., I.iii.2 (I.137).
[3] T.M.S., I.iii.3 (I.148). [4] T.M.S., I.iii.2 (I.130).
[5] T.M.S., I.iii.3 (I.147). [6] W.N., V.i.3.art.3 (II.315).

which are open to them for obtaining the respect of mankind, but also, presumably, because of the fact that they will judge their fellows, whom they resemble in situation and character, by imagining their own behaviour in similar circumstances.

A man in the lower ranks of society, who does not so easily obtain the attention of other men, and who would be ruined by behaviour common to those in the higher ranks of society, has to pursue a different route to such respect and fortune as he can hope to obtain; he must tread the path of 'humble modesty and equitable justice'[1] and obtain the approbation of mankind 'by industry, by patience, by self-denial'.[2] If he ever hopes to distinguish himself, 'he must acquire superior knowledge in his profession, and superior industry in the exercise of it. He must be patient in labour, resolute in danger, and firm in distress . . . probity and prudence, generosity and frankness, must characterize his behaviour'.[3] Mere propriety is not sufficient to obtain the attention of other men; this he can achieve only by extraordinary virtue and wisdom. And so he adheres to the 'austere' morality, as it is called in the *Wealth of Nations*; this is the same as the 'uncorrupted' morality which is Smith's main subject in the *Moral Sentiments*. It is the morality of those whose dominant motive is the desire for wealth and the status which it brings; rich men are able to give way to the love of ease and develop a different style of life and different social norms:

'A man of large revenue, whatever may be his profession, thinks he ought to live like other men of large revenues; and to spend a great part of his time in festivity, in vanity, and in dissipation.'[4]

This way of attracting the attention of their fellows is not open to the average person.

The existence of these two moralities raises the question: which did Smith consider to be the correct or truly moral one? On the surface the answer is clear: by saying that austere morality is concerned with virtue and wisdom while the liberal morality takes an easy view of vice, and by calling men's disposition to respect the great a 'corruption' of their moral sentiments, he seems to be favouring the former against the latter, This has led to many accusations that he cannot make such a distinction without going beyond the bounds of his own moral theory, for he must be assuming some standard, not based on sympathy, to choose between the two moralities. This need not, however, be admitted; at least, not yet. Smith defends his designation of austere morality as *the* morality, primarily on linguistic grounds:

[1] T.M.S., I.iii.3 (I.148).　　[2] T.M.S., I.iii.2 (I.130f.).
[3] T.M.S., I.iii.2 (I.134).　　[4] W.N., V.i.3.art.3 (II.338).

this is what is usually talked of in 'moral' terms, that is using the terminology of virtue and vice, good and evil, right and wrong. Moreover the two 'moralities' can be distinguished in other ways; we have seen that he believes them to be phenomenologically different although he does not go into an analysis of this difference between admiration for virtue and admiration for wealth. A hint of how this could be developed occurs in his discussion of the shame and remorse sometimes felt by a powerful man who fails to gain the respect and esteem of his equals,[1] which indicates that we should look for an analysis of the difference between moral and non-moral approbation in his discussion of conscience and guilt. Smith does not, however, follow this up, although it is worth noting that he associates the emotions of shame and remorse with the respect and esteem, or lack of it, of one's equals; it would appear that there is an important empirical difference between the factors which determine attitudes of approval and disapproval between equals and those which operate between different social ranks or classes.[2]

Smith also comments on variations in the moral standards of different groups which are not connected with their relative social status. These result from the fact that 'normal' behaviour varies with the type of environmental opportunities which are available to different groups of people. Different economic circumstances produce different patterns of behaviour, and hence different ideas about what constitutes normal or expected conduct. For instance the austere morality reflects the fact that hard work is the only means for attaining security for those in the 'middling and inferior stations of life':

'The success of such people, too, almost always depends upon the favour and good opinion of their neighbours and equals; and without a tolerably regular conduct these can very seldom be obtained. The good old proverb, therefore, That honesty is the best policy, holds, in such situations, almost always perfectly true. In such situations, therefore, we may generally expect a considerable degree of virtue; and, fortunately for the good morals of society, these are the situations of by far the greater part of mankind.'[3]

This passage suggests the idea that austere morality obtains the approval of one's equals in a situation where this approval is necessary both to obtain any sympathy whatever, and to make a living. Together these needs for mutual sympathy and material welfare help to explain why the standards of austere morality evolve and why they are adhered to. It also suggests an important line of thought

[1] T.M.S., I.iii.3 (I.158).   [2] T.M.S., I.iii.3 (I.151).
[3] T.M.S., I.iii.3 (I.151).

about the relationship between moral and economic behaviour which has caused so much controversy amongst interpreters of Smith. In this chapter Smith declares that it is only 'a small party, who are the real steady admirers of human wisdom and virtue' and that 'The great mob of mankind are the admirers and worshippers, and, what may seem more extraordinary, most frequently the disinterested admirers and worshippers, of wealth and greatness.'[1] That is to say, virtue gains but little attention and, in itself, would have little effect on behaviour if it did not happen to coincide with the means by which most of mankind are best able to reach comparative wealth and reputation. This in itself is enough to show that Smith does not say, in the *Moral Sentiments*, either that sympathy leads exclusively to unselfish conduct, or that self-interest is not the ruling passion in human behaviour.

IV. PRUDENCE

While taking more than a passing interest in the existence of a distinct morality typical of the wealthy and powerful class in any society, Smith concentrates most of his attention on the austere morality of the ordinary citizen; the man who has to work hard for the approval of his equals. Apart from the virtue of self-control, the main types of virtue and vice in this morality are divided into those concerning prudence, benevolence and justice.[2] We shall deal with the first two of these in the remainder of this chapter and leave the more complex virtue of justice until the next chapter. This will provide us with sufficient examples of how Smith shows moral rules to be the outcome of the interaction of 'normal', instinctive behaviour and the laws of sympathy.

The virtue of prudence derives, in the first place, from the fact that 'The preservation and healthful state of the body seem to be the objects which Nature first recommends to the care of every individual'.[3] He justifies this statement by pointing to the appetites of hunger and thirst, bodily pleasure and pain, heat and cold; they are all 'lessons delivered by the voice of Nature herself, directing him [man] what he ought to chuse and what he ought to avoid'.[3] Nature's lessons are repeated by early training during which children are urged to take care of themselves; this is something they also learn to do as a consequence of their own experience that some things are pleasant and others painful. As a result, the normal person comes to pay great attention to 'what is called his external fortune'.[4]

[1] T.M.S., I.iii.3 (I.148). [2] T.M.S., VI.Conclusion (II.188).
[3] T.M.S., VI.i. (II.50). [4] T.M.S., VI.i (II.51).

One of these early lessons teaches men that the advantages of external fortune not only satisfy their bodily wants but also receive the respect and admiration of other men, consequently,

'The desire of becoming the proper objects of this respect, of deserving and obtaining this credit and rank among our equals, is, perhaps, the strongest of all our desires.'[1]

The attitude of the spectator thus reinforces man's natural desire to improve his own material condition, and, especially in commercial society, this results in the fact, that:

'The care of the health, of the fortune, of the rank and reputation of the individual, the objects upon which his comfort and happiness in this life are supposed principally to depend, is considered as the proper business of that virtue which is commonly called Prudence.'[2]

Moreover, because greater suffering is caused by a fall from fortune than simply its absence, men fear for the future, and are constantly searching for security. Smith outlines the qualities of person required to obtain this security in his own type of society: competence, hard work, sincerity, reserve, caution and common sense.[3] These are all qualities which call for a certain amount of foresight, but this is an ability that does not come naturally to men, who all tend to be under the sway of immediate impulses. However, the spectator, being free from these impulses, feels as much concern for the future as for the present condition of the agent. In order to obtain the spectator's approval, the agent attempts to control his natural impulse for immediate gratification and tries instead to act in his own long-term interests. The virtue of prudence, therefore, requires the discipline of spontaneous self-regarding impulses and the sacrifice of present to future self-interest.[4]

As regards the self-regarding passions in general, the laws of sympathy apply to them in the normal way, It is easier for the spectator to sympathize with an individual's joy at his own good fortune than with the sorrow caused by his ill-fortune; although the spectator, being human, may feel envious of extreme good fortune. On the other hand, great griefs stir the imagination more than small personal misfortunes which, to the spectator, usually appear tiresome.[5]

To make this convincing Smith would have to show more clearly

---

1 T.M.S., VI.i (II.51).   2 T.M.S., VI.i (II.52).
3 T.M.S., VI.i (II.53ff.); cf. VII.ii.3 (II.294): 'The habits of œconomy, industry, discretion, attention, and application of thought'.
4 T.M.S., VI.i (II.58).   5 T.M.S., I.ii.5 (I.93-101).

that differences in the internal and external environmental circumstances of individuals and groups affect their estimation of prudential conduct. Hints of this approach do appear when he asserts that in countries such as sixteenth-century Italy, where arrest for criminal offences is much less than certain, it is not considered imprudent to commit crime, and adds a note to the effect that, while injustice perpetrated by ordinary people may be considered imprudent it may not be so when done by wealthy and powerful men like Caesar Borgia who can escape the consequences of their acts.[1] These examples are scarcely sufficient to establish his theory, but they indicate the lines of empirical investigation which are relevant.

An important point for Smith's general moral theory emerges in his attempt to account for the fact that prudence, even when exhibited to the extreme degree which a wise and judicious man attains, 'is regarded as a most respectable, and even, in some degree, as an amiable and agreeable quality, yet it never is considered as one, either of the most endearing, or of the most ennobling of the virtues. It commands a certain cold esteem, but seems not entitled to any very ardent love or admiration.'[2] This can be explained, on Smith's theory, by the fact that, since prudential acts only affect the individual himself, they do not awake any response of gratitude in a third person, and there is, therefore, no sympathetic gratitude and no tendency to ascribe merit and reward to prudential behaviour. Similarly the lack of prudence excites no sympathetic resentment, and so 'Mere imprudence, or the mere want of the capacity to take care of one's-self, is, with the generous and humane, the object of compassion; with those of less delicate sentiments, of neglect, or, at worst, of contempt, but never of hatred or indignation.'[3] It is only when prudence is combined with other virtues, and the ability to calculate for one's own benefit is turned to the pursuit of the good of others, that it becomes fully admired, praised and rewarded. This is the reason why it is sometimes not regarded as a virtue at all.

V. BENEVOLENCE

By arguing that prudence normally obtains the cool approbation of the spectator Smith has also presented his main argument against the assertion that virtue consists solely of benevolence, a view he attributes to Hutcheson. Smith agrees with Hutcheson to the extent that he acknowledges benevolence to have a particularly important place amongst the virtues; it easily obtains not only approbation

---

[1] T.M.S., VI.i (II.63f.).   [2] T.M.S., VI.i (II.60f.); cf. III.6 (I.436).
[3] T.M.S., VI.i (II.62).

but warm praise and enthusiastic reward.[1] This, of course, he can explain by means of the double sympathy which it arouses, both by its own hedonic tone, for benevolence is always amiable and pleasant, and by the pleasure it affords to its recipients:

'Generosity, humanity, kindness, compassion, mutual friendship and esteem, all the social and benevolent affections, when expressed in the countenance or behaviour . . . please the indifferent spectator upon almost every occasion.'[2]

The spectator, therefore, reinforces men's natural benevolent impulses.[3] However, Smith argues that there can be excess of benevolence which the spectator, although he is indulgent towards such a rare phenomenon, cannot wholly go along with it.[4] Hutcheson is therefore accused of inadequate empirical observation, for although the view 'that virtue consists in benevolence is a notion supported by many appearances in human nature',[5] it is not consistent with the fact that men approve of prudence, or the fact that they consider that there can be an excess of benevolence as well as a deficiency; nor does it account for the fact that men approve of a greater degree of benevolence being shown towards those who stand in special relationship to the agent than to those who have no particular relationship to him. Smith explains Hutcheson's failure to observe these facts by saying that he has been misled by his erroneous deduction from the belief that the deity is motivated solely by benevolence to the conclusion that men ought, in imitation, to base their own actions entirely on this principle. He shows this to be unacceptable theological naturalism which ignores the difference in situation between a self-sufficient perfect being on the one hand and 'so imperfect a creature as man' on the other.[6] Observation shows that men must act on selfish motives for much of the time and Smith humanely concludes that:

'The condition of human nature were peculiarly hard, if those affections, which, by the very nature of our being, ought frequently to influence our conduct, could upon no occasion appear virtuous, or deserve esteem and commendation from any body.'[6]

Smith's positive analysis of what men believe to be the proper degree of benevolent action can be approached, as with prudence, by considering first what he considers are the natural and instinctive benevolent motives which guide normal behaviour, and, secondly,

[1] T.M.S., VII.ii.3 (II.287). [2] T.M.S., I.ii.4 (I.88).
[3] T.M.S., VI.iii.2 (II.134) and VI.Conclusion (II.187).
[4] T.M.S., VII.ii.3 (II.296) and I.ii.4 (I.91).
[5] T.M.S., VII.ii.3 (II.286). [6] T.M.S., VII.ii.3 (II.297).

how the impartial spectator views these motives after they have passed through his scrutiny. Of the latter we have already said enough. Benevolence is agreeable both to the agent and to those affected by his behaviour, and is therefore readily sympathized with and encouraged by the spectator;[1] there is thus little or no need for the agent to control his benevolent impulses and bring them into line with what the spectator can approve of, since this approval will be forthcoming for all the normal instinctive expressions of benevolence. The chief part of his analysis of benevolence therefore consists in a discussion of the order in which individuals and groups are 'recommended by Nature to our care and attention'[2] by the benevolent instincts, which exist independently of the approbation of the impartial spectator.

Smith notes that:

'After himself, the members of his own family, those who usually live in the same house with him, his parents, his children, his brothers and sisters, are naturally the objects of his warmest affection.'[2]

To explain this he introduces an important expansion of his laws about the operations of sympathy by saying that a man feels most benevolence towards members of his family because 'he is more habituated to sympathize with them'.[3] By this he means that frequent close contact with others increases a man's ability to imagine himself in their position, for 'He knows better how every thing is likely to affect them, and his sympathy with them is more precise and determinate, than it can be with the greater part of other people. It approaches nearer, in short, to what he feels for himself'.[3] This does not prove that a person will feel more benevolent towards those with whom he lives and works, since the increased ability to enter into their feelings may reveal more disagreement than agreement, and Smith shows that he is aware of the extreme discord that can exist amongst families.[4] Yet, although gaps are missing in the argument, we can rescue Smith to some extent by saying that intimate knowledge of another person may remove some barriers towards mutual sympathy and therefore it is likely to be the case that the agent in such a situation will not have to moderate his passions to the same degree as is necessary with strangers because the family spectator can take more account of how he feels as an individual with his own particular peculiarities of behaviour. Smith also argues that benevolence can arise out of sympathy, particularly in the case of

---

[1] T.M.S., I.ii.4 (I.90). [2] T.M.S., VI.ii.1 (II.69).
[3] T.M.S., VI.ii.1 (II.70). [4] T.M.S., II.ii.4 (I.91).

pity;[1] and this is in accordance with what he says about frequency of contact increasing benevolent affections. But it must be said that he seems to have overlooked the possibility that such intimate relations will produce more hatred than love.

Despite this, there is much to be said for his argument that the 'natural affection' of the family is based rather on prolonged close contact than upon any instinct that follows from common ancestry. He conceives 'natural affection as more the effect of the moral than the supposed physical connection between the parent and the child',[2] although, in this particular relationship, there is some ground for assuming a natural instinct to protect children. 'Habitual sympathy' also explains the fact that all groups of people who are exposed to any large degree of face-to-face contact develop an affection for each other:

'Colleagues in office, partners in trade, call one another brothers, and frequently feel towards one another as if they really were so.'[3]

This applies also to those who live in the same neighbourhood, since 'we respect the face of a man whom we see every day, provided he has never offended us'.[3] Other natural objects of our benevolent affections are those who have shown us kindness, those with whom we have a great deal in common and choose as our friends, and those whom we respect because of their greatness and power, or feel deep pity for on account of their unfortunate circumstances.[3] As well as these individual categories of men, Smith goes on to explain patriotism by means of the same principle: we love our own country more than others primarily because, after our family and friends, our countrymen are those for whom we have most habitual sympathy. Moreover, our own interests as well as though of our family and friends are bound up with the fate of our country, therefore prudence as well as benevolence prompts us to patriotism as well as to hatred of those neighbouring nations which threaten our own country.[4]

These examples indicate how Smith uses the fact that a particular type of behaviour is normal to explain why it is considered morally virtuous. Normal behaviour is what the impartial spectator expects; it is how he would behave himself, and unless some peculiarities of the working of sympathy affect his judgments (which they rarely do

[1] T.M.S., I.i.1 (I.4).
[2] T.M.S., VI.ii.1 (II.82); cf. (II.78); Smith uses this argument to observe that 'The education of boys at distant great schools, of young men at distant colleges, of young ladies in distant nunneries and boarding-schools, seems, in the higher ranks of life, to have hurt most essentially the domestic morals, and consequently the domestic happiness, both of France and England.'
[3] T.M.S., VI.ii.1 (II.83-92).   [4] T.M.S., VI.ii.2 (II.93-112).

in the case of benevolence) this is the behaviour with which he agrees and, therefore, of which he approves. Illustrating this by reference to family affection, Smith writes:

'Relations being usually placed in situations which naturally create this habitual sympathy, it is expected that a suitable degree of affection should take place among them. We generally find that it actually does take place; we therefore naturally expect that it should; and we are, upon that account, more shocked when, upon any occasion, we find that it does not. The general rule is established, that persons related to one another in a certain degree, ought always to be affected towards one another in a certain manner, and that there is always the highest impropriety, and sometimes even a sort of impiety, in their being affected in a different manner.'[1]

It is in the observation and reporting of these facts and the explanation of them in terms of habitual sympathy that Smith provides the answer to those who say that universal benevolence is an important motive in human affairs; although he agrees that 'we cannot form the idea of any innocent and sensible being, whose happiness we should not desire',[2] in practice, as he observes, we are affected by the immediate presence of family, friends, neighbours, fellow-workers and countrymen, and exhibit more benevolence towards them than towards men in general. Indeed, such universal benevolence is an extension of benevolence felt for particular persons and is not the motive from which we exercise our benevolent affections in particular cases.

Smith's analysis of benevolence, with his explanation of the content of the relevant moral rules, fits well with his general theory. It ties together many aspects of the theory in a consistent manner and accords with the observed facts to a tolerable degree. Of particular interest are the comments he makes concerning the variable content of these moral rules, especially the contrast between the morality of pastoral and commercial countries which foreshadow the later sociological contrast between community and association. In pastoral countries where security depends on the defence of local neighbourhoods, men 'have more intercourse with one another than with the members of any other tribe', and a strong affectional relationship between members of the extended family is developed, which often includes whole clans or tribes. He comments that:

'It is not many years ago that, in the Highlands of Scotland, the Chieftain used to consider the poorest man of his clan, as his cousin

---

[1] T.M.S., VI.ii.1 (II.73).   [2] T.M.S., VI.ii.3 (II.113).

and relation. The same extensive regard to kindred is said to take place among the Tartars, the Arabs, the Turkomans, and, I believe, among all other nations who are nearly in the same state of society in which the Scots Highlanders were about the beginning of the present century.'[1]

It is the need for mutual protection that keeps these extended families together, but in commercial societies this is no longer necessary, and 'They soon cease to be of importance to one another; and, in a few generations, not only lose all care about one another, but all remembrance of their common origin.'[2] This is a trend 'longer and more completely established in England than in Scotland'. Smith also argues that there is, on the whole, more benevolence in commercial societies than in primitive ones since, although benevolence is always highly esteemed, it is not the normal expected behaviour amongst those whose individual needs are not tolerably satisfied. These are interesting examples of the way in which he is able to show that the laws of sympathy lead to different types of normal expected behaviour and therefore to variations between moral standards in different types of society.

[1] T.M.S., VI.ii.1 (II.80f.).   [2] T.M.S., VI.ii.1 (II.81).

CHAPTER 9

JUSTICE

Justice is the main topic which provides a common factor for the *Moral Sentiments*, the *Lectures on Jurisprudence* and the *Wealth of Nations*. In this last book the aspect of justice which features most prominently is the form and expense of the administration of law; the *Lectures* contains a good deal of material on the history of the various functions of government, amongst which the maintenance of justice is the most fundamental, but, in itself, it contains no more than hints of Smith's theory of justice. It is only in the *Moral Sentiments* that any real attempt is made to provide a theory to explain the nature and content of the rules of justice. In some ways this represents the climax of the whole work. Smith thought that he had something new to say about the nature of justice. He also considered it to be the most important virtue and he continually emphasized both that a sound system of justice is necessary for the development of commercial society and that some degree of justice is essential for the very existence of any type of society:

'Society may subsist, though not in the most comfortable state, without beneficence; but the prevalence of injustice must utterly destroy it.[1]

But at the same time Smith rather sidesteps a full discussion of the topic by saying that it is to be the subject of another work: his projected study of law and government. The *Moral Sentiments* is intended only to lead up to his study of 'natural jurisprudence; concerning which it belongs not to our present subject to enter into any detail'.[2] This may account for the relatively large number of loose ends in his account of justice and help to explain the occasional failure to fit this virtue into his general theory which mark his writings in this field. Nevertheless the contents of the *Lectures on Jurisprudence* would suggest that Smith's projected work would have taken for granted that the *Moral Sentiments* had provided a sufficient analysis of the main facts about human nature and society

[1] T.M.S., II.ii.3 (I.215).   [2] T.M.S., VI.ii.Introd. (II.67).

which are necessary to explain the main features of justice, leaving him free to go on and show how these led both to basic similarities and to predictable variations in the systems of law which exist or have existed in different societies.[1] Read in the light of the *Moral Sentiments*, the *Lectures on Jurisprudence* give us some idea as to how he would have set about this task, and it is, therefore, possible to get some indication of the way in which Smith's theory of morality can be applied and tested in the sphere of justice as well as of morality in general.

I. THE LEGAL DEFINITION

From the standpoint of moral theory, the initial difficulty to be overcome, in order to appreciate Smith's theory of justice, is the fact that he takes it to be a purely legal concept; the rules of justice either are, or ought to be, laws. By this I do not mean that he excludes it from the sphere of morality—there is never any doubt that justice is a moral virtue—but that he does not consider its non-legal applications and restricts his consideration of justice to the moral content of the law. Smith realizes that this requires justification and, in fact, he takes more care over his definition of justice than over any other of his principal concepts. He distinguishes three meanings which he has come across in different languages and which he, therefore, considers must have some 'natural affinity'. The first meaning, which he equates, after Aristotle, with 'commutative justice', is the one he adopts:

'In one sense we are said to do justice to our neighbour when we abstain from doing him any positive harm, and do not directly hurt him, either in his person, or in his estate, or in his reputation.'[2]

He rejects, probably on the grounds that they are too broad and do not represent 'what is peculiarly called justice',[3] two other meanings:

'In another sense we are said not to do justice to our neighbour unless we conceive for him all that love, respect, and esteem, which his character, his situation, and his connexion with ourselves, render suitable and proper for us to feel, and unless we act accordingly.'[4]

This he calls distributive justice and argues that, since it amounts to

---

[1] Cf. L.J., p. 152 and p. 9.   [2] T.M.S., VII.ii.1 (II.207).
[3] T.M.S., II.ii.1 (I.203); cf. VII.ii.1 (II.209).   [4] T.M.S., VII.ii.1 (II.207f.).

giving praise, reward and assistance to every person to whom it is due, it encompasses all the social virtues, including benevolence; it can only, therefore, be a metaphorical use of the term. And, thirdly, he distinguishes and rejects another meaning of 'justice', attributed to Plato, in which it is equivalent to the sum of all virtues; in this sense justice is the same as his own concept of propriety and has to do with proper government of all the affections.[1] The definition he adopts is more specific and, as he says, essentially negative; the just act is the act which causes no injury to a person other than the agent and therefore, in contrast to benevolence, 'does no real positive good':

'Mere justice is, upon most occasions, but a negative virtue, and only hinders us from hurting our neighbour.'[2]

It is not so much that justice is a virtue, for justice, in itself, gains little approbation and inspires no reward,[3] as that injustice is a serious vice. The unjust act causes positive harm to definite individuals.[4] The rules of justice, therefore, consist mainly of a series of prohibitions, laying down the things a person may not do to others either in the pursuit of his own self-interest or in order to benefit a third party.[5]

Smith is right to try and restrict the term 'justice' to its distinctive meaning, so that to call an act just is to assess it in relation to one but not all moral standards. But, unfortunately, the meaning he adopts is out of line with the general consensus of present-day philosophy which regards justice as roughly synonymous with fairness, especially in relation to the distribution of those things which men wish either to avoid or to receive. On this view, justice gives rise to rights to receive certain things as well as rights not to be injured, and is not restricted to legal obligations. But Smith considered that the obligation to be fair in distributing benefits was nothing like so strict as the obligation to avoid injuring others, and it was because of this that he wished to mark off the latter from the former. That he then gave it the title of justice can be explained from his legal interests which led him to assume that justice 'proper' was a legal concept. Since he considered that 'the end of justice is to secure from injury'[6] and thus preserve the peace of society, his negative definition of justice suited him well. The tradition here is that of Grotius and Pufendorf, coming through Hutcheson: Smith is dealing with what they called 'perfect rights', which correspond to

---

[1] T.M.S., VII.ii.1 (II.207 and 209f.). [2] T.M.S., II.ii.1 (I.202f.).

[3] Cf. T.M.S., II.ii.1 (I.203). [4] Cf. T.M.S., II.ii.1 (I.196f.).

[5] Cf. T.M.S., II.ii.2 (I.207). [6] L.J., p. 5.

duties the performance of which may justifiably be compelled, as distinct from 'imperfect rights' which may not be compelled.[1] The former concern jurisprudence, for, as Smith says, 'Those who write upon the principles of jurisprudence, consider only what the person to whom the obligation is due, ought to think himself entitled to exact by force'.[2] These he considers to be rights in the true sense, whereas the latter belong only to morals and are rights in a metaphorical sense; they lack the stricter obligation which he credits Hume with having noticed attaches to legal rights, that is rights which *ought* to be, and, Smith assumes, for the most part are, safeguarded by law.[3] Distributive justice, which, for Smith, deals only with the allocation of benefits, lacks this strict obligation; it is a species of beneficence, and

'Beneficence is always free, it cannot be extorted by force, the mere want of it exposes to no punishment,'[4]

but,

'There is however another virtue, of which the observance is not left to the freedom of our own wills, which may be extorted by force, and of which the violation exposes to resentment, and consequently to punishment. This virtue is justice: the violation of justice is injury: it does real and positive hurt to some particular persons, from motives which are naturally disapproved of.'[5]

This constitutes Smith's first main contention regarding justice: it concerns those duties which may properly be exacted by force, and the violation of which may rightfully be punished; taken together with the assertion that all such duties are duties not to injure other people, this amounts to the bold generalization that all proper duties, embodied in the civil and criminal law, are duties to refrain from injuring others. This proposition is one which he sets out to prove, from the content of actual laws, in the *Lectures on Jurisprudence*.

Smith's legal preoccupations also help us to understand why he made his second important generalization about justice; he alleges that the laws of justice can be determined with complete precision.

---

[1] Cf. Hutcheson, *An Inquiry Concerning the Original of our Ideas of Virtue or Moral Good* (1725), in D, D. Raphael, *British Moralists*, §353.

[2] T.M.S., VII.iv (II.366).

[3] T.M.S., VII.iv (II.397): 'In no country do the decisions of positive law coincide *exactly*, in every case, with the rules which the natural sense of justice would dictate'. (My italics).

[4] T.M.S., II.ii.1 (I.194).   [5] T.M.S., II.ii.1 (I.196f.).

In general he believed that no precise moral rules could be laid down in advance, but:

> 'The rules of justice are accurate in the highest degree, and admit of no exceptions or modifications, but such as may be ascertained as accurately as the rules themselves.'[1]

In the case of other virtues the agent has to adapt moral rules to particular circumstances and exercise his own judgment as to the proper course of action. But the rules of justice can not only be stated with precision; it is actually wrong for a person to attempt to modify these rules in accordance with his estimation of each situation and so adapt them to the peculiar circumstances of each particular act: the laws of justice are not only exact, they 'admit of no exceptions'. Smith draws the analogy between the laws of justice and the rules of grammar: both can be stated precisely, and must be followed in detail in all cases, but, on the other hand, they represent only the essential preliminary requirements of good literature in the one case and proper conduct on the other.[2] The example he gives is that of a debt: its amount, and usually its duration, are precisely and rigidly determined.[3] Plausible as this particular example, and others relating to contracts, may be, Smith does not succeed in showing how it applies to all other laws, and it would be difficult to see how he could do so; in determining what is to count as an injury, for instance, it is hard indeed to know how to make a precise assessment of harm done to someone's reputation or the 'injury' involved in restricting his economic freedom. When considering the law in general, Smith's confidence that the precise content and application of the law can be determined with precision represents more a feature of an ideal legal system than a legal reality.

II. RESENTMENT

The explanation for these views, which Smith hoped that he would eventually be able to justify in full, takes us back to his doctrine of merit, and in particular to the view that demerit is judged by the spectator's indirect sympathy with the resentment of a person affected by the action of another.[4] Resentment is the key emotion in Smith's analysis of justice. It is the emotion felt by a person towards the object, usually another person, which causes him to suffer; it is an emotion which urges men to retaliate, to 'return evil for evil':

> 'It prompts us to beat off the mischief which is attempted to be done to us, and to retaliate that which is already done.'[5]

[1] T.M.S., III.6 (I.439). [2] T.M.S., VII.iv (II.359). [3] T.M.S., III.6 (I. 440).
[4] Cf. p. 112. [5] T.M.S., II.ii.1 (I.196).

The unifying theme in Smith's discussion of justice is the attempt to trace all laws back to the various causes of resentment in society and to explain these laws by reference to this resentment in the modified form in which it is felt by the impartial spectator.

Prior to all morality and law, men naturally resent certain things being done to them; the spectator sympathizes with this resentment if it is reduced to a level into which he can enter. This reduction is necessary because resentment is an unpleasant emotion and because the spectator fears for the safety of the person who is its object; moreover, the spectator does not sympathize unless he disapproves of the motive of the agent, and this disapproval is not forthcoming if the agent has been provoked by an injury which has been done to him for which he is making retaliation:

'Proper resentment for injustice attempted, or actually committed, is the only motive which, in the eyes of the impartial spectator, can justify our hurting or disturbing in any respect the happiness of our neighbour . . . The wisdom of every state or commonwealth endeavours, as well as it can, to employ the force of the society to restrain those who are subject to its authority, from hurting or disturbing the happiness of one another. The rules which it establishes for this purpose, constitute the civil or criminal law of each particular state or country. The principles upon which those rules either are, or ought to be founded, are the subject of a particular science, of all sciences by far the most important, but hitherto, perhaps, the least cultivated, that of natural jurisprudence.'[1]

Because resentment incites men to be the direct cause of harm to those who have injured others, it is the passion which prompts punishment. If the resentment is shared by the spectator then the punishment is justified.[2] The spectator approves of this immediately, without any calculation of its utility, merely by considering the injury which has been inflicted. Resentment is rarely aroused except by observing or imagining an actual injury, and this explains why the law forbids the infliction of injury but does not require positive acts which benefit others, for while failure to act may result in grievous harm it does not arouse the resentment which is forthcoming when the agent is seen to bring about that injury.

The difficulties which arise in connection with this theory of justice are similar to those we have already noted in assessing the

[1] T.M.S., VI.ii (II.66f.).
[2] L.J., p. 136. 'Injury naturally excites the resentment of the spectator, and the punishment of the offender is reasonable as far as the indifferent spectator can go along with it. This is the natural measure of punishment.'

empirical usefulness of the concept of the impartial spectator. How is it possible to discover what men 'naturally' resent since in all actual cases the resentment men feel is affected by their knowledge of their legal rights and duties? Swabey puts this objection in an extreme form by saying that 'Resentment . . . presupposes a notion of rights which have been violated'.[1] But while it is certainly true that men sometimes resent injuries purely because they infringe their acknowledged rights, it is surely wrong to say that they always resent injuries simply because they are violations of their rights; they also resent the injury itself. The idea of a right which has been broken is not part of the meaning of 'resentment', and, although the two ideas are closely related in practice, it is possible to conceive of resentment, although not of the justification of resentment, in the absence of any rights or duties. The real difficulty is to know what that resentment would be. Smith simply has to assume that immediate and strong reactions normally felt by most people when they are affected by the actions of others are a guide to 'natural', that is pre-moral and pre-legal, resentment. But the difficulties in tracing all laws back to this simple form of resentment might well have been one of the reasons why his jurisprudence never reached its completed state.

In the *Moral Sentiments* the example into which Smith goes at most length in order to demonstrate the connection between resentment and the law, concerns the 'Influence of Fortune upon the Sentiments of Mankind'.[2] He argues that, although most people, when considering the matter in the abstract, will agree that only the intended consequences of acts should be punished, nevertheless the law of negligence does take account of the actual consequences which normally result from the intention in question. For instance gross negligence, as 'if a person should throw a large stone over a wall into a public street' because it is the sort of action which could be expected to cause injury, is punished even if no injury results, but it is punished much more severely if someone is actually injured.[3] Similarly if, through an unlucky chance, an action which would normally be considered blameless, results in injury, then, although no punishment is exacted, compensation may be required.[4] He illustrates this with many examples drawn from classical history and the laws of different countries.

The explanation for the existence of these laws is an 'irregularity'

[1] W. C. Swabey, *Ethical Theory from Hobbes to Kant*, p. 185.

[2] T.M.S., II.iii (I.230ff.). This is also mentioned briefly in the L.J., p. 15; cf. p. 113.

[3] T.M.S., II.iii.2 (I.258ff.).   [4] T.M.S., II.iii.2 (I.260).

of sentiment which affects all judgments of merit and demerit, an irregularity which arises from the fact that gratitude and resentment are immediate reactions in those who receive, or observe someone receiving, benefits or injuries.[1] These feeling are aroused even when the cause of the benefits or injuries is inanimate, but they quickly diminish if it is seen that the cause was not a responsible agent who was aware of the consequences of his actions. Although gratitude and resentment are immediate responses they develop into complex feelings which include the desire that the cause of the benefit or injury should be capable of feeling the pleasure of reward and the pains of punishment and of knowing that he enjoys or suffers them upon account of his past conduct. While a person may, therefore, feel a 'shadow of resentment' towards a stone over which he has stumbled, experience leads him to know that there is little satisfaction to be found in expressing such resentment and, on reflection, the feeling fades away, although, owing to its initial strength, it never entirely loses its force.[2] The same is true, to a lesser extent, when the cause of the injury is another person's minor carelessness: resentment still occurs, even though it is modified on reflection, although no resentment would have been felt had no injury resulted from the act; in such cases some 'atonement' is felt to be necessary.

This is one example of the way Smith fulfils his object of explaining a certain feature of the law by showing that it follows from a fact about resentment. The 'irregularity' in question accounts for the pervasiveness of similar laws of negligence in different countries, and it can also explain certain variations between different types of society: for instance, it is in barbarous societies, where there is little opportunity for reflection, that spontaneous resentment is least checked and the laws of negligence are consequently severe with respect to unintended consequences.[3]

III. THE RIGHTS OF MAN

The *Lectures on Jurisprudence* set out to be more systematic in their treatment of justice, but they begin from the doctrine of the *Moral Sentiments* that the gravity of the crime depends on the extent of the resentment naturally felt by the person affected, modified by the various laws of sympathy as they apply to an observer. The various

[1] T.M.S., II.iii.Intro. (I.233).
[2] T.M.S., II.iii.1 (I.234ff.). Cf. L.J., p. 153, where he describes resentment as 'a very indiscriminating principle'.
[3] T.M.S., II.iii.2 (I.253).

types of perfect right correspond, therefore, to the ways in which one may injure another:

'As the greater and more irreparable the evil that is done, the resentment of the sufferer runs naturally the higher; so does likewise the sympathetic indignation of the spectator, as well as the sense of guilt in the agent.'[1]

Smith deals first with those rights which every person has simply 'as a man', which are subdivided according to whether the injuries are to (1) his body, (2) his reputation, or (3) his estate. A man may suffer injuries 'in his body by wounding, maiming, murdering, or by infringing his liberty'.[2] The degree of bodily injury determines the degree of the crime:

'Death is the greatest evil which one man can inflict upon another, and excites the highest degree of resentment in those who are immediately connected with the slain. Murder, therefore, is the most atrocious of all crimes which affect individuals only.'[1]

The sympathetic resentment here is, of course, with the imagined resentment of the slain;[3] in lesser injuries the resentment caused may be actually observed. Smith thinks that these rights are obviously based on resentment and require no lengthy explanation,[4] and certainly it is not difficult to draw up a list of bodily injuries in ascending order of gravity, but how is it possible to make precise comparisons between these injuries and, for instance, restrictions on liberty, especially when this is taken to include freedom to participate in economic activities without governmental restrictions?[5] This is the sort of difficulty with which Smith simply does not deal.

Secondly, a man may be injured 'in his reputation, either by falsely representing him as a proper object of resentment or punishment, as by calling him a thief or robber, or by depreciating his real worth and endeavouring to degrade him below the level of his profession'.[6] Smith explains this by bringing in the supposition, which is fundamental to his theory of sympathy, that an essential element in human happiness is the praise, attention and respect of one's fellow-men; an attack on a person's reputation endangers this respect and is, therefore, deeply resented. Moreover, it will be remembered that the spectator sympathizes more with imaginative than with bodily pains[7] and, since a person's reputation is closely

---

[1] T.M.S., II.ii.2 (I.208); cf. L.J., p. 137. [2] L.J., p. 5.
[3] T.M.S., II.i.2 (I.172). [4] L.J., p. 8.
[5] Cf. W.N., IV.ix (II.208). [6] L.J., p. 5.
[7] Cf. p. 98f.

bound up with what he imagines that other people think about him, the spectator's sympathetic resentment is, in this case, almost as high as the original feeling of the person who has been insulted. As a particular example of this Smith points out that, while lying is not a crime, the law protects the person who is falsely accused of lying. Men are naturally credulous and desire to be told the truth, and they resent it when they discover that they have been told a lie.[1] But they have an even stronger desire to be respected and, if possible, to become leaders within their society; as this is not possible if they are thought to be liars, the resentment they feel when they are accused of this practice is exceptionally strong. If such a charge is believed it has dire consequences for the man accused, since he is cut off, not only from leadership, but from 'any sort of ease, comfort, or satisfaction in the society of his equals'.[2] Mere lying is not therefore considered a crime, but an accusation of lying, if untrue, may render a man liable to the criminal law, since it is an important injury to a person's reputation.

However, when the expectations set up by verbal communication are very strong, even honesty may be a legal duty, and this is the basis for the law of contract: 'The foundation of contract is the reasonable expectation, which the person who promises raises in the person to whom he binds himself; of which the satisfaction may be extorted by force'.[3] Similarly,

'That obligation to performance which arises from contract is founded on the reasonable expectation produced by a promise, which considerably differs from a mere declaration of intention. Though I say I have a mind to do such a thing for you, yet on account of some occurrences do not do it, I am not guilty of breach of promise. A promise is a declaration of your desire that the person for whom you promise should depend on you for the performance of it. Of consequence the promise produces an obligation, and the breach of it is an injury.'[4]

Resentment, Smith argues, varies according to the degree of damage done by non-performance of a contract and the 'reasonableness' of the expectation that it would be kept: by this he means the degree of doubt there is concerning the commitment of the person who promised; thus a solemn oath, or a promise in writing, is more binding than a more casual verbal promise; he shows this to be reflected in both English and Roman law.

The law of contract is, in fact, part of Smith's third division

[1] T.M.S., VII.iv (II.382).   [2] T.M.S., VII.iv (II.385).
[3] L.J., p. 7.   [4] L.J., pp. 130f.

within those rights which the individual possesses 'as a man'; it relates to the ways in which a man can be injured 'in his estate'. Estate covers 'real rights' to do with property and 'personal' rights 'such as are all debts and contracts, the payment or performance of which can be demanded only from one person'.[1] The right to property is in many ways the most important of all since it is the one which is most likely to be violated in a commercial society and its defence is, therefore, the main function of government.[2] Smith explains the right to property by pointing to the natural resentment that all men feel when they are deprived of things which they are accustomed to having the exclusive use of. Actual possession produces the expectation of continued possession, and since the spectator goes along with his expectation he also shares the resentment which arises in the person whose expectations are thwarted through the intervention of some other person. 'To be deprived of that which we are possessed of, is a greater evil than to be disappointed of what we have only the expectation';[3] actual possession, therefore, especially when this possession has taken time and trouble, builds up in the possessor what Smith calls a 'reasonable expectation',[4] (by which he means an expectation which is shared by the spectator) that he will continue to possess it. The main ways of acquiring property are by 'occupation, or the taking possession of what formerly belonged to nobody' and 'prescription, which is a right to a thing belonging to another arising from long and uninterrupted possession'.[5] Expectation which is strong enough to be the basis of a right to property is also built up by 'accession, when a man has a right to one thing in consequence of another, as of a horse's shoes along with the horse,'[5] and 'succession' or inheritance, which he explains by reducing it to a form of acquisition by prescription and occupation;[6] and, finally, property may also be acquired by 'voluntary transference' which requires 'first a declaration of the intention both of the person who transfers, and of him to whom it is transferred: second, the actual delivery of the thing'.[7]

Smith assumes that the natural expectations built up in these various ways account for the laws of property which can be observed to exist in all but the earliest forms of society. But he emphasizes that his theory can also account for the variations between the property laws of different societies, and the *Lectures on Jurisprudence*, especially in the fuller report recently discovered by Professor

[1] L.J., p. 6.   [2] Cf. W.N., V.i.2 (II.231).
[3] T.M.S., II.ii.2 (I.208).   [4] L.J., p. 108.
[5] L.J., p. 107.   [6] L.J., pp. 113ff.
[7] L.J., p. 125.

Lothian, contain many illustrations of the different ways of acquiring property in different types of society.[1] In a society of hunters there are no settled habitations and no need for much in the way of property, but the continued possession of animals by those who have killed them in the hunt, a form of occupation, would be expected; a hunter does not need to fence off and cultivate a piece of land and therefore he has no occasion for resentment at not being able to do so, but with the development of agriculture it becomes natural for each to cultivate the land nearest to his habitation and so by occupation and accession acquire the exclusive use of the land for himself: the longer possession continues, and the more work the labourer puts in on that piece of land, the greater his expectation of keeping it for himself. With the emergence of crafts, together with the division of labour, new expectations are created, and in commerical society there develops a vast complex of property laws corresponding to these expectations.

IV. THE DIVERSITY OF LEGAL CODES

Any complete explanation of the laws which hold in particular countries requires reference, therefore, to the economy of that country; the impartial spectator is affected by his knowledge of what it is like to live under a particular economic system; his assessment of reasonable resentment includes, it will be remembered, the consideration of how he would react in such a situation, and this can only be known to him if he understands the economic forces at work in the situation; he cannot, for instance, know if resentment is proportional to the degree of theft unless he knows the value of the object stolen, and this requires familiarity with the economy of that particular country, since what is valued under one system may not be under another. This means that Smith's discussion of justice is open-ended, in that, if he is to fill out his generalizations about sympathetic resentment and show how they explain the laws of different societies, he has to give an account of the basic economy of each country. Much of the *Lectures on Jurisprudence* are therefore taken up with tracing the development of societies from one sort of economy to another and demonstrating the corresponding changes in their law. Of particular importance here is the fact that the various orders and ranks of a society are determined by, or at least vary according to, the type of economy which exists in a particular society. The *Moral Sentiments* explains the distinction of ranks by reference to men's tendency to admire the rich and the powerful, but

[1] Cf. L.J., pp. 107-53.

it is necessary to go beyond this and show, by reference to the source of wealth in each society, why there is a particular system of ranks in each society. This in turn, affects what type of government establishes itself in each society, which influences both the content of the law and the way in which it is administered. This aspect of justice is dealt with in the *Wealth of Nations*.[1]

Many variations between the laws of different countries can be explained by showing how Smith's analysis of the moral sentiments would lead us to expect different laws in different economic and political systems as being quite 'natural'. Other variations are accounted for by giving a special reason why the system of natural jurisprudence has not been fully implemented in a particular country. Smith assumes that the alleged connections between resentment and the law are, in fact, only tendencies, which may be thwarted and, consequently, sometimes remain unfulfilled. For instance he admits that the laws of natural jurisprudence will exist only 'in all well-governed states'.[2] The standpoint of the impartial spectator will not prevail where there is no effective legislature or no judges to execute the law. Even when governments are established they are often unable to repress powerful sectional interests and tend to ignore the rules of justice when they conflict with their interest as governors:

'Sometimes what is called the constitution of the state, that is, the interest of the government; sometimes the interest of particular orders of men who tyrannize the government, warp the positive laws of the country from what natural justice would prescribe.'[3]

This seems to come near to the admission that it is only in a society of equals that the rules of natural justice will emerge, and Smith explicitly denies that such a society is possible. However he indicates that even a tyrant has an interest in maintaining order and knows that this is best done by administering the law in accordance with the sentiments of the people, which means in accordance with the attitudes of the impartial spectator.[4]

The lack of a good system of government is not the only thing which can prevent the full implementation of natural justice. It is also affected by the 'rudeness and barbarism of the people'. We have already discussed the meaning of these terms in connection with

[1] Cf. W.N., III.iv (I.435f.) and V.i.2 (II.231ff.).

[2] T.M.S., VII.iv (II.396).

[3] T.M.S., VII.iv (II.396); for instance, the laws which slave-owners pass to govern the behaviour of slaves (cf. L.J., p. 96 and p. 102), and the bias against women in the laws of adultery drawn up by men. (cf. L.J., pp. 74ff.).

[4] Cf. L.J., p. 31.

ordinary moral rules;[1] the characterization is largely an economic one: barbarians are hunters and shepherds, commercial society is 'civilized'. But here the important factor is the influence which these different ways of life have upon the sensibility of those involved in them. In barbaric society men are not so capable of refined emotions and this, of course, affects the reactions of the spectator in this society, and so:

'In some countries, the rudeness and barbarism of the people hinder the natural sentiments of justice from arriving at that accuracy and precision which, in more civilized nations, they naturally attain to.'[2]

An interesting example of this occurs in Smith's explanation of some variations in domestic law connected with marriage. The duty of fidelity on the part of a wife to her husband, and, to a lesser degree, of husband to wife, is based, according to Smith, on jealousy. Whatever its utility in caring for children, the institution of marriage is directly supported by the fact that the spectator sympathizes with the husband's feelings of jealousy.[3] Jealousy, however, depends on the sentiment of love, which is not an emotion that can be felt by barbarians. This means that 'in those countries where the manners of the people are rude and uncultivated, there is no such thing as jealousy',[4] and, consequently, there are no laws which enforce monogamous marriage.

V. JUSTICE AND UTILITY

Sometimes Smith contrasts men's 'natural rights' to the protection of body and reputation with the 'acquired rights' of estate, in order to bring out that the right to a particular piece of property has to be explained by reference to the manner in which it was acquired.[5] More often he talks of 'natural rights' as those which belong to a person simply 'as a man', in contrast with 'adventitious rights' as those which belong to a man in virtue of some special relationship he has as a member of a family or a state.[6] However, all rights are natural in the sense that they are to be traced back to resentments which are not themselves explained by reference to the law, and are therefore 'antecedent to the institution of civil government'.[7] In a

[1] Cf. p. 144.   [2] T.M.S., VII.iv (II.396).
[3] Cf. L.J., pp. 73ff.   [4] L.J., p. 75.
[5] L.J., p. 107.
[6] This is clearly brought out in the report of lectures delivered in 1762-3, discovered recently by Professor J. M. Lothian.
[7] T.M.S., II.ii.1 (I.199); cf. L.J., p. 15.

few cases laws are the consequences of arbitrary decisions of law-makers (Smith gives as an example the rules of affinity in blood relations[1]), but, on the whole, law is a consequence and not a cause of 'natural' rights and duties.

Hume contrasted the 'natural' with the 'artificial' in order to argue that justice is an artificial virtue in the sense that it is founded on men's reflections concerning its utility.[2] Smith is adamant that justice is, on Hume's definition, a natural virtue. Throughout his discussion of legal rules he is anxious to show not only that their origin and continued existence can be explained by the spectator's sympathetic resentment, but that this renders irrelevant and misconceived all attempts to account for such rules by their utility. He denies that men administer punishment because they are aware of its usefulness in deterring crime, reforming the wrongdoer and reducing the criminal's opportunities for repeating the offence;[3] on the contrary, 'resentment seems best to account for the punishment of crimes'.[4] Similarly he denies that contracts are binding or that property is sacrosanct because men acknowledge the usefulness of such arrangements. Appeals to utility are nearly always rationalizations of practices which are caused by spontaneous feeling.

Smith's main argument against Hume is simply to reiterate his conviction that his own explanation is quite sufficient to account, in detail, for the wide variety of positive laws that have been enacted in different countries. In addition, he points out that all men have a deep sense of injustice in particular cases, but few of them are aware of the general utility of justice; moreover, exceptions to the laws of justice are not permitted even when they are shown to be useful; so far, he says, are ordinary people from basing their regard for justice on calculations of its utility for society, that they believe injustice will be punished in an after-life which, he considers, can have no effect on social utility.[5]

Smith does not deny that justice is useful both for the individual concerned in particular instances and for society in general; we have already seen how he alleges that propriety and utility coincide, and justice is the supreme example of this; it is the most useful of all virtues and the punishment of injustice has all the beneficial consequences which are attributed to it. But this utility, he submits, while it may provide the basis for a final explanation, is not one of the efficient causes of justice.[6]

Yet there is a certain ambivalence in Smith's statements about the

[1] L.J., p. 88.   [2] *Treatise* (ed. by Selby-Bigge), III.ii.1 (p. 484).
[3] T.M.S., II.ii.3 (I.213ff.).   [4] L.J., p. 152.
[5] T.M.S., II.ii.3 (I.288f.).   [6] Cf. Chapter 10, especially pp. 217ff.

relationship between justice and utility; in some places he seems to imply that considerations of utility do affect the content and application of the rules of justice. It is not only that arguments based on an appeal to beneficial consequences have some effect in bolstering up the natural sense of justice; he also asserts that it is because men are aware of the utility of punishments that they carry out, long after the crime has passed and the resentment it provoked has died down, punishments which were initially determined by fierce resentment. This would not take place were it not for 'consideration of the general interest of society'.[1] Moreover, as we shall see, awareness of the public utility of justice is one of the factors which influence men to obey their governments.[2] Very often too, in the *Lectures on Jurisprudence* Smith's appeal to what is 'reasonable' in particular circumstances has the appearance of an explanation in terms of the conscious efforts of men to safeguard the general interests of society.[3]

It almost seems that he was in two minds about the relationship of utility and justice, suggesting that while, on the whole, utilitarian reflection simply confirms the natural sentiments of justice, on occasions it may result in laws which are in conflict with these sentiments. A similar clash appears, although in a somewhat different form, in the opposition of immediate moral sentiments to those which are based on reflection about the past; we have already noted that the immediate 'animal resentment' of men requires compensation to be paid by a man who unwittingly and unluckily injures another; Smith notes that 'This task would surely never be imposed upon him, did not even the impartial spectator feel some indulgence for what may be regarded as the unjust resentment of that other'.[4] He hedges here by saying that such a sentiment *may* be regarded as unjust, and, with similar hesitation, he talks of the 'fallacious sense of guilt, if I may call it so', felt by the person who has caused unintended harm to another;[5] he also speaks, less equivocally, of the 'perhaps natural, though no doubt most unjust resentment' of the injured person.[6] This is not in itself a conflict between natural sentiments and utility, but it illustrates how Smith was prepared to admit that reflection does modify those spontaneous feelings of resentment on which he usually relies for his explanations of the law.

But even here he does not allow that reflection has much influence on the content of law. In this same discussion of the law of negligence he points out that, while public utility would suggest that punishment

---

[1] T.M.S., II.ii.3 (I.221).   [2] Cf. p. 208.
[3] Cf. L.J., p. 58.   [4] T.M.S., II.iii.2 (I.263).
[5] T.M.S., II.iii.3 (I.272).   [6] T.M.S., II.iii.3 (I.271).

for gross negligence, which does not result in injury, should be just as severe as when actual harm is caused by such negligence, this is not in fact the case.[1] This is because resentment is roused only by the sight of harm being inflicted and the law is consequently lenient with regard to carelessness which, by good fortune, harms nobody. Reflection on what might have happened has, therefore, very little effect on the content of the law and, on the whole, the same is true in the case of reflection about the actual and possible future consequences of action. However, in this latter case he is more ready to allow exceptions:

'Upon some occasions, indeed, we both punish and approve of punishment, merely from a view to the general interest of society, which, we imagine, cannot otherwise be secured. Of this kind are all the punishments inflicted for breaches of what is called either civil police, or military discipline. Such crimes do not immediately or indirectly hurt any particular person; but their remote consequences, it is supposed, do produce, or might produce, either a considerable inconveniency, or a great disorder in the society.'[2]

He takes as his example the case of a sentinel who falls asleep at his post and endangers a whole army. Smith seems unable to make up his mind whether the severe punishments inflicted for such offences are unjust or not. 'The natural atrocity of the crime seems to be so little' and yet 'This severity may, upon many occasions, appear necessary, and, for that reason, just and proper. When the preservation of an individual is inconsistent with the safety of a multitude, nothing can be more just than that the many should be preferred to the one.'[2]

The interesting thing here is that he is unsure whether such punishments should be called just, but is prepared to admit that utilitarian reflection does have an important influence on the content of the law in such instances. He tries to turn this to his own advantage by saying that not only are such instances rare, but that, when they do occur, we approve of the punishment with reluctance, and regard the sentinel, for instance, as 'an unfortunate victim, who, indeed, must, and ought to be, devoted to the safety of numbers'.[3] This contrasts with the enthusiastic approval that accompanies the execution of a murderer.

Smith admits more than he need do in this discussion of the laws

[1] L.J., p. 152.
[2] T.M.S., II.ii.3 (I.226f.). Cf. L.J., p. 136. See also Smith's views on the capital crime of exporting wool (L.J., p. 136).
[3] T.M.S., II.ii.3 (I.228).

of military discipline. There is no necessity for him to say that the sentinel's punishment is just because men approve of it. Justice is *only one* standard by reference to which laws may be assessed. In this case it would be possible for him to say that the sentinel's punishment is expedient but not just, and that the expediency is so great that it outweighs the requirements of justice. That Smith sometimes regards the matter in this light can be seen from his attitude towards beneficial exceptions to the system of natural liberty. He notes, for instance, that it can be dangerous for a small state to permit unlimited exportation of corn, and remarks:

'To hinder . . . the farmer from sending his goods at all times to the best market, is evidently to sacrifice the ordinary laws of justice to an idea of public utility, to a sort of reasons of state; an act of legislative authority which ought to be exercised only, which can be pardoned only in cases of the most urgent necessity.'[1]

This is in line with the often noted fact that the requirements of public utility can conflict with the duty of treating individuals justly. It is utility, not justice, which entails that one man should be sacrificed in the interests of the many. This point was sometimes obscured for Smith by his assumption that justice is *the* legal virtue as far as the criminal law goes; expediency he reserves for the economic functions of the state. To admit that this is not the case would mean, of course, that he would have to give up his claim that he is able to explain *all* civil and criminal laws by tracing them back to sympathetic resentment, but it might have made his conclusions about justice less paradoxical and uncertain.

Professor Raphael suggests that it was the same dubiety about the justice of the sentinel's punishment that led him to drop an argument he used, in a lecture delivered prior to the publication of the *Moral Sentiments*, which states that 'punishment . . . which exceeds the demerit of the crime is an injury to the criminal'.[2] This argument coincides with the doctrine of the *Moral Sentiments* that the only justification for injuring another person is retaliation for the injuries committed by that person, and that the degree of the spectator's resentment is the measure of the severity with which crimes are punished. It is an argument which would have provided more useful ammunition in favour of his retributive theory of punishment. But Professor Raphael points out that, since Smith considered the sentinel's punishment to be just, he would have had to admit that,

[1] W.N., IV.v (II.48).
[2] D. D. Raphael, 'Adam Smith and "The Infection of David Hume's Society"', *Journal of the History of Ideas*, vol. XXX, no. 2 (1969), p. 240.

in this instance, a 'just' punishment was also an injury and therefore deserved punishment in return. Smith would have been able to avoid this contradictory conclusion if he had been prepared to say that the sentinel's punishment is approved on the grounds of its expediency and not because it is just.

Despite these loose ends in Smith's theory of justice it is still clear that he was prepared to admit that utilitarian reflection has some effect in determining the content of the law, and it would seem that he himself welcomes the fact that immediate resentment is occasionally subordinated to considerations of utility. This will become even more evident when we have discussed the principles which lie at the basis of his political philosophy.

CHAPTER 10

POLITICS AND PRINCIPLES

The thesis that Smith's theory of morality is essentially a scientific one should not be taken to imply that he does not endorse any moral and political principles of his own. By and large he accepts, as morally justified, the norms which it is his main purpose to explain. His own moral convictions can be seen in the arguments which he uses to justify his confidence in the judgments of the impartial spectator. These convictions are also apparent in the moral assumptions he brings to bear on the political issues of his day and in the recommendations he makes concerning the general conduct of politics. This is not to say that the arguments which he uses to justify his moral and political principles are the same as those which he uses to explain why certain principles are generally accepted. At least they do not correspond to the efficient causes of moral and political principles; although, as we shall see, they do often correspond to the final causes of such principles, or, in other words, to the purposes which are unwittingly served by these efficient causes.

Despite all that Smith has to say against utility as the explanation for the ordinary person's moral and political attitudes, his own normative moral and political philosophy turns out to be, in the end, a form of utilitarianism. It is because men, by following their spontaneous moral sentiments, play their part in a system which is conducive to the happiness of mankind, that Smith recommends that these moral sentiments should continue to serve as guides for conduct. They find their justification in the fact that they are a means towards the production of general happiness. Similarly, when it comes to giving political advice, he relies on the principle of utility to provide the basis on which political decisions ought to be made. For the most part utility dictates that politicians should leave well alone, but this is by no means always the case. Sometimes it is necessary for them to intervene in the natural social processes for the benefit of human happiness. Utility, or the production of happiness, is thus the principle by reference to which he judges that both the natural moral sentiments and the system of natural liberty are desirable. It is also the principle behind his suggestions for refining these sentiments and correcting such defects as may remain even when the condition of natural liberty has been established. We may, therefore, say that, with respect to his own normative philosophy, utility is his supreme moral and political principle.

I. THE THEORY OF GOVERNMENT

Smith's theory of government is the meeting place for his scientific theory of society and his own practical recommendations; it is, therefore, a good point from which to start a consideration of the normative and metaphysical beliefs which lie behind his science of society. The four functions which Smith allocates to government are 'justice, police, revenue and arms'; 'The object of justice is security from injury, and it is the foundation of civil government. The objects of police are the cheapness of commodities, public security and cleanliness'; revenue concerns taxes raised to defray the expenses of government, and the fourth purpose of government is to maintain an army for external defence.[1] The powers of government are legislative, judicial and federal (the power of making war and peace);[2] its main method of operation is, therefore, the law, which Smith defines as the command of the sovereign.[3] He has a deep interest in the development of different types of government in different societies, which he explains partly by economic and partly by military factors.[4] He himself favoured a type of mixed government, corresponding to the constitution of Britain in his own day, which combined a representative legislature, on a limited franchise, with a hereditary monarchy. The descriptions which he gives of the development of government in its various functions are of great sociological interest in themselves, but, from the point of view of the discussion of the relationship between his sociological theory and his normative philosophy, they are only a background for his analysis of political obligation. It is in his analysis of the reasons why men do obey, or ought to obey, their governments that we can discern his own political philosophy.

Government exists where there is law; a law is a commandment whose observance can be enforced; whenever one person or group of persons can successfully get their decisions accepted as law, they constitute a government.[5] Smith sees that this makes the question of the citizens' obligation to obey the commands of the sovereign central to the study of politics, and, in order to answer this question,

[1] L.J., pp. 3f.   [2] L.J., p. 17.   [3] T.M.S., III.5 (I.413).
[4] L.J., pp. 14-55.   [5] L.J., p. 15.

he finds it necessary to discuss the duties of the sovereign towards the subject. When Smith asks why men 'enter into' civil society, he is still primarily asking a factual question: he wants to know what 'induces men to obey'[1] their government. Because he treats it as a factual question he has no difficulty in rejecting the theory that men obey because of some contract entered into either by themselves or their forbears, for, as he says, (1) men obey where the contract is unknown, (2) they do not give the contract as the reason why they obey, (3) they are not aware of giving their consent, and (4) in those instances where there is a contract, as in the case of resident aliens, this does not result in any trust being placed in the persons who have made the contract to obey.[2] However, it becomes clear that it is not *only* a factual question which he is asking when he includes amongst the objections to the contract theory the moral argument that a person ought not to be bound by a promise made by his ancestors: he goes on to ridicule the notion of tacit consent by saying that most people have no real chance to leave their country and:

'To say that by staying in a country a man agrees to a contract of obedience to government is just the same with carrying a man into a ship and after he is at a distance from land to tell him that by being in the ship he has contracted to obey the master.'[3]

In concluding, therefore, that 'the foundation of a duty cannot be a principle with which mankind is entirely unacquainted'[3] Smith appears to be making the psychological point that we cannot have a motive of which we are totally unaware, and the moral point that a man cannot be obliged to obey a contract into which he did not explicitly enter.

His own theory of political obligation is, likewise, a mixture of descriptive and normative theory. Men obey, he argues, because of 'the principles of authority and utility';[4] the first relates to those characteristics of men which make others accept them as superior and worthy of being obeyed, and the second to the subjects' awareness of the private and public utility of the functions of government. It is the principle of authority which has most in common with the doctrine of the *Moral Sentiments* where Smith tends to play down the importance of utility and rely on laws of social psychology to explain men's behaviour.

The four characteristics which give authority are age, long possession of power, wealth, and mental or physical abilities. The first is explained by arguing that the imagination connects the ideas of age

[1] L.J., p. 10. [2] L.J., pp. 11ff.
[3] L.J., p. 12. [4] L.J., p. 9; cf. W.N., V.i.1 (II.232ff.).

with those of wisdom and experience which, to some extent, makes age just as effective as the possession of ability in obtaining authority. In so far as these qualities are admired in themselves, rather than as means to fulfilling the useful functions of government, they come under the principle of authority. But of more importance than either age or wisdom is the long possession of power; this is explained by the association of ideas, and, in particular, by relating it to the expectations and resentments of mankind: we have seen how many rights, especially property rights, arise out of the expectations which an established practice or possession forms in men's minds and the consequent resentment which is aroused by the frustration of these expectations. This is applied to the possession of political power; men are prepared to accept the commands of those who have always given them orders but will reject those of the 'upstart'. Wealth is the fourth, and most important, authority-conferring characteristic; this we have already examined in detail when considering the 'origin and distinction of ranks',[1] and it is necessary, here, only to add that Smith considers the possession of wealth to be the main factor which attracts the respect of other men and to remind ourselves that this is not primarily a matter of the subject's economic dependence on the rich but of the ability of the rich to obtain the admiration and sympathy of the poor on account of the ease with which men sympathize with the imagined pleasures of the wealthy. This source of authority alone is, according to Smith, 'upon ordinary occasions, sufficient to govern the world'.[2]

If the principle of authority is the one which leads men to obey rulers without question, then that of utility induces them to obey because they appreciate the purposes which government serves, particularly its role in maintaining justice and peace in society, for not only does government protect the rich against the poor, but 'by civil institutions the poorest may get redress of injuries from the wealthiest and most powerful'.[3] This is not primarily a sense of private or individual utility, since political obligation may oblige men to act against their own interests:

'It is the sense of public utility, more than of private, which influences men to obedience. It may sometimes be for my interest to disobey, and to wish government overturned, but I am sensible that other men are of a different opinion from me, and would not assist me in the enterprise. I therefore submit to its decision for the good of the whole.'[3]

This does not, in fact, contradict Smith's view of the minor place

[1] Cf. p. 172.　　[2] T.M.S., I.iii.2 (I.131).　　[3] L.J., p. 10.

which benevolence holds in the pantheon of motives, since he hints
that private utility would hold more sway if the individual was in a
position to conduct an individual rebellion.

The principle of utility is on a par with that of authority as an
explanation for obedience; it acts as a further support for the
principle of authority and may, indeed, incorporate the principle of
authority in so far as men become aware of the utility of blind
obedience to rulers.[1] Smith even suggests some sociological generalizations about the relative weight of the two principles in different types
of civil society:

'In all governments both these principles take place in some degree,
but in a monarchy the principle of authority prevails, and in a
democracy that of utility. In Britain, which is a mixed government,
the factions formed some time ago, under the names of Whig and
Tory, were influenced by these principles, the former submitted to
government on account of its utility and the advantages which
they derived from it, while the latter pretended that it was of divine
institution, and to offend against it was equally criminal as for a
child to rebel against its parent.'[2]

But, from the philosophical point of view, the principles are not on
the same level, since the principle of utility is used to evaluate the
principle of authority. It is clear that Smith does not consider that
the principle of authority is self-justifying. He notes, for instance,
that it is irrational because it depends on an illusion, created by the
imagination, which runs counter to our ordinary moral judgments:

'That kings are the servants of the people, to be obeyed, resisted,
deposed, or punished, as the public conveniency may require, is the
doctrine of reason and philosophy; but it is not the doctrine of
Nature. Nature would teach us to submit to them for their own
sake, to tremble and bow down before their exalted station, to
regard their smile as a reward sufficient to compensate any services,
and to dread their displeasure, though no other evil were to follow
from it, as the severest of all mortifications.'[3]

On the other hand he points out the usefulness of the principle of
authority in promoting the stability and hence the happiness of
society.

It would appear, therefore, that Smith elevates the principle of

[1] T.M.S., I.iii.2 (I.127).
[2] L.J., p. 11. This quotation reveals Smith's preferences both for Whigs against
Tories and for utility against authority.
[3] T.M.S., I.iii.2 (I.128).

utility into *the* principle of his normative theory of political obligation. Men ought to obey their rulers in so far as their government is effective in producing public happiness by sustaining the internal and external peace of a country; in the end, this is the standard by which all governments must be judged. Such a principle, of course, entails that when a government fails to fulfil these purposes it should cease to command men's obedience (although the principle of authority may still produce *de facto* obedience), and Smith is willing to allow that 'Whatever be the principle of allegiance, a right of resistance must undoubtedly be lawful, because no authority is altogether unlimited.'[1] However, this right of rebellion is severely limited; frequent rebellions lead to instabilities which make it difficult to re-establish *de facto* authority, presumably because it makes it impossible to rely on the principle of long possession. Therefore, on the basis of the principle of utility itself, Smith concludes that, while 'no government is quite perfect', nevertheless 'it is better to submit to some inconveniences than make attempts against it'.[2] But the right to rebel does exist, and Smith argues unequivocally for the justice of the Revolution against James II on the grounds that he ignored the rights of Parliament. Yet even in this case he is primarily concerned to explain *why* the Revolution occurred, namely because James aroused 'the most furious passions, fear, hatred, and resentment',[3] and 'plainly showed his intention to change the religion of the country, which is the most difficult thing in the world',[4] so that men overcame their 'habitual sense of deference'[3] and rose in rebellion.

II. UTILITY AND THE STATESMAN

The principle of utility does not only determine the limits of obligatory obedience to political authority, it is also the principle which Smith uses, in conjunction with his sociological theory, to guide the decisions of statesmen. Rulers ought to act so as to secure the happiness of their citizens. It seems to have been Smith's own conviction that 'All constitutions of government . . . are valued only in proportion as they tend to promote the happiness of those who live under them.'[5] This may be demonstrated by looking in turn at what he has to say about the four purposes of government.

The most important function of government is to enforce the rules of natural justice. In Chapter Nine we saw that Smith does not

---

[1] L.J., p. 68. Here the word 'authority' is clearly used in a *de jure* sense.
[2] L.J., p. 69.   [3] T.M.S., I. iii.2 (I.128).
[4] L.J., p. 71.   [5] T.M.S., IV.1 (I.468).

consider that men in general seek justice for its utility. But it was also noted, in the same chapter, that Smith does not deny that justice has utility. In his final explanation of the sentiments on which the sense of justice is based, Smith emphasizes that justice is essential to the security and thus to the happiness of society:

'Justice . . . is the main pillar that upholds the whole edifice. If it is removed, the great, the immense fabric of human society, that fabric which to raise and support seems in this world, if I may say so, to have been the peculiar and darling care of Nature, must in a moment crumble into atoms. In order to enforce the observation of justice, therefore, Nature has implanted in the human breast that consciousness of ill-desert, those terrors of merited punishment which attend upon its violation, as the great safeguards of the association of mankind, to protect the weak, to curb the violent, and to chastise the guilty.'[1]

Thus resentment is useful because it accomplishes 'all the political ends of punishment; the correction of the criminal, and the example to the public'.[2]

Smith's definition of justice is particularly suited to utilitarian interpretations (especially the negative formulation of utilitarianism which advocates the minimization of pain), since it is to do with the prevention of harm or injury, and it is clear that, for all he has to say against utility as the immediate ground of the sentiments of justice, he regards the government's duty to enforce justice as a particular case of its duty to promote the happiness, or at least to ward off the unhappiness, of its subjects:

'The wisdom of every state or commonwealth endeavours as well as it can, to employ the force of the society to restrain those who are subject to its authority, from hurting or disturbing the happiness of one another.'[3]

Smith expects that, even in the case of politicians, it will always be immediate resentment against injustice which leads men to support the laws of justice, but in so far as it becomes a matter of debate as to whether or not the state should enforce the rules of natural justice, it is to the principle of utility that Smith considers all men, and especially statesmen, will have recourse. We have seen, in the last chapter, that in certain aspects of justice, such as the infliction of punishment after due judicial processes,[4] and the enforcement of laws of military discipline,[5] Smith notes, probably with approval, that

---

[1] T.M.S., II.ii.3 (I.215f.).   [2] T.M.S., II.i.1 (I.166).
[3] T.M.S., VI.ii (II.66f.).   [4] Cf. p. 201.   [5] Cf. p. 202.

considerations of utility have a place. When it comes to the general philosophical justification of all sentiments of justice, this appeal to the production of happiness and the prevention of pain is used to validate all the rules of natural justice. Apart from the immediate injuries which the administration of justice prevents, it has other, less direct but extremely important, consequences. It is indicated, in the *Wealth of Nations*, that justice is useful in promoting prosperity; indeed it is an essential requirement for the development of commercial society:

'Commerce and manufactures can seldom flourish long in any state which does not enjoy a regular administration of justice, in which the people do not feel themselves secure in the possession of their property, in which the faith of contracts is not supported by law, and in which the authority of the state is not supposed to be regularly employed in enforcing the payment of debts from all those who are able to pay.'[1]

It is, therefore, the principle of utility that lies behind Smith's recommendation that all governments should enforce the laws of natural justice. And the same principle explains his willingness to allow that, under certain circumstances, it is even right for the government to compel acts of positive benevolence; in some cases, if it is necessary for 'promoting the prosperity of the commonwealth',[2] the magistrate may make laws concerning conduct which was neither right nor wrong before these laws were made. Moreover, Smith frequently insists that it is the statesman's duty to revise the law when it is hindering social development.[3]

It is less clear whether Smith thought that justice, in the sense of fairness, could conflict with utility in the sense of the maximization of happiness and the minimization of pain. The immediate moral sentiments prompt men to feel resentment at injuries being inflicted on *anyone*, which seems to imply that justice protects the happiness of all men equally.[4] Apart from the sentinel example, Smith does not give much consideration to clashes between fairness and utility; he tends to assume that there is no conflict between them: the sovereign owes 'justice and equality of treatment' to 'all the different orders of his subjects',[5] but there is no suggestion that this equality is incompatible with the useful consequences of enforcing the rules of justice. Although his arguments in favour of aristocracy would seem to suggest that he considers that the few should be preferred to the many, it should be remembered that he justified the division of

---

[1] W.N., V.iii (II.445).   [2] T.M.S., II.ii.1 (I.201).
[3] W.N., III.ii (I.408).   [4] Cf. p. 172.   [5] W.N., IV.viii (II.171).

society into ranks because of the contribution this makes to the stability of society[1] and thus to the happiness of all its members. Moreover, we have seen that Smith does not believe that prosperity does bring great happiness, whatever men's imaginations may indicate to the contrary. He seems to think that the essential requirements of a happy life are open to all and clearly approves that this should be so.[2] On the other hand, while he accepts a limited equality of distribution as inevitable and desirable,[3] he is more concerned with equality of opportunity, the removal of restrictions on the individual's chances to make the most of his own abilities and virtues.[4] In this process considerations of merit and demerit lead to justified inequalities. This is part of justice in so far as a person rightly resents being deprived of the fruits of his labours. It is possible therefore, to argue that Smith would put considerations of fairness above the production of greater quantities of happiness as such, but he himself did not feel that he had to choose between these two goals.

The second function of government, namely police, is mainly concerned with the 'cheapness of commodities', and is the central topic of the *Wealth of Nations*. It is, of course, Smith's most famous doctrine that all governments should allow the natural workings of the economy to operate without state intervention. This thesis is partly supported by saying that restrictions on the economic liberty of the subject are unjust, but Smith's main argument is along the lines that government inaction, outside the sphere of justice, is the best means to promote high consumption and therefore the general happiness.[5] For, although Smith realizes that in some ways commercial society reduces men's opportunities for self-development,[6] he is in no doubt that, on the whole, it is greatly beneficial. His advocacy of the system of natural liberty is ultimately based on an assessment of its utility in increasing *per capita* consumption. The fact that this is so can be seen in his willingness to consider exceptions to the policy of non-intervention.[7] On the whole he distrusts governments as inefficient and self-interested, but he sees that in certain matters

[1] T.M.S., I.iii.2 (I.127).
[2] T.M.S., III.3 (I.369): 'In the most glittering and exalted situation that our idle fancy can hold out to us, the pleasures from which we propose to derive our real happiness, are almost always the same with those which, in our actual, though humble station, we have at all times at hand, and in our power.'
[3] W.N., I.viii (I.88).
[4] Cf. W.N., I.x.2 (I.136) and IV.ix (II.208).
[5] Cf. W.N., IV.ii (I.478).
[6] Cf. W.N., V.i.3 art. 2 (II.303).
[7] Many examples of this are given by Jacob Viner, 'Adam Smith and Laissez-Faire' in *Adam Smith, 1776-1926*, pp. 138-54.

some government action is necessary for the general welfare; for instance, every government has 'the duty of erecting and maintaining certain public works and certain public institutions, which it can never be for the interest of any individual, or small number of individuals, to erect and maintain'.[1]

Smith is prepared to consider each case for government intervention in economic life on its own merits; in discussing certain regulations concerning banking, for example, he concludes that:

'Such regulations may, no doubt, be considered as in some respect a violation of natural liberty. But those exertions of the natural liberty of a few individuals, which might endanger the security of the whole society, are, and ought to be, restrained by the laws of all governments; of the most free as well as the most despotical.'[2]

In fact the system of natural liberty is not so much an absence of all state-supported institutions as the presence of those institutions which are best adapted to make the self-interested actions of individual men work to the advantages of all.[3] Laws which prevent the self-interest of particular groups, such as merchants, from thwarting the checks and balances of open competition are justified.[4] Some state aid for education,[5] and control over religion,[6] are deemed advisable to counter the adverse effects of the division of labour and religious fanaticism. Despite the difficulties inherent in such a task, the statesman has the duty of doing everything in his power to promote the prosperity of the nation. In particular he has to keep laws relating to economics up to date. Restrictions and practices which were useful in their day, such as monopolies and inheritance according to the rules of primogeniture, had, in Smith's time, ceased to fit the changed economic conditions and he therefore recommends their abolition.[7]

The third function of government, the collection of revenue, is subordinate to its other functions in that the revenue is required in order that these other activities can be carried on. But even here utility comes in when he recommends that taxes be gathered in such a way as to raise the maximum revenue while doing as little harm as possible to the economic life of the nation,[8] although he also stresses that taxes should be 'equal', by which he means a propor-

---

[1] Cf. W.N., IV.ix (II.209).   [2] W.N., II.ii. (I.344f.).

[3] Cf. Nathan Rosenberg, 'Some Institutional Aspects of the *Wealth of Nations*', *Journal of Political Economy*, vol. XLVIII, pp. 557-70.

[4] Cf. W.N., I.xi (I.278).   [5] Cf. W.N., V.i.3. art.2 (II.302).

[6] Cf. W.N., V.i.3. art.3 (II.317).   [7] Cf. W.N., III.ii (I.408).

[8] Cf. W.N., V.ii.2 (II.351).

tional equality according to which those who have most at stake in the successful functioning of government, that is, those with most property, should pay most.[1] The final purpose of government is that of seeing to external defence by the provision of an army. This is an end to which Smith was prepared to sacrifice economic freedoms,[2] as he considered it to be a necessary condition of all justice and prosperity that each country should be secure from invasion and defeat in war.

It is not difficult to draw up a list of the many different ways in which Smith's advice to statesmen is governed by his utilitarian presuppositions. In addition to the clear tasks of administering justice and seeing to the security of the nation, there are numerous instances where he is anxious to see governments act in order to correct the defects of the natural order. Yet it should still be remembered that Smith sets strict limitations on the extent to which far-sighted human action can 'turn away the arrow which is aimed at the head of the righteous'.[3] Many of the malfunctionings which he mentions are not such as can be remedied. In the case of government action there is, in addition, the danger that attempts to improve the lot of mankind may lead to disaster because politicians do not realize the intricacy of the mechanism with which they are dealing. Smith comes out strongly against what he calls the 'spirit of system' which leads men to change the constitution and laws of society according to some elaborate plan of their own; he realizes the constant temptation for politicians to hold out schemes for the dramatic improvement of society:

'The leaders of the discontented party seldom fail to hold out some plausible plan of reformation which, they pretend, will not only remove the inconveniences and relieve the distresses immediately complained of, but will prevent, in all time coming, any return of the like inconveniences and distresses'.[4]

Moreover,

'The great body of the party are commonly intoxicated with the imaginary beauty of this ideal system, of which they have no experience.'[4]

Such plans, Smith believes, always under-rate the natural forces at work in society and over-estimate the power of government to alter the natural course of events.

In contrast to the man of system, he sets out a picture of the wise statesman which is an eloquent and balanced statement of Burkean

---

[1] Cf. W.N., V.ii.2 (II.350). [2] Cf. W.N., IV.ii (I.484).
[3] T.M.S., III.5 (I.421). [4] T.M.S., VI.ii.2 (II.107).

conservatism, and shows that Smith's alleged complacent optimism is sometimes mixed with more than a tinge of pessimism:

> 'The man whose public spirit is prompted altogether by humanity and benevolence, will respect the established powers and privileges even of individuals, and still more those of the great orders and societies, into which the state is divided. Though he should consider some of them as in some measure abusive, he will content himself with moderating, what he often cannot annihilate without great violence. When he cannot conquer the rooted prejudices of the people by reason and persuasion, he will not attempt to subdue them by force . . . He will accommodate, as well as he can, his public arrangements to the confirmed habits and prejudices of the people; and will remedy as well as he can, the inconveniences which may flow from the want of those regulations which the people are averse to submit to. When he cannot establish the right, he will not disdain to ameliorate the wrong; but like Solon, when he cannot establish the best system of laws, he will endeavour to establish the best that the people can bear.'[1]

This is not to say that statesmen are never to make radical changes in the law or even in the constitution of the state. In normal times the loyal support of the constitution is the best means to make 'our fellow-citizens as safe, respectable and happy as we can', but in disturbed times,

> 'even a wise man may be disposed to think some alteration necessary in that constitution or form of government, which, in its actual condition, appears plainly unable to maintain the public tranquillity. In such cases, however, it often requires, perhaps, the highest effort of political wisdom to determine when a real patriot ought to support and endeavour to re-establish the authority of the old system, and when he ought to give way to the more daring, but often dangerous spirit of innovation.'[2]

The ordinary politician cannot be expected to rise to these heights and act purely with regard to the general interest of society. Men's desire for power and selfish interest, together with normal human short-sightedness, make them unable to act effectively from humanity and benevolence. However, Smith thinks that there is one motive which may indirectly lead men to promote the general welfare. This takes us back to his own peculiar theory of utility, namely that men are fascinated by any machine or system which shows a nice adjust-

[1] T.M.S., VI.ii.2 (II.108ff.).   [2] T.M.S., VI.ii.2 (II.104f.).

ment of means to ends; in the realm of politics it is possible to rouse men to great political and administrative tasks by interesting them in intricate means rather than beneficial ends. This motive accounts for a good deal of the useful acts of politicians.[1]

Even if it is admitted that in the sphere of politics utility is Smith's over-riding moral principle, this does not automatically establish that this is so in non-political matters. But the whole weight of his discussion of final causation would suggest that, in all matters of individual and social morality, utility is the ultimate ground on which he approves of the ordinary moral sentiments. Justice, of course, is part of morality, and this we have already discussed. Prudence is a virtue which clearly promotes the happiness of the individual, and given that each person is best suited to look after his own interests, the practice of prudential behaviour throughout a society would undoubtedly promote the general happiness.[2] Smith makes a point of stressing that benevolence is naturally felt most strongly for those whom we are best able to help and gets weaker and weaker as the persons concerned become more and more remote from our sphere of influence.[3] The restricted nature of the benevolent affections which are approved of by the impartial spectator is ultimately justified by the fact that society is benefited most by each endeavouring to promote the welfare of those whom he is in the position of being able to help. Here, as elsewhere, Smith notes, and approves, the fact that 'Nature' intends the happiness of mankind.[4] Because Smith's statements about final causation reveal his own moral principles, this does not imply that he did not regard these statements as primarily assertions of final causation; he clearly regarded it as explanatory to say that a particular causal process exhibits the purpose of God. But, having demonstrated this, he took a certain satisfaction in being able to sit back and admire the handiwork of God, and this admiration includes approval of the principle on which God is seen to act; it is because God is a utilitarian[5] that we can say that Smith's own moral presuppositions are utilitarian.

III. CONTEMPLATIVE UTILITARIANISM

To argue that Smith is a utilitarian seems paradoxical in view of his recurrent criticism of utilitarianism. But these criticisms are all

---

[1] Cf. W.N., IV.i (I.469ff.).   [2] Cf. pp. 178ff.   [3] Cf. pp. 182ff.
[4] Cf. T.M.S., VI.ii.Intro. (II.68).
[5] T.M.S., VI.ii.3 (II.118): 'The administration of the great system of the universe... the care of the universal happiness of all rational and sensible beings, is the business of God'.

directed at those who argue that utility can explain the origin of moral judgments or that it ought to be the principle by which men make their day-to-day moral choices. Those who fail to distinguish between Smith's theory of the causes of moral judgments and his practical advice to the ordinary moral agent on the one hand, and his own normative philosophy on the other, inevitably misrepresent his ultimate moral principles.[1]

It is true that he did not think that utility is the basis of everyday moral judgments; for while these judgments take into account the immediate consequences of acts, even this is secondary to the assessment of the appropriateness of an act to its situation. Nor did he think that utility *ought* to be the conscious basis of ordinary moral judgments; men's calculations concerning future consequences are too inaccurate, and they would tend, especially where their own interests are involved, to use considerations of utility as excuses to make exceptions in their own favour.

Sometimes it does appear that Smith commends a form of rule-utilitarianism, in that, although particular acts are to be judged by whether or not they conform to the appropriate moral rules, the rules themselves are to be assessed according to their consequences. For instance, he says that, in assessing the utility of justice, we should consider the consequences of a certain type of behaviour becoming general throughout a society.[2] But he considers that the origin of general rules is to be found in judgments concerning particular acts and that appeal to such judgments is a more effective way of justifying these rules than presentation of calculations about their utility. Such calculations may provide ultimate justification for moral rules but they are uncertain everyday supports for these rules.

Utility is, however, the principle which is necessary for the guidance of those who have to consider the total system of society, whether as scientists, philosophers, or statesmen.[3] It is the principle which provides many final explanations, and which enables us to make ultimate assessments concerning the soundness of ordinary moral judgments and the value of the whole mechanism of society; it is also the principle according to which political reforms ought to be conducted, and on which the citizen ought to base his decisions about political obligation, when this is in doubt.

---

[1] Cf. A. L. Macfie, *The Individual in Society*, pp. 45-8. Macfie, having pointed out that Smith criticizes Hume's theory of utility, concludes that 'Utility for him [Smith] was not basic.'   [2] T.M.S., II.ii.3 (I.223).

[3] It is because the ordinary person is unable to make accurate utilitarian calculations that Smith considers politics to be a specialist occupation and does not favour a universal franchise.

Utility is, therefore, very much *the* meta-principle for Smith. It is to be found at the basis of his whole moral outlook, but it operates most typically at the level of contemplation, when men adopt a God's-eye-view of society, enter into His universal benevolence and feel admiration and approval for what they observe. At this level of reflection utility provides the key to the interpretation of God's creation. For, as we have seen, Smith considers God to be a utilitarian[1]; probably a rule-utilitarian. God considers the general consequences of types of conduct and arranges it so that men habitually act in such a way as to maximize the general happiness. But, of course, God is a utilitarian whose situation is so unlike that of men that it is difficult to compare His utilitarianism with that of human beings. For instance, God does not, presumably, have to choose between His own happiness and that of other beings, and therefore many of the problems of justice versus utility, or private versus public utility, do not arise.

But we can ask whether it is *only* happiness that God wishes for men. Here the relevant quotations are equally divided between those that speak of the 'happiness and perfection of the species', and those that mention only human happiness.[2] It seems, therefore, that there is some hint of ideal utilitarianism present in what is predominantly a hedonistic utilitarian theory. 'Perfection' may simply mean the multiplication of the species, but it is much more likely to refer to the Stoic idea of man's place in the total system of the universe. It is at this point that Smith's moral ideals merge with his aesthetic or contemplative principles. The 'perfectly virtuous' man acts in accordance with 'the rules of perfect prudence, of strict justice, and of proper benevolence',[3] and it is this 'perfection of human nature' which 'can alone produce among mankind that harmony of sentiments and passions in which consists their whole grace and propriety'.[4] The perfection of the species thus serves to promote the harmony of society as an integral part of the total system which God has created. It is through virtuous behaviour that men become completely adapted to the workings of the social mechanism, a mechanism which they can, to some extent, appreciate and admire. It is clear that Smith did not consider that this concept of perfection

---

[1] Cf. T.M.S., III.5 (I.413f.): 'The happiness of mankind, as well as of all other rational creatures, seems to have been the original purpose intended by the Author of nature.'

[2] Cf. T.M.S., II.iii.3 (I.267): 'Man was made . . . to promote . . . the happiness of all'; T.M.S., III.5 (I.421): 'The same great end, the order of the world, and the perfection and happiness of human nature'; and T.M.S., II.iii.3 (I.265).

[3] T.M.S., VI.iii (II.120).   [4] T.M.S., I.i.5 (I.47).

conflicted with the ideal of human happiness, since the essential elements of human happiness include the approval of society and of conscience, which can only be obtained by virtuous conduct.

It will be remembered that Smith's analysis of utility includes the aesthetic appreciation of a well-functioning machine in which more attention is paid to means than to ends.[1] This applies to man's appreciation of God's human creation:

'When we consider such actions as making a part of a system of behaviour which tends to promote the happiness either of the individual or of the society, they appear to derive a beauty from this utility, not unlike that which we ascribe to any well-contrived machine.'[2]

This brings out the extent to which Smith regarded utility as a principle for directing contemplation rather than an immediate moral guide; it involves an aesthetic appreciation of the design as well as approval of the product. In practical terms it may involve making small improvements in the machine, thus rendering it even more pleasing to behold, and also more beneficial to mankind, but, for most people, its logical implications are that they should concern themselves with their own affairs and adopt an attitude of detachment, even resignation, with respect to the wider world. It certainly does not mean that they should be utilitarians in the manner in which God is a utilitarian, acting in order to achieve the happiness of all men; it is the lot of relatively weak and powerless human beings to look to their own happiness and the welfare of a few close friends and relations; by so doing they promote God's plan for bringing about the general happiness in the manner for which they are best equipped. As politicians, and occasionally as subjects, they may be called upon to transcend this limited outlook and act according to their estimation of the happiness of a whole nation. But to reflect on the happiness of *all* mankind is something that should almost always be reserved for the social scientist, and the philosopher.

---

[1] Cf. pp. 116ff.   [2] T.M.S., VII.iii (II.356).

CHAPTER 11

THE THEOLOGICAL CONTEXT

Whatever the precise nature of Smith's own moral principles, the fact that he does endorse some of the norms which feature in his study of morality raises the issue of their philosophical justification. What arguments does he deploy to establish their validity? It is at this point that those critics of Smith who complain that he does not provide an adequate basis for morality come into their own; as long as he was only describing and explaining how men come to hold their moral opinions, then these criticisms could be ignored; but when Smith passes, as he does occasionally, from explanation to recommendation, such criticisms become apposite.

Unfortunately, Smith seems largely unaware that he has this problem on his hands; he appears to have felt little need to justify what was, to him, the obvious legitimate authority of most moral rules. It would be wrong to criticize him too severely for this; he had other problems to tackle which were quite sufficient to keep him fully occupied. And it is not so much that he was blind to problems of philosophical justification as that he thought that doubts about the authenticity of ordinary moral rules could be easily allayed; they arose, he thought, from mistaken explanatory theories and misleading half-truths. It is also clear that he considered that his own studies of morality vindicated, rather than undermined, the authority of normal moral standards. If we can discover why he believed that his own moral convictions, and, by implication, the moral judgments of the ordinary person, were strengthened by his empirical theory, then this will bring to light the grounds of his confidence, both in the moral judgments of his own society, and in his own reflective moral principles.

I. META-ETHICS

We cannot say that, at the end of the day, Smith brings in some intuitive type of reason, or a superior type of moral faculty, to provide the ultimate justification of the moral principles he accepts as binding. Being, by temperament and occupation, a reflective person, he assumes that moral judgments based on reflection are superior to the unthinking responses of the ordinary person, although he rarely admits any conflict between the two. But reflection is simply a further deployment of the human faculties which feature in, and help to explain, the development of all moral judgments. Even when he says that some people are able to adopt the most ideal of all spectator standpoints and take, as it were, a God's-eye-view of human life, and so feel something of the universal benevolence which he attributes to the Deity,[1] Smith does not think that this is achieved by means of some special access to knowledge of good and evil. It is simply a wider application of the same feelings that are present in the ordinary spectator when he is contemplating the welfare of any innocent person.

Similarly, we have seen in his analysis of conscience that, while he accepts that some obligations feel more authoritative than others, even the most authoritative of them do not emanate from a source different in kind from that which explains every other moral obligation: the same laws of sympathy and spontaneous behaviour account for the whole range of moral experience. This means that Smith is open to the objection that, by tracing all moral duties back to their source in some modification of sympathetic feelings, he deprives these duties of the authority they would require to have if they were to be the source of binding obligations. Feelings themselves, it is said, have no authority; they simply exist. These feelings may compel men to act, but they cannot oblige them. It would seem that Smith's scientific explanation of the ordinary moral consciousness makes the task of philosophical justification extremely difficult.

The *Moral Sentiments* demonstrates little real concern for such justification. When Smith considers other moral theories he regards them as rival scientific theories which call in doubt his own theory of morality. His criticisms of alternative theories concentrate on showing them to be inaccurate or unnecessary as scientific explanations. Thus Hutcheson's moral sense theory which, Smith says, asserted that 'the principle of approbation is founded on a peculiar power of perception, somewhat analagous to the external senses', is dismissed because it cannot explain the fact that men morally approve and disapprove of the moral judgments of others, and also because it is unnecessary to invent a new 'sense' to explain what can be shown to result from a combination of familiar faculties. After summarizing his own theory he throws out a challenge:

[1] T.M.S., VI.ii.3 (II.114); cf. p. 181.

'I should be glad to know what remains, and I shall freely allow this overplus to be ascribed to a moral sense, or to any other peculiar faculty, provided any body will ascertain precisely what this overplus is.'[1]

This confidence in the completeness of his own scientific theory seems to have blurred his awareness of the need for a philosophical justification of moral rules.

But Smith does realize that there are philosophers who deny that there is any 'real' distinction between right and wrong by arguing that men are mistaken when they consider themselves to be under binding moral obligations, that is obligations which they cannot justifiably get out of simply by repudiating them. For instance, he attacks Mandeville for reducing all morality to self-love, and cites him as the chief exponent of 'licentious systems' which do not 'suppose that there is any real and essential distinction between vice and virtue'.[2] Smith retorts that Mandeville confused vanity with 'the desire of doing what is honourable and noble'[3] and says that he has been misled by the fact that 'there are some of our passions which have no other names except those which mark the disagreeable and offensive degree'[4] into thinking that any action is selfish if it involves any degree whatsoever of a passion which is selfish when present to an extreme degree. It is 'the great fallacy of Dr Mandeville's book to represent every passion as wholly vicious, which is so in any degree and in any direction,'[5] and it is on account of this fallacy that he is able to argue with some plausibility that there is no 'real virtue'.[6]

However convincing such a reply may be to a theory which says that there is no difference in experience between selfishness and altruism, or between proper and improper degrees of the passions, Smith has done nothing in this rejoinder beyond reiterating that there are moral rules which govern human conduct and that these are felt to have an authority different in kind from that of selfish desires. Mandeville's position may not be compatible with ordinary moral experience, but to show this is not to provide a philosophical justification for that experience. While Smith was aware that theories such as those of Hobbes and Mandeville provide a problem for those who wish to uphold the moral standards of their society, he did not see the inadequacy of his own theory in this respect. Because he saw no problem in declaring sentiment to be the basis of all

---

1 T.M.S., VII.iii.3 (II.356).   2 T.M.S., VII.ii.4 (II.300).
3 T.M.S., VII.ii.4 (II.308).   4 T.M.S., VII.ii.4 (II.316).
5 T.M.S., VII.ii.4 (II.317).   6 T.M.S., VII.ii.4 (II.319).

moral judgments, he assumed that philosophers like Cudworth, who argued that men derive their knowledge of right and wrong from reason, were simply mistaken about the function of that faculty which, it will be remembered, Smith associates with the ability to reason inductively.

Nevertheless there are some elements of philosophical justification in the *Moral Sentiments*. There are a few appeals to the fact that the *de jure* authority of moral rules is 'obvious', which could be interpreted as an appeal to self-evidence or common sense, although these are usually associated with an assertion of the alleged function of moral sentiment in controlling other sentiments which, in turn, is related to the theological argument that the rules of morality are the commandments of God; these arguments owe a good deal to Butler, and Smith also reflects Butler's view that the obvious authority of moral rules is a fact which is independent of any particular analysis of the moral faculty:

'Upon whatever we suppose that our moral faculties are founded, whether upon a certain modification of reason, upon an original instinct, called a moral sense, or upon other principle of our nature, it cannot be doubted, that they were given us for the direction of our conduct in this life. They carry along with them the most evident badges of this authority, which denote that they were set up within us to be the supreme arbiters of all our actions, to superintend all our senses, passions and appetites, and to judge how far each of them was either to be indulged or restrained.'[1]

This quotation contains all the strands of his argument concerning the authority of moral rules. In the first place there is the appeal to what 'cannot be doubted'. But this is not an ultimate appeal to some rational intuition, for it is linked to the assertions that the moral faculty does in fact arbitrate within and between all other faculties, and this, in turn, is vindicated by the claim that this is the function which the Deity intended it to fulfil. This train of argument rests on the assumption that the world is a unified mechanism and on the belief that the justification of its constituent parts consists in demonstrating their place within the whole. Unfortunately for Smith, such an argument has to take for granted the goodness of the mechanism as a whole, and since this cannot be done without drawing on the very moral principles which he is required to justify, the argument is, in the end, circular. However, it is to Smith's theological beliefs that we must trace his confidence in the trust-

[1] T.M.S., III.5 (I.410).

worthiness of the reflective moral consciousness, and it is important, therefore, to examine the nature and status of these beliefs.

II. ORTHODOXY

It is exceedingly difficult to unravel the inter-connections between Smith's moral theory and his theological beliefs, but some attempt at this is required if we are to be able to indicate in what sense Smith's normative moral theory is dependent on his theistic metaphysics. Smith writes that there is 'an opinion which is first impressed by nature, and afterwards confirmed by reasoning and philosophy, that those important rules of morality are the commands and laws of the Deity, who will finally reward the obedient, and punish the transgressors of their duty';[1] this makes it look as if he thought that men's motives for acting with propriety are prudential fear of divine punishment and the hope of rewards in a life-to-come. But, in fact, he says that this belief is simply an 'enhancement' of a respect for the rules of duty which is originally rooted in men's experience of the pangs and rewards of conscience. It is these 'vice-gerents of God within us' who 'never fail to punish the violation of them [moral rules], by the torments of inward shame, and self-condemnation: and, on the contrary, always reward obedience with tranquillity of mind, with contentment, and self-satisfaction'.[2] Smith argues that belief in a life-after-death is largely based on the expectations which arise from these operations of conscience, which give rise to the hope that goodness will receive the reward and evil the punishment which they so often fail to obtain in this world. Moral rules thus have a 'natural' (pre-theological) authority of their own in the sense that men's motive for obeying moral rules is not a prudential regard to a future life but to the rewards and punishments of conscience itself. In discussing the situation of a person who has a guilty conscience on account of an undiscovered crime, Smith asserts that 'though he could be assured that no man was ever to know of it, and could even bring himself to believe that there was no God to revenge it, he would still feel enough of both these sentiments [horror and remorse] to embitter the whole of his life'.[3]

But, if theological considerations of this sort do not explain men's submission to the authority of conscience, did Smith regard them as fundamental for the philosophical defence of ordinary moral

[1] T.M.S., III.5 (I.407).   [2] T.M.S., III.5 (I.413).
[3] T.M.S., III.2 (I.297).

sentiments? To answer this question it is necessary to know whether or not Smith believed in a life-after-death. There is some evidence that he did. He argues forcibly that it is natural for men to hold such a belief, and suggests that it is only because some religious persons have suggested such bizarre criteria for attaining future rewards that it could have been exposed to ridicule.[1] Smith considers it to be a natural belief for several reasons: it is prompted by the weakness of men, who fear their approaching death; it is suggested by man's conception of the dignity of human life, and it offers comfort to those who are suffering difficulties and disappointments in this life;[2] but most of all, as we have seen, it is a natural implication of moral experiences: it comforts those who themselves feel something of the Deity's benevolence but lack his power to aid their fellow-men,[3] and, more fundamentally, it is a necessary postulate if men are to reconcile their ideas of justice with the actual distribution of rewards and punishments which they perceive in this life:

'Nature teaches us to hope, and religion, we suppose, authorises us to expect, that it [injustice] will be punished, even in a life to come. . . . The justice of God, however, we think, . . . requires that he should hereafter avenge the injuries of the widow and the fatherless, who are here so often insulted with impunity.'[4]

But did Smith himself accept the teaching of nature and religion? As far as the latter is concerned, we can say that he places no weight on revealed religion. In an age when at least the outward form of Christianity was a prudent garb for anyone with a modicum of worldly ambition, a man's religious affirmations did not always reveal his true beliefs, and it is to be expected that commentators should speculate about the extent to which the friend and admirer of David Hume might share the latter's agnosticism. In the atmosphere of his time, Smith's silence on matters of revealed religion is strong evidence that he was less than enthusiastic on its behalf. On the other hand, his occasional references to orthodox religious

[1] T.M.S., III.2 (I.327-30).
[2] T.M.S., III.2 (I.325): '. . . a hope and expectation deeply rooted in human nature; which can alone support its lofty ideas of its own dignity; can alone illumine the dreary prospect of its continually approaching mortality, and maintain its cheerfulness under all the heaviest calamities to which, from the disorders of this life, it may sometimes be exposed'.
[3] Cf. T.M.S., VI.ii.3 (II.114).
[4] T.M.S., II.ii.3 (I.228f.). N.B. 'We suppose' occurs in the third and subsequent editions, instead of 'we think' in the first and second editions (1st edn, p. 202).

beliefs have led some to claim that he was, at least in his early days, an orthodox Christian believer. The arguments, on both sides, draw partly on somewhat scanty and inconclusive biographical evidence, but mainly on the overt references to religion found in his works; for instance, it is pointed out that some passages in the first edition of the *Moral Sentiments* seem to accept the doctrines of revealed religion, but that these are often toned down in later editions by the addition of such qualifying phrases as 'we suppose'.

The only contribution which I wish to make to this debate is to suggest that these later modifications, and the withdrawal in the sixth edition of a passage on the atonement which appears to endorse a specifically Christian belief, might well have been the result of Smith's desire to correct misinterpretation of the original passages rather than of any change of belief on his part. We have already seen Smith's interest in explaining religious doctrines, and it is possible to interpret all his references to reveal religion as attempts to explain its causes and not to draw on revelation for supporting evidence. Like many natural theologians, he was always pleased to point out where his beliefs agreed with the tenets of orthodox religion, but his over-riding aim was to show that his theories could explain the doctrines of revealed religion, and so demonstrate the variety of phenomena to which his hypotheses are relevant. It is possible that, when he discovered that these attempts at explanation had been misinterpreted and taken as affirmations of 'sound' religious doctrine, he decided to modify their wording in such a way as to bring out more clearly his purpose in mentioning the religious doctrines in question; but at the same time he would make sure that he could not be accused of attacking these doctrines; this would account for the addition of phrases like 'we suppose' or 'we imagine', to his original statements.

The few uses he makes of orthodox terminology, as when he speaks of 'the great law of Christianity',[1] 'our Saviour',[2] and 'the inspired writers',[3] are also to be found in contexts where he is explaining and not affirming religious belief. Similarly, the passage on the atonement, withdrawn in the sixth edition of the *Moral Sentiments*, was probably intended as an attempt to explain a religious belief by tracing it to a fact about the moral sentiments, in this case the sense of demerit; Smith writes that:

'If we consult our natural sentiments, we are apt to fear, lest before the holiness of God, vice should appear more worthy of

[1] T.M.S., I.i.5 (I.47).   [2] T.M.S., III.6 (I.448).
[3] T.M.S., II.i.5 (I.189).

227

punishment than the weakness and imperfection of human virtue can ever seem to be of reward.'[1]

He then shows how this natural sense of unworthiness leads man to feel the need for a forgiveness he does not deserve:

'He . . . naturally fears, lest the wisdom of God should not, like the weakness of man, be prevailed upon to spare the crime, by the most importune lamentations of the criminal. Some other intercession, some other sacrifice, some other atonement, he imagines, must be made for him, beyond what he himself is capable of making, before the purity of the divine justice can be reconciled to his manifold offences. The doctrines of revelation coincide, in every respect, with those original anticipations of nature; and, as they teach us how little we can depend on the imperfections of our own virtue, so they show us, at the same time, that the most powerful intercession has been made, and that the most dreadful atonement has been paid for our manifold transgressions and iniquities.'[2]

This passage is the chief evidence for those who regard Smith as a back-sliding orthodox believer. But it is interesting to note that Smith's hypothetical penitent 'imagines' that some atonement must be made. This seems to indicate a psychological necessity which Smith feels that he is able to account for, an interpretation which is supported by another passage, not withdrawn in the sixth edition, which mentions the idea of atonement in relation to the attitude of criminals to their punishment:

'By acknowledging their guilt, by submitting themselves to the resentment of their offended fellow-citizens, and, by thus satiating that vengeance of which they were sensible that they had become the proper objects, they hoped, by their death to reconcile themselves, at least in their own imagination, to the natural sentiments of mankind; to be able to consider themselves as less worthy of hatred and resentment; to atone, in some measure, for their crimes.'[3]

If Smith was not concerned to endorse the doctrine of the atonement in the first place, then we cannot say that he withdrew the passage because his belief had waned. Nor, on my view, can we argue that it was withdrawn because, as he is reported to have said, it was 'unnecessary and misplaced',[4] since, as an apt illustration of

---

[1] T.M.S. (1st edn), II.ii.3 (p. 204).
[2] T.M.S. (1st edn), II.ii.3 (pp. 205f.).   [3] T.M.S., III.2 (I.298).
[4] Rev. John Sinclair, *Memoirs of the Life and Works of Sir John Sinclair*, vol. II, p. 40.

his theory, it is certainly not misplaced, although it may not, perhaps, be strictly necessary. It could be that he objected to the fact that a passage which he had intended to be an explanation of religious belief should have been interpreted as an affirmation of it.

This fits with his other references to religion, in the *Essays*, where he traces the origin of religion to fear and scarcity, and, as we have seen, indicates that monotheism is a natural consequence of the development of science.[1] Again, Millar's report of the content of his natural theology lectures would lead us to suppose that he paid at least as much attention to explaining as to evaluating religious doctrines, for he is said to have 'considered the proofs of the being and the attributes of God, and those principles of the human mind upon which religion is founded'.[2]

These comments on Smith's attitude towards orthodox religion are intended to justify the view that he did not rely on revealed religion to provide a justification for the authority of moral rules. There is no reason, for instance, to think that he accepted the belief in a benevolent and just god and the doctrine of an after-life on the authority of Christian doctrine, and then used these beliefs to underpin moral obligations. Indeed I have argued that it is likely that he had reservations about the doctrine of a life-after-death. In one passage Smith mentions that 'the virtuous man who has the misfortune to doubt of it [a life-after-death], cannot possibly avoid wishing most earnestly and anxiously to believe it'.[3] This would not seem to square with Hume's reported attitude, but it can, perhaps, be taken as an indication of Smith's own ambivalent position. If this is so, he would appear to have been more certain about the binding nature of moral duties than about the prospect of a Day of Judgment, in which case he would not wish to press the idea that moral obligation finds its ultimate justification in the prudential obligation to prepare for such an event. He is happy to explain orthodox belief and to show how it is functional for the individual and for society, but it cannot be said that he is prepared to allow it philosophical currency.

However, the idea of a life-after-death may not be the religious belief which is crucial for the support of morality. It is possible that a limited natural theology, accepting only the existence of a benevolent creator, is sufficient for this purpose. Smith shows his awareness of this possibility when he outlines two types of answer to the question: why ought we to obey the will of the Deity?

[1] Cf. p. 33f.   [2] Cf. p. 18.   [3] T.M.S., III.2 (I.326).

'It must either be said that we ought to obey the will of the Deity because he is a Being of infinite power, who will reward us eternally if we do so, and punish us eternally if we do otherwise: or it must be said, that independent of any regard to our own happiness, or to rewards and punishments of any kind, there is a congruity and fitness that a creature should obey its creator, that a limited and imperfect being should submit to one of infinite and incomprehensible perfections.'[1]

The first answer, he says, would make virtue consist in prudence, the second would make it a species of propriety, 'since the ground of our obligation to obedience is the suitableness or congruity of the sentiments of humility and submission to the superiority of the object which excites them'.[2]

This latter could be interpreted as Smith's own view, although he is more interested in classifying it as a theory of virtue than with accepting or rejecting it as an argument. But would it serve his purpose? If the duty to obey the Deity is based on an apprehension of the propriety of such obedience, then we cannot rely on this argument to justify judgments of propriety in general, since the argument would then be circular. Moreover Smith's belief in the existence of God depends, to some extent, on inferences from moral experience. Moral rules are commands; therefore, he assumes, there must be a commander: the world produces morally desirable phenomena; therefore, it is argued, there must be a benevolent God who has created it.

III. THE ARGUMENT FROM DESIGN

It would seem that, both in his arguments for the existence of God and in the arguments he uses which might indicate why he considered that God should be obeyed, Smith draws on those very moral sentiments for which we are seeking a philosophical justification. It would be possible to compromise at this point and defend Smith by arguing that, at this level of metaphysical argument, it is wrong to expect any straightforward uni-directional inference from premises to conclusions; rather we should be prepared to consider a set of mutually supporting affirmations which together provide a convincing theory.

Thus it could be said that, although one cannot rigorously argue either from moral experience to theistic belief, or from the premise

---

[1] T.M.S., VII.ii (II.298).   [2] T.M.S., VII.ii (II.299).

that God exists to the conclusion that moral rules should be obeyed as His commands, nevertheless, the facts of the moral life readily fit into a theistic interpretation of the world, and a belief in God underpins men's most firmly held moral beliefs, so that together morality and religion can provide a coherent and satisfying view of the human condition. This may well be how it appeared to Smith. Yet to gain a proper appreciation of his position it is necessary to realize that Smith's main argument for God's existence is not a moral one. His theism is largely based on the argument from design; this argument enabled him to arrive, without circularity, at the view that moral rules are the commands of God; he thought that he had grounds for believing in God which did not depend on the authenticity of these same moral rules.

It is true that the argument from design can presuppose morality in so far as it stresses that the mechanism of nature produces the sort of results we would expect from a *benevolent* God, and Smith does frequently point out, in his analyses of final causes, that God, or Nature, does intend the happiness of mankind. But the main foundation for the argument from design is simply the intricate workings of the machine itself. It will be remembered that in his interpretation of 'why utility pleases' Smith emphasizes that utility is valued not only because of the results it produces, but because of the nice adjustment of means to ends which is exhibited in its operation.[1] This seems to have been the semi-aesthetic appreciation which Smith felt with regard to the workings of nature, and he considered that, in demonstrating the hidden mechanisms at work in society, he had added to our knowledge of the intricate interconnections to be found in just one aspect of the creation, and so reinforced the conclusion that:

'In every part of the universe we observe means adjusted with the nicest artifice to the ends which they are intended to produce.'[2]

This is the manner in which science, including the science of morals, supports the non-moral form of the argument from design, simply by demonstrating, in ever-increasing detail, the fact that there is order and unity to be found throughout the universe. Science displays the design for our wonder and contemplation, and from this contemplation arises the conviction that such artifice implies an artificer, and that the precise adjustment of means to ends is the product of the wisdom of God.[3] Even the argument that men ought to obey the Deity because it is fitting that they should do so can be interpreted,

[1] Cf. pp. 116ff.   [2] T.M.S., II.ii.3 (I.216f.).   [3] Cf. pp. 60ff.

not as a point about moral propriety, although it is at least that, but also as an expression of the desire that men should co-operate with the plan of the universe, and by obeying the creator, make their own contribution to the harmonious workings of the total system.

One common objection to the argument from design is its unverifiable nature. It is not possible, it is argued, to say what a disordered world would be like, and therefore there is no conceivable observable circumstance which could disprove the existence of God. Smith would not agree with this, since he does not argue from the fact of *any* order, but from the assertion of the sort of order which scientific research exhibits, namely one in which the operations of a great variety of phenomena can all be traced to the workings of a few simple principles, for, as he says 'the system of human nature seems to be more simple and agreeable when all its different operations are in this manner deduced from a single principle'.[1] Most of the *Moral Sentiments* is taken up with exhibiting the laws of sympathy as one such unifying factor. Thus, while he might accept that *any* order implies a creator, he would insist that the implication becomes more compelling as the order is shown to be more comprehensive and complex, and the extent to which this is the case is a matter to which empirical evidence is relevant. No doubt the inference still remains problematical, but this must be so if it is a metaphysical conclusion which is being drawn: that is a conclusion about science rather than within it.

Smith certainly accepted the argument from design, if only in the sense that his mind worked within its general presuppositions. He shared, though not in its most extreme forms, the Stoics' vision of a harmonious universe in which everything has its place and its part to play. We cannot say what he thought of the arguments of Hume's *Dialogue concerning Natural Religion*, for he never seems to have come to grips with its attack on the analogy between the world and an artefact, upon which the argument from design is based. As a result, he was shielded from any real uncertainty about the desirability of following the dictates of reflective conscience, and he shows no signs of radical doubt concerning the soundness of the ordinary person's spontaneous moral judgments. It is possible to overemphasize his confidence in 'the economy of nature'; in terms of the hopes and fears of individual human beings, his attitude is one of resignation rather than jubilation. He seldom glories in the human lot, although he considers it more than bearable. But these anxieties and doubts about human destiny do not shake his general conviction

---

[1] T.M.S., II.ii.3 (I.218).

that the world as a whole exhibits a design and an order which rightly evokes man's wonder and admiration. It is this conviction which lies behind his confidence in the authority of moral rules and explains his lack of concern with the details of the philosophical justification of his own moral principles.

CONCLUDING ASSESSMENT

Even if we find it difficult to accept the inference from the postulate of an ordered universe, to the conclusion that there must be an Author of Nature, we may accept that, if the argument from design has any validity, then Smith was correct in his belief that the more detailed and intricate the 'design' the more convincing the argument becomes. Can we also accept that he made a reliable and useful contribution to our knowledge of human society as one part of nature's 'immense machine'? This question has interest and importance even if we reject Smith's theological assumptions, for if he did succeed in demonstrating that society is a type of system and that sympathy is one key to the understanding of that system, then he has made an impressive contribution to social science. There is no reason why Smith's social science should not be separated from his natural theology in this way; and, if this is done, then primacy must go to the former, since this is where his own original work is to be found.

Our study of the *Moral Sentiments*, and its relationship to Smith's other writings and to his reported lectures, has put us in the position of being able to make some sort of assessment of his attempt to approach the science of society through the study of morality. As his own analysis of sound scientific method is remarkably modern, there is no reason why this assessment should not be made by reference to his own standards of scientific merit.

His first criterion of a good scientific theory is that it should connect, or render more coherent, a large number of apparently dissimilar phenomena. Smith must certainly be commended for the width of his endeavours in this direction. He uses the concept of sympathy to explain, not only ordinary moral judgments, but the respect for authority which lies at the root of political obedience, the motives which explain men's efforts to achieve wealth and power beyond the requirements of bodily comfort and safety, the basis of family affection and patriotism, and the entire content of the civil and criminal law. Many of these phenomena, especially insatiable

234

worldly ambition and the acceptance of social inequalities, although very familiar, are such as may strike a reflective person as being rather odd, and in need of explanation.

Smith's attempt to provide a unified explanation for all of them constitutes in itself a considerable intellectual achievement. It is, perhaps, the strongest point in favour of his theory of sympathy that it not only allows for, but actively suggests, connections between many different aspects of social behaviour; for instance, the desire for recognition explains not only economic motivation but the limits which the rules of justice place on worldly ambition: men only admire the wealthy if they have no resentment concerning the way that wealth was obtained, so that the ambitious man is defeating his own purposes if he commits detectable injustices. Similarly Smith explores the relations between economics and morality, between morality and law, between economics and politics, between morality and religion, between science and economics; and all this is within an historical framework which allows for, and to some extent explains, social change and development. Of particular interest are his explorations of the relationships between social class and morality and his study of the effects of custom on morality and law. These demonstrate both the wide-ranging scope and the unifying potential of his theory of imaginative sympathy.

Smith's second and third criteria of a good scientific theory are that it should be simple and that it should employ a mechanism which is familiar. Sympathy would seem to meet both these requirements. However, the rather unusual concept of sympathy which Smith uses in his theory, and the complexities which he introduces in its exposition, make it rather less simple and familiar than it might have been. In fact the simple principle of sympathy turns out to be a good deal less than straightforward. It is not an emotion and therefore cannot be easily compared with the force of gravity in the science of astronomy. The desire for harmony of sentiment is a standing motive in Smith's account of human behaviour, but the processes by which men are able or fail to achieve this harmony break down into a multiplicity of activities. There is thus no one single force of attraction which unites men in society in the way that the planets are held in their orbits by the force of gravity. Sympathy, that 'power with which the mind is manifestly endowed', turns out to be described by a variety of different laws connected with man's imaginative faculties which are by no means all simple. Smith adds to them as he goes along, and there is no reason why more should not be introduced to account for any further phenomena that appear to require explanation. However, although the early simplicity of his theory is rather overshadowed by its later complexities, he does not have recourse to any principles which are not reasonably familiar.

The requirement that a theory should not introduce mysterious causal forces, or unfamiliar explanatory principles, probably makes more sense in the social than in the natural sciences, and it is one of the merits of Smith's theory that he does not appeal to problematical mental processes or occult social forces. His originality lies in the way in which he uses a relatively small number of generalizations about human nature and human society to build up his picture of the manner in which agreed moral standards develop. Beginning with the premise that human experience is, in an important sense, essentially private, he goes on to show how individuals come to partake in a social reality which appears to them to have order and stability and which provides the basis for social cohesion.

The need for a theory to fit the observed facts is Smith's final criterion by which to evaluate a scientific theory. It is at this point that our most serious doubts must be expressed. It is not that his generalizations are manifestly false, for many of them are reasonably convincing. But it is very difficult to see how they could be rigorously tested, since they are not sufficiently open to falsification. Despite the many examples he uses to justify his generalizations, they are far from adequate. Individually they depend, too often, on a particular interpretation of ambiguous social phenomena, and together they sometimes have more the appearance of a random collection of anecdotes than of a systematic attempt to examine counter, as well as confirming, instances of his empirical hypotheses.

Smith failed to live up to his own high standards of precision. In spite of his attempts to formulate the laws of sympathy in the mathematical terms made familiar by the science of physics, these laws cannot, in fact, be stated in precise, quantitative terms. For instance, the claim that men can sympathize more with those who are normally near to them and least with those farthest removed from them may indicate a general tendency but not a precise proportional relationship. It may seem rather unfair to press this point in view of the little progress that social scientists have made in this respect up to the present time. But these are his own standards and, as he rightly emphasized, the claims that one theory is to be preferred to another on scientific grounds is closely tied to its power of providing precise, testable predictions.

This deficiency is particularly noticeable in his concept of 'nature' which has been discussed at length. In spite of its fundamentally empirical orientation it is given too many different applications, some of which cannot be used with any precision in empirical observation. When it simply means 'normal' or 'average', then this is acceptable and useful provided it is made clear to which groups of people he is referring. But when it means 'pre-moral', 'pre-legal', or 'pre-social', then it often leads to unverifiable propositions about features of human nature which are not now observable and which probably never did exist in their 'original' form. Too much of Smith's theory rests on assertions about the raw material of human nature which becomes shaped by individual and social experience. A certain amount of this is necessary in any social theory which takes individual and social development seriously. But one difficulty with genetic social models is that they often refer to processes which cannot be repeated. In the case of the development of individuals a certain amount of repetition can be observed, but we cannot start with the isolated ingredients of pre-social man and reconstruct, in practice as well as theory, the course of human history. Smith thought that the 'natural' propensities of man could still be observed in spontaneous desires, and in temptations to act against the dictates of the impartial spectator, but sometimes he has recourse to unsubstantiated speculations about the fundamental or 'original' ingredients of human nature. Again, it is hardly fair to blame Smith for these difficulties, which are still with us. But it must be emphasized that he was, by modern standards, over-confident in his conviction that he had discovered the essential nature of man and the essence of social relationships.

Even if we are left with some suggestive and interesting hypotheses rather than with a tested and comprehensive theory, it is impossible not to admire the observation, the insight, and the sheer industry and perseverance which are displayed in Smith's theory of morality. The task he set himself was an impossibly large one. To study the morality of a society is not to study an isolated phenomenon, rather it is to investigate the substance and interconnections of all aspects of social life; it is not, therefore, an easily delineated subject-matter, and it is to Smith's credit that he attempted to follow out his theories in so many different areas. But this makes for an unmanageably large undertaking and inevitably leaves him with too many over-simplified generalizations and tantalizing loose ends. In his attempt to be comprehensive he often becomes vague and over-extended.

Present-day criticisms of Smith's standing as a social scientist partly reflect changes in the expected standards of empirical evidence, but, to a large extent, they simply demonstrate the difficulties inherent in any attempt to create a science of society. For its time, the *Moral Sentiments* must be regarded as a considerable achievement; it is a great advance on the over-individualistic approach of many of Smith's contemporaries: he had a strong grasp of the importance of attending to the social environment in the explanation of human behaviour; his theory of conscience, for instance, is a brave attempt to combine psychological and sociological explanation. The *Moral Sentiments* is certainly a much more important book than is realized by those who dismiss it on the grounds that it is philosophically uninteresting. The more it is read and pondered as a work of social science, the more its true worth will be accepted. It remains a model in its theoretical intentions, even if it falls short in the execution; and even in its execution it is often plausible and nearly always interesting.

Many modern works in social science spend too much time expounding their methodological approach and too little time doing anything significant with it. Smith makes the opposite error of taking his method too much for granted. He did not lack a methodological framework, but he did fail to make it explicit, and he has suffered misinterpretation and neglect in consequence. Properly understood, the *Moral Sentiments* deserves greater attention than it has received, not least by those who wish to study the *Wealth of Nations*. For, far from going back on the ideas he had worked out in the *Moral Sentiments*, Smith's more famous work takes many of these ideas for granted. We can discover Smith's basic explanation of economic motivation and the social framework within which economic activity takes place only by a correct analysis of the *Moral Sentiments*. However, quite apart from its significance for the understanding of the *Wealth of Nations*, the *Moral Sentiments* is able to stand on its own as an impressive and important book of which Adam Smith was rightly proud.

BIBLIOGRAPHY

Bonar, J. *The Moral Sense*. New York: Allen and Unwin, 1930.
Bonar, J. *A Catalogue of the Library of Adam Smith*, 2nd edn, London: Macmillan, 1932.
Brandt, R. B. *Ethical Theory: the problems of normative and critical ethics*, Englewood Cliffs: Prentice-Hall, 1959.
Brown, T. *Lectures on Ethics*, Edinburgh: William Tait, 1846.
Bryson, G. E. *Man and Society: the Scottish inquiry of the eighteenth century*, Princeton: the University Press, 1945.
Buckle, H. T. *History of Civilization in England* (1857-61), new edition, London: Oxford University Press, 1904.
Clark, J. M., Douglas, P. H., Hollander, J. B., Morrow, G. R., Palyi, M. and Viner, J. *Adam Smith, 1776-1926*, Chicago: the University Press, 1928.
Cropsey, J. *Polity and Economy*, The Hague: Martinus Nijhoff, 1957.
Farrer, J. A. *Adam Smith*, London: Sampson Low, Marston, Searle and Rivington, 1881.
Haldane, R. B. *Life of Adam Smith*, London: Walter Scott, 1887.
Halévy, E. *Growth of Philosophical Radicalism*, translated by Mary Morris, London: Faber and Faber, 1928.
Jouffroy, T. S. *Introduction to Ethics, including a critical survey of moral systems*, translated by W. H. Channing, 2 vols, Boston: Hilliard, Gray & Coy, 1841.
Lange, F. A. *History of Materialism*, London: Trubner, 1881.
Laurie, H. *The Scottish Philosophy*, Glasgow: James Maclehose, 1902.
Leslie, T. E. C. *Essays in Political and Moral Philosophy*, Dublin: Hodges, Foster and Triggis, 1879.
McCosh, J. *The Scottish Philosophy*, London: Macmillan, 1875.
Macfie, A. L. *The Individual in Society*, London: Allen and Unwin, 1967.
Meek, R. L. *Economics and Ideology*, London: Chapman and Hall, 1967.
Morrow, G. R. *The Ethical and Economic Theories of Adam Smith*, New York: Longmans, 1921.
Popper, K. *The Logic of Scientific Discovery*, London: Hutchinson, 1959.
Prior, A. N. *Logic and the Basis of Ethics*, Oxford: Clarendon Press, 1949.
Rae, J. *Life of Adam Smith* (1895) with an introductory 'Guide to John Rae's *Life of Adam Smith*' by Jacob Viner, New York: Kelley, 1965.
Raphael, D. D. (ed.) *British Moralists*, 2 vols, Oxford: the University Press, 1969.

Roll, E. *A History of Economic Thought*, London: Faber and Faber, 1938.

Scheler, M. *The Nature of Sympathy* (1913), translated by Peter Heath: London: Routledge and Kegan Paul, 1954.

Schneider, H. W. (ed.) *Adam Smith's Moral and Political Philosophy*, Chicago: Phoenix Books, 1967.

Schumpeter, J. A. *History of Economic Analysis*, New York: Oxford University Press, 1954.

Selby-Bigge, L. A. *British Moralists*, Oxford: Clarendon Press, 1897.

Sidgwick, H. *Outlines of the History of Ethics* (1886), 6th edn, London: Macmillan, 1931.

Small, A. W. *Adam Smith and Modern Sociology*, Chicago: the University Press, 1907.

Sorley, W. R. *Ethics of Naturalism*, London: Blackwood, 1885.

Stephen, L. *History of English Thought in the Eighteenth Century*, 3rd edn, 2 vols, London: Smith, Elder and Co., 1902.

Swabey, W. C. *Ethical Theory from Hobbes to Kant*, London: Vision Press, 1961.

Taylor, O. H. *A History of Economic Thought*, New York: McGraw-Hill, 1960.

Veblen, T. *The Place of Science in Modern Civilization* (1919), New York: Russell and Russell, 1961.

West, E. G. *Adam Smith*, New York: Arlington House, 1969.

Westermarck, E. *Ethical Relativity*, London: Kegan Paul, Trench and Trubner, 1932.

INDEX

Printed in the United States
by Baker & Taylor Publisher Services